Praise for *Configuration Management Best Practices*

"Understanding change is critical to any attempt to manage change. Bob Aiello and Leslie Sachs's *Configuration Management Best Practices* presents fundamental definitions and explanations to help practitioners understand change and its potential impact."

—*Mary Lou A. Hines Fritts, CIO and Vice Provost Academic Programs, University of Missouri-Kansas City*

"Few books on software configuration management emphasize the role of people and organizational context in defining and executing an effective SCM process. Bob Aiello and Leslie Sachs's book will give you the information you need not only to manage change effectively but also to manage the transition to a better SCM process."

—*Steve Berczuk, Agile Software Developer, and author of* Software Configuration Management Patterns: Effective Teamwork, Practical Integration

"Bob Aiello and Leslie Sachs succeed handsomely in producing an important book, at a practical and balanced level of detail, for this topic that often 'goes without saying' (and hence gets many projects into deep trouble). Their passion for the topic shows as they cover a wonderful range of topics—even culture, personality, and dealing with resistance to change—in an accessible form that can be applied to any project. The software industry has needed a book like this for a long time!"

—*Jim Brosseau, Clarrus Consulting Group, and author of* Software Teamwork: Taking Ownership for Success

"A must read for anyone developing or managing software or hardware projects. Bob Aiello and Leslie Sachs are able to bridge the language gap between the myriad of communities involved with successful Configuration Management implementations. They describe practical, real world practices that can be implemented by developers, managers, standard makers, and even Classical CM Folk."

— *Bob Ventimiglia, Bobev Consulting*

Configuration Management Best Practices

Practical Methods that Work in the Real World

Bob Aiello and Leslie Sachs

✦ Addison-Wesley

Upper Saddle River, NJ • Boston • Indianapols • San Francisco
New York • Toronto • Montreal • London • Munich • Paris • Madrid
Capetown • Sydney • Tokyo • Singapore • Mexico City

Many of the designations used by manufacturers and sellers to distinguish their products are claimed as trademarks. Where those designations appear in this book, and the publisher was aware of a trademark claim, the designations have been printed with initial capital letters or in all capitals.

The authors and publisher have taken care in the preparation of this book, but make no expressed or implied warranty of any kind and assume no responsibility for errors or omissions. No liability is assumed for incidental or consequential damages in connection with or arising out of the use of the information or programs contained herein.

The publisher offers excellent discounts on this book when ordered in quantity for bulk purchases or special sales, which may include electronic versions and/or custom covers and content particular to your business, training goals, marketing focus, and branding interests. For more information, please contact:

U.S. Corporate and Government Sales   (800) 382-3419

corpsales@pearsontechgroup.com

For sales outside the United States please contact:

International Sales
international@pearson.com

Visit us on the Web: informit.com/aw

Library of Congress Cataloging-in-Publication Data

Aiello, Bob, 1958-
  Configuration management best practices : practical methods that work in the real world / Bob Aiello, Leslie A. Sachs.
    p. cm.
  ISBN 978-0-321-68586-5 (pbk. : alk. paper) 1. Information technology--Management. 2. Configuration management. I.
  Sachs, Leslie A., 1961- II. Title.
  T58.64.A35 2010
  004.068'5--dc22
                            2010022175

ISBN-13: 978-0-321-68586-5
ISBN-10: 0-321-68586-5

Text printed in the United States on recycled paper at R.R. Donnelley in Crawfordsville, Indiana.

First printing August 2010

Editor-in-Chief
Karen Gettman

Acquisitions Editor
Chris Guzikowski

Senior Development Editor
Chris Zahn

Managing Editor
Kristy Hart

Project Editor
Jovana San Nicolas-Shirley

Copy Editor
Keith Cline

Indexer
Erika Millen

Proofreader
Sheri Cain

Cover Designer
Gary Adair

Compositor
Gloria Schurick

Dedicated to Benjamin K. Sachs

Those who met Ben did not easily forget the soft-spoken, yet articulate engineer with the deep blue eyes and gracious manner. Respected by family, friends, and business associates alike, he was known for his remarkable intelligence, integrity, and passion for excellence. Ben is also remembered fondly by the many people whose lives he touched with his warmth, kindness, and generosity. His successful career provided ample evidence to support the firm belief that "doing the right thing" will inevitably result in better quality, higher productivity, increased shareholder value, and more satisfied, loyal customers. Ever the promoter of good corporate citizenship, Ben combined his high morals and ethical standards with a natural optimism to create win-win resolutions for even the most challenging situations. Both our personal and professional development have been tremendously enhanced as a result of his wisdom and loving guidance.

Thank you, Dad, for never passing up the opportunity to enthusiastically express both your confidence in our abilities and pride in our accomplishments and for so eagerly sharing your infectious joy in living!

Bob Aiello and Leslie Sachs

Contents

Preface   xxi
Introduction   xxxiii

PART I THE CORE CM BEST PRACTICES FRAMEWORK 1

Chapter 1 Source Code Management 3
    Terminology and Source Code Management 5
Goals of Source Code Management 5
Principles of Source Code Management 6
1.1 Why Is Source Code Management Important? 6
1.2 Where Do I Start? 7
1.3 Source Code Management Core Concepts 9
    1.3.1 Creating Baselines and Time Machines 9
    1.3.2 Reserved Versus Unreserved Checkouts 10
    1.3.3 Sandboxes and Workspaces 11
    1.3.4 Variant Management (Branching) 11
    1.3.5 Copybranches Versus Deltas 12
    1.3.6 How to Handle Bugfixes 12
    1.3.7 Streams 14
    1.3.8 Merging 15
    1.3.9 Changesets 16
1.4 Defect and Requirements Tracking 16
1.5 Managing the Globally Distributed Development Team 17
1.6 Tools Selection 19
    1.6.1 Open Source Versus Commercial 21
    1.6.2 Product Maturity and Vendor Commitment 21
    1.6.3 Extensibility and Open API 22
    1.6.4 Don't Overengineer Your Source Code
           Management 22
1.7 Recognizing the Cost of Quality (and Total Cost of
    Ownership) 23
    1.7.1 Building Your Source Code Management Budget 24

1.8 Training 24

     1.8.1 The "Bob Method" for Training 24

1.9 Defining the Usage Model 25

1.10 Time to Implement and Risks to Success 26

1.11 Establishing Your Support Process 26

1.12 Advanced Features and Empowering Users 27

Conclusion 27

Chapter 2 Build Engineering 29

    Goals of Build Engineering 30

    Principles of Build Engineering 30

2.1 Why Is Build Engineering Important? 31

2.2 Where Do I Start? 32

2.3 Build Engineering Core Concepts 32

     2.3.1 Version IDs or Branding Your Executables 32

     2.3.2 Immutable Version IDs 33

     2.3.3 Stamping In a Version Label or Tag 33

     2.3.4 Managing Compile Dependencies 33

     2.3.5 The Independent Build 34

2.4 Core Considerations for Scaling the Build Function 34

     2.4.1 Selling the Independent Build 35

     2.4.2 Overengineering the Build 35

     2.4.3 Testing Your Own Integrity 36

     2.4.4 Reporting to Development Can Be a Conflict

        of Interest 37

     2.4.5 Organizational Choices 37

2.5 Build Tools Evaluation and Selection 38

     2.5.1 Apache Ant Enters the Build Scene 38

     2.5.2 Of Mavens and Other Experts 38

     2.5.3 Maven Versus Ant 39

     2.5.4 Using Ant for Complex Builds 39

     2.5.5 Continuous Integration 40

     2.5.6 CI Servers 40

     2.5.7 Integrated Development Environments 40

     2.5.8 Static Code Analysis 41

     2.5.9 Build Frameworks 41

2.5.10 Selecting Your Build Tools 41

2.5.11 Conducting the Bakeoff and Reaching Consensus .. 42

2.6 Cost of Quality and Training 42

2.7 Making a Good Build Better 42

2.7.1 "Bob-Proofing" Your Build 43

2.7.2 Test-Driven Builds 43

2.7.3 Trust, But Verify 43

2.7.4 The Cockpit of a Plane 44

2.8 The Role of the Build Engineer 44

2.8.1 Know What You Build 45

2.8.2 Partner with Developers 46

2.8.3 Drafting a Rookie 46

2.9 Architecture Is Fundamental 46

2.10 Establishing a Build Process 47

2.10.1 Establishing Organizational Standards 47

2.11 Continuous Integration Versus the Nightly Build 47

2.12 The Future of Build Engineering 48

Conclusion 48

Chapter 3 Environment Configuration 49

Goals of Environment Configuration Control 50

Principles of Environment Configuration Control 51

3.1 Why Is Environment Configuration Important? 51

3.2 Where Do I Start? 51

3.3 Supporting Code Promotion 52

3.4 Managing the Configuration 52

3.4.1 Which Database Are You Using? 53

3.4.2 Did That Trade Go Through? 53

3.4.3 How About a Few Tokens? 54

3.4.4 Centralizing the Environment Variable Assignment .. 55

3.5 Practical Approaches to Establishing a CMDB 55

3.5.1 Identify and Then Control 56

3.5.2 Understanding the Environment Configuration 56

3.6 Change Control Depends on Environment Configuration 56

3.7 Minimize the Number of Controls Required 57

3.8 Managing Environments 57

3.9 The Future of Environment Configuration 57

Conclusion 58

Chapter 4   Change Control 59

Goals of Change Control 60

Principles of Change Control 60

4.1 Why Is Change Control Important? 61

4.2 Where Do I Start? 61

4.3 The Seven Types of Change Control 61

4.3.1 A Priori 62

4.3.2 Gatekeeping 62

4.3.3 Configuration Control 62

4.3.4 Change Advisory Board 63

4.3.5 Emergency Change Control 64

4.3.6 Process Engineering 64

4.3.7 Senior Management Oversight 64

4.4 Creating a Change Control Function 65

4.5 Examples of Change Control in Action 65

4.5.1 The 29-Minute Change Control Meeting 66

4.5.2 Change Control at the Investment Bank 66

4.5.3 Change Control at the Trading Firm 67

4.5.4 Forging Approvals 69

4.6 Don't Forget the Risk 69

4.7 Driving the CM Process Through Change Control 69

4.8 Entry/Exit Criteria 70

4.9 After-Action Review 71

4.10 Make Sure That You Evaluate Yourself 71

Conclusion 71

Chapter 5   Release Management 73

Goals of Release Management 74

Principles of Release Management 74

5.1 Why Is Release Management Important? 75

5.2 Where Do I Start? 75

5.3 Release Management Concepts and Practices 76

5.3.1 Packaging Strategies That Work 76

5.3.2 Package Version Identification 76

      5.3.3 Sending a Release Map with the Release 77

      5.3.4 What Does Immutable Mean? 77

    5.4 The Ergonomics of Release Management 77

      5.4.1 Avoiding Human Error 78

      5.4.2 Understanding the Technology 78

      5.4.3 Tools from Build Engineering 79

      5.4.4 Avoiding Human Error 79

      5.4.5 My Own Three-Step Process 79

      5.4.6 Too Many Moving Parts 80

    5.5 Release Management as Coordination 80

      5.5.1 Communicating the Status of a Release 80

      5.5.2 Don't Forget the Release Calendar 80

      5.5.3 RM and Configuration Control 81

    5.6 Requirements Tracking 81

    5.7 Taking Release Management to the Next Level 81

      5.7.1 Using Cryptography to Sign Your Code 82

      5.7.2 Operating Systems Support for Release Management 82

      5.7.3 Improving Your RM Process 82

  Conclusion 83

Chapter 6 Deployment 85

  Goals of Deployment 86

  Principles of Deployment 86

  6.1 Why Is Deployment Important? 87

  6.2 Where Do I Start? 87

  6.3 Practices and Examples 87

      6.3.1 Staging Is Key 87

      6.3.2 Scripting the Release Process Itself 89

      6.3.3 Frameworks for Deployment 89

      6.3.4 What If Bob Makes a Mistake? 89

      6.3.5 More on the Depot 90

      6.3.6 Auditing Your Release 90

  6.4 Conducting a Configuration Audit 91

  6.5 Don't Forget the Smoke Test 92

  6.6 Little Things Matter a Lot 92

  6.7 Communications Planning 92

      6.7.1 Announcing Outages and Completed Deployments ... 93

6.8 Deployment Should Be Delegated 93

6.9 Trust But Verify 93

6.10 Improving the Deployment Process 93

Conclusion 94

PART II ARCHITECTURE AND HARDWARE CM 95

Chapter 7 Architecting Your Application for CM 97

Goals of Architecting Your Application for CM 98

7.1 Why Is Architecture Important? 99

7.2 Where Do I Start? 99

7.3 How CM Facilitates Good Architecture 99

7.4 What Architects Can Learn From Testers 99

      7.4.1 Testing as a Service to the Developers 100

7.5 Configuration Management–Driven Development (CMDD) . 101

7.6 Coping with the Changing Architecture 101

7.7 Using Source Code Management to Facilitate Architecture ... 102

7.8 Training Is Essential 102

7.9 Source Code Management as a Service 103

7.10 Build Engineering as a Service 103

Conclusion 103

Chapter 8 Hardware Configuration Management 105

Goals of Hardware CM 106

8.1 Why Is Hardware CM Important? 106

8.2 Where Do I Start? 107

8.3 When You Can't Version Control a Circuit Chip 107

      8.3.1 A Configuration Item by Any Other Name 107

      8.3.2 Version Control for Design Specifications 108

8.4 Don't Forget the Interfaces 108

8.5 Understanding Dependencies 108

8.6 Traceability 108

8.7 Deploying Changes to the Firmware 109

8.8 The Future of Hardware CM 109

Conclusion 109

PART III   THE PEOPLE SIDE OF CM 111

Chapter 9   Rightsizing Your Processes 113

Goals of Rightsizing Your CM Processes 114

9.1 Why Is Rightsizing Your Processes Important? 115

9.2 Where Do I Start? 115

9.3 Verbose Processes Just Get in the Way 116

9.4 SPINs and Promoting the CMM 117

9.5 Disappearing Verbose Processes 117

9.5.1 Agile Processes Just Work 118

9.5.2 Open Unified Process 118

9.5.3 Getting Lean 119

9.5.4 An Extremely Brief Description That I Hope
Motivates You to Take a Closer Look at Lean
Software Development 119

9.6 The Danger of Having Too Little Process 120

9.7 Just-in-Time Process Improvement 120

9.8 Don't Overengineer Your CM 120

9.9 Don't Forget the Technology 121

9.10 Testing Your Own Processes 121

9.11 Process Consultation 122

9.11.1 Transparency That Is Genuine 122

9.12 Create a Structure for Sustainability 122

Conclusion 123

Chapter 10   Overcoming Resistance to Change 125

Goals of Overcoming Resistance to Change 126

10.1 Why Is Overcoming Resistance to Change Important? 127

10.2 Where Do I Start? 127

10.3 Matching Process to Culture 127

10.4 Mixing Psychology and Computer Programming 129

10.5 Process Improvement from Within 129

10.6 Picking Your Battles 131

10.7 Fostering Teamwork 131

10.8 Why Good Developers Oppose Process Improvement 132

10.9 Procedural Justice 132

10.10 Input from Everyone 132

10.11 Showing Leadership 133

10.12 Process Improvement People May Be the Problem 133

10.13 Combining Process and Technology Training 134

10.14 Listening to the Rhythm 135

10.15 Processes Need to Be Tested 136

10.16 Baby Steps and Process Improvement 136

10.17 Selling Process Improvement 137

10.18 What's in It for Me? 137

10.19 Process Improvement as a Service 137

10.20 Guerrilla Tactics for Process Improvement 138

Conclusion 139

**Chapter 11 Personality and CM: A Psychologist Looks at
the Workplace 141**

Goals of Understanding Personality: What's in It for Me? 142

11.1 Personality Primer for CM Professionals 144

11.2 What Do CM Experts Need to Consider in
Terms of Personality? 146

   11.2.1 Communication Styles 147

   11.2.2 Do Men and Women Use and Interpret
Language Differently? 147

   11.2.3 Effective Consultation 148

   11.2.4 Verifying the Message 148

   11.2.5 Information Processing Preferences 149

   11.2.6 Birth Order at Work 150

   11.2.7 Firstborns as Leaders 150

   11.2.8 The Middle-Born Compromiser 151

   11.2.9 The Youngest as Initiator 151

   11.2.10 The Only Child 151

   11.2.11 Being Yourself 152

11.3 Applying Psychology to the Workplace 152

   11.3.1 Effective Teamwork Begins at Home 153

   11.3.2 Volleyball or Effective Collaboration 153

   11.3.3 Embedding Build Engineers and Testers in
the Development Team 153

   11.3.4 Blackbox Versus Whitebox Versus Graybox 154

11.3.5 Group Dynamics That Can Damage the
Organization 154

11.3.6 Where CM and QA Fit In 154

11.4 Family Dynamics! 155

11.4.1 Indecisiveness 155

11.5 Workplace Culture and Personality 156

11.5.1 Personality and Structure 156

11.5.2 We Already Invented All the Good Ideas 157

11.5.3 Loose Cannons Who Don't Want to Comply 157

11.5.4 Enforcing Process, While Still Keeping the
Train Moving 158

11.5.5 Formulas for Success 158

11.5.6 Caveats 159

Conclusion 159

Chapter 12   Learning From Mistakes That I Have Made 161

Goals of Learning from Mistakes 162

12.1 Why Is It Important to Learn from Our Mistakes? 162

12.2 Where Do I Get Started? 162

12.3 Understanding Our Mistakes 163

12.4 The Mistakes I Have Made 163

12.4.1 Missing the Big Picture 163

12.4.2 Writing Release Automation Can Be Challenging . 164

12.4.3 Thinking That a Good Process Will Carry Itself ... 165

12.4.4 Failing to Gain Consensus 165

12.4.5 Failing to Show Leadership for CM 165

12.4.6 Becoming Part of the Problem 165

12.4.7 Forgetting to Ask for Help 166

12.5 Turning a Mistake into a Lesson Learned 166

12.5.1 Clarifying What I Need to Get the Job Done 166

12.5.2 Getting the Training That I Need 167

12.6 Common Mistakes That I Have Seen Others Make 167

12.6.1 Ivory Tower 167

12.6.2 Failing to Get Technical and Hands-On 167

12.6.3 Not Being Honest and Open 168

Conclusion 168

PART IV   COMPLIANCE, STANDARDS, AND FRAMEWORKS 169

Chapter 13   Establishing IT Controls and Compliance 171

Goals of Establishing IT Controls and Compliance 172

13.1 Why Are IT Controls and Compliance Important? 173

13.2 How Do I Get Started? 173

13.3 Understanding IT Controls and Compliance 174

    13.3.1 Sarbanes-Oxley Act of 2002 174

    13.3.2 Management Assessment of Internal Controls 174

    13.3.3 Committee of Sponsoring Organizations 175

    13.3.4 Cobit as a Framework for IT Controls 176

    13.3.5 What Does It Mean to Attest to And Report
            on the Assessment Made by the Management? 176

    13.3.6 Health Insurance Portability and Accountability
            Act of 1996 177

    13.3.7 When the GAO Comes Knocking 177

    13.3.8 Results of the Audit 178

    13.3.9 GAO Reports on NARA's Configuration
            Management Practices 179

    13.3.10 ERA Configuration Management Plan 179

    13.3.11 Areas for Improvement 180

    13.3.12 Understanding the Results of the Audit 180

    13.3.13 Office of the Comptroller of the Currency 181

13.4 Essential Compliance Requirements 181

    13.4.1 Providing Traceability of Requirements to
            Releases 182

    13.4.2 Production Separation of Controls 182

13.5 The Moral Argument for Supporting CM Best Practices 182

13.6 Improving Quality and Productivity Through Compliance . 183

13.7 Conducting a CM Assessment 183

    13.7.1 Assessment First Steps 184

    13.7.2 Listen First Regardless of How Bad the
            Situation Appears 184

Conclusion 185

Chapter 14   Industry Standards and Frameworks 187

Goals of Using Industry Standards and Frameworks 188

14.1 Why Are Standards and Frameworks Important? 188

14.2 How Do I Get Started? 189

14.3 Terminology Required 189

    14.3.1 Configuration Item 189

    14.3.2 Configuration Identification 190

    14.3.3 Configuration Control 190

    14.3.4 Interface Control 190

    14.3.5 Configuration Status Accounting 191

    14.3.6 Configuration Audit 191

    14.3.7 Subcontractor/Vendor Control 192

    14.3.8 Conformance Versus Noncompliance 192

14.4 Applying These Terms to the Standards and Frameworks .. 193

14.5 Industry Standards 193

    14.5.1 IEEE 828—Standard for Software Configuration
Management Plans 193

    14.5.2 ISO 10007—Quality Management Systems—
Guidelines for Configuration Management 195

    14.5.3 ANSI/ITAA EIA-649-A—National Consensus
Standard for Configuration Management 196

    14.5.4 ISO/IEC/IEEE 12207 and 15288 196

14.6 Industry Frameworks 196

    14.6.1 ISACA Cobit 197

    14.6.2 CMM/CMMI 207

    14.6.3 itSMF's ITIL Framework 208

    14.6.4 SWEBOK 214

    14.6.5 Open Unified Process (OpenUP) 215

    14.6.6 Agile/SCRUM 216

Conclusion 217

Index **219**

Preface

Configuration management (CM) plays a critical role in any technology development effort. I have been involved with implementing and supporting CM for more than 25 years, and much of what I am about to discuss comes directly from my own personal experience. I have implemented and supported each of these CM practices, often with the agreement that I could be woken in the middle of the night if my processes/automation did not work as expected. As an instructor, I have taught industry-strength CM tools to 900+ technology professionals (again with the offer that they got my home phone number upon successfully completing my class). My colleagues and students have consistently indicated that my passion and love for this discipline has always been abundantly clear. It is my view that configuration management consists of six functional areas:

1. Source code management

2. Build engineering

3. Environment configuration

4. Change control

5. Release engineering

6. Deployment

I have searched for, but never found, any single book (or even a series of books) that covered all of these functional areas. Most CM books are either too narrowly focused on one key area (such as building code with Ant) or so "ivory tower" that they did not give me enough information on how to really implement these functions in a practical real-world environment. It's nice to point out the need to "maintain control of all configuration items," but unless you tell me exactly how to do that in a practical and realistic way, the advice is not truly usable. It is my intent both to cast a wide net on the CM practices that you need to understand and to provide enough detail so that you know not only what each CM function entails, but, just as important, *how* to implement each of the CM functions. I expect that my readers will hold me to that commitment. The URL of our supporting website is http://cmbestpractices.com.

The Traditional Definition of Configuration Management

Configuration management, or in this context, software configuration management (SCM), has a traditional definition consisting of four specific functions:

1. Configuration identification

2. Change control

3. Status accounting

4. Configuration audit

These functions have long been described in industry standards and frameworks and obviously viewed as essential to any valid configuration management effort. Although I agree completely that these functions are correct and essential, I find their terminology to be difficult for many technology professionals to understand and appreciate. In this book, I discuss the traditional CM functions, and I suggest a framework for understanding and implementing configuration management in a way that I believe reflects current industry practices. Specifically, I show the relationship between the four classic functions and the six functions of source code management, build engineering, environment configuration, change control, release engineering, and deployment, which I believe more closely reflects the way that CM is actually done on a day-to-day basis. This is an important focus of my efforts to make configuration management best practices more approachable and practical for technology professionals to enjoy as part of their own process-improvement efforts.

Terminology and CM

Configuration management, like many other disciplines, suffers from the use of confusing terminology. I am not going to solve that problem in this book, but I do endeavor to at least not make the situation worse. The acronym SCM has been used to refer to both source code management and, more recently, software configuration management. One of my most knowledgeable colleagues has prevailed upon me to not make the situation worse, so I use the SCM acronym only to refer to the broader software configuration management, which is a specialization of configuration management (as opposed to hardware configuration management discussed in Chapter 8, "Hardware Configuration Management"). Similarly, the acronym CI is used to refer to both configuration items and continuous integration. CM terminology can be quite confusing. I can't do much about the confusion caused by this dual use of CI as an acronym, as it is pervasive, but I do what I can to be as clear as possible. There are similar challenges with regard to the terms configuration control and release management. I do my best to present a clear explanation of these terms and, more importantly, explain how to implement these practices in a real-world setting. Once again, I hope that you will join me online if you want to discuss the use of these terms as well as their evolution. This is an exciting time for configuration management because many technology professionals are recognizing that CM impacts everything from IT service management (ITSM) to the entire Agile ALM. Whenever possible, I endeavor to use the definitions in the IEEE's SEVOCAB: Software and Systems Engineering Vocabulary, which, at the time of this writing, can be found at www.computer.org/sevocab.

Why I Love CM

I love CM because it is a creative and exciting endeavor that can significantly add value by improving quality and productivity in any technology project. Not only do I discuss what I have learned, but I also relate the combined experience of thousands of CM experts who have kindly shared their own expertise and best practices with me over the years that I have been engaged in this work. I owe each of these fine colleagues a debt of gratitude for all that they have shared with me. I have written and published many articles on configuration management and thoroughly enjoyed the feedback that I have received (especially when those supplying it disagreed with me and offered other practical approaches to solving thorny CM-related problems). I anticipate that this book will also generate considerable interaction with my colleagues, especially through the supporting http://cmbestpractices.com website that I have created. Please visit this website for up-to-date information on the topics that we discuss in this book as well as to give me feedback about your own experiences with implementing configuration management.

Why I Wrote This Book

I wrote this book to share my expertise and experience with implementing all aspects of CM in realistic business, engineering, and government environments.

I hope that you find this information to be practical, comprehensive, and helpful in implementing CM in a variety of real-world situations.

Some topics in CM are evolving so quickly that writing a book on them would be a daunting task. For example, as I write this Preface, my "day job" is to implement IBM's latest Application Lifecycle Management (ALM) solution, which includes a brand new source code management and automated workflow solution. Therefore, for this book, I discuss how to select a CM tool in only general terms, but restrict tool-specific comments to my supporting website (http:// cmbestpractices.com/tools) so that the information can be kept current and accurate. I also hope that you hold me accountable for the accuracy of every word that I write because I have very strong personal views that CM is essential on a moral, ethical, and theological basis. Although CM is not my "religion," doing honest and high-quality work is certainly part of my religious belief system. I also view spreading CM best practices as being a model for good corporate citizenship. I have been very active in the virtual community that develops and supports configuration management as well as other aspects of application development. On any given day, you can see technology professionals providing each other with substantial assistance without regard for whether they work for competing organizations. The community is truly culturally diverse, multilingual, and universal in its respect for and acceptance of others. I am proud to be part of this work and wish my efforts to promote CM best practices to be part of a wider movement to promote effective IT controls, responsible business leadership, and good corporate citizenship resulting in greater services and value for everyone who shares this increasingly tiny world that we live in. To say this in another way, I believe that every government agency, financial services firm (including banks, hedge funds, and insurance firms), along with firms that are in the medical, pharmaceutical, and defense (and every other) industry should be required to implement proper IT controls to protect the public who rely on their services as well as shareholder value. I wrote this book, in part, to help transition this effort from being a burden to instead being a journey in improving productivity and quality. It is my belief that implementing IT controls, including CM best practices, in a pragmatic way should result in higher profitability for the members of the firms, their shareholders, and the public which depends upon their services.

Classroom Materials

Students and college professors are also welcome to contact us with regard to supporting materials (such as lecture slides, course curriculum, etc.) for the classroom. Where feasible, it is our intent to offer to visit and lecture in educational settings that adopt this book for classroom instruction purposes. Please contact Leslie Sachs who will coordinate these efforts.

Who Should Read This Book

Technology professionals including development managers, system architects, developers, systems engineers, hardware engineers, quality assurance, quality engineering, operations engineers, and technology project managers will all benefit from the information in this book. CTOs, IT auditors, and corporate managers will especially enjoy the sections on establishing IT controls and compliance. Whether you are an Agile enthusiast or working with a classic waterfall lifecycle, this book will help you get your job done better. CM is all about good corporate citizenship. The news media love to report instances of corporate greed and incompetence among those who have a responsibility for providing and maintaining technology for the public good. CM best practices help ensure that the global economy runs smoothly, ATMs work correctly, air traffic control systems remain online, and so on. If you want your technology development efforts to be more efficient and to yield higher-quality products, this book is for you.

How to Read This Book

You should at least skim the Introduction because it will give you an overview of the CM functions and their overall linkages. You should also feel free to skip to the area that you need help with next. I have endeavored to write each chapter so that it can be read and used separately. In practice, this has often been how I implemented CM. For example, I have often skipped directly to solving the most urgent problems (as indicated by the customer) without being rigid about the order of implementing CM functions. That said, there are some dependencies, and I do my best to describe them, too.

How This Book Is Organized

This book is organized into 14 chapters divided into four parts. Part I consists of six chapters covering source code management, build engineering, change control, environment configuration, release engineering, and deployment. Part II covers architecture and hardware CM, and Part III covers the essential people issues that you need to know to effectively implement CM best practices. Part IV covers compliance and the standards (such as IEEE, ISO, EIA) and frameworks (such as ITIL, Cobit, CMMI) needed to establish effective IT controls. What follows in the next section is a short description of each chapter.

Part I: The Core CM Best Practices Framework

Six chapters make up the core CM best practices framework.

Chapter 1: Source Code Management

Source code management is an essential starting point for any configuration management function. In this chapter, we discuss the requirements for an effective source code management effort and some of the core concepts. In source code management, you make sure that you know where all the artifacts needed by your application are located and that they are all properly identified and can be managed effectively. If we were baking a cake, then source code management would help you ensure that you have all the correct ingredients on hand and in the proper amount.

Chapter 2: Build Engineering

Build engineering includes the compilation of all the configuration items that go into release. Your build engineering practices need to be efficient, reliable, and repeatable. Build engineering also includes procedures for building in the essential version IDs that are required for configuration identification. Build engineering involves mixing the batter and baking the cake itself.

Chapter 3: Environment Configuration

Environment configuration involves handling the compile and runtime changes necessary for the promotion of code from development to QA to production. It also includes the configuration and management of the requirements. Environment configuration ensures that you have the shelf ready to show off the great cake that you baked.

Chapter 4: Change Control

There are seven functions in change control: evaluating requests for change, gatekeeping (such as promotion), configuration control, emergency change control, process changes, advising on the downstream impact of a potential change, and senior management oversite of change control. Change control decides when the cake is baked and ready to be taken from the oven and sent to the happy person who will enjoy the cake.

Chapter 5: Release Management

Release management involves packaging the configuration items into components that can be reliably promoted and deployed as needed. Release management is effectively putting your cake into the nice box with the open window so that others can see and appreciate the fine work that you have done.

Chapter 6: Deployment

Deployment should be a narrowly defined function of promoting the prepackaged release to QA or production as needed. This is effectively putting your cake on the truck to be delivered to your consumers. (Make sure that you get my home address correct for delivery.)

This completes the first part of the book, covering what I view as being the essential core CM competencies necessary for any CM function. I am really getting hungry now, so I have to stop using a cake as a metaphor for CM. The rest of the chapters make up the eight supporting functions that are also important for the implementation of an effective CM effort.

Part II: Architecture and Hardware CM

Architecture and hardware also are candidates for CM.

Chapter 7: Architecting Your Application for CM

This is an often-overlooked aspect of configuration management and involves recognizing the interrelationship between application architecture and configuration management. The essential nature of CM is the same whether you are implementing it on a mainframe or your favorite handheld device. But the actual procedures will vary significantly based on the architecture of your application. So, implementing CM on a WINTEL platform may be very different from on a UNIX/Linux platform using Java SOA or C++. This chapter is about understanding that relationship. This chapter is also about how CM helps implement excellent architecture. CM best practices help your team to develop excellent application and systems architecture.

Chapter 8: Hardware Configuration Management

I need to write an entire book on hardware configuration management. There just isn't enough recognition of its value and importance in the CM field. I have been frequently asked to write about hardware CM. This chapter begins what I am sure will be a longer journey.

Part III: The People Side of CM

You can't afford to ignore the people side of any business or organizational endeavor. CM is no different. I have been involved and observed many successful efforts to implement CM best practices. In the situations where the results were less than acceptable or even truly a failure, it was almost always due to people issues. This chapter gives you very practical advice from real world experiences on how to deal with the people side of CM. This is a very important part of the book for your success.

Chapter 9: Rightsizing Your Processes

My whole career has been focused on implementing process improvement. I have learned that too much process is just as bad as not enough. This chapter is about finding the right balance and implementing *just enough* process to get the job done.

Chapter 10: Overcoming Resistance to Change

Having a great process does not help anyone if you can't get your team to accept the process and actually start working in a new and better way. This chapter is about overcoming resistance to change and getting the team to accept and enjoy the new way of doing things.

Chapter 11: Personality and CM: A Psychologist Looks at the Workplace

Leslie Sachs takes the lead in this chapter as she describes the essential people skills that you need to be effective in implementing CM best practices. I get scared when I read Leslie's work because she seems to always be eavesdropping on my conversations. Read this chapter if working with people is important to you.

Chapter 12: Learning From Mistakes That I Have Made

I have made lots of mistakes in my career. I have achieved a lot, yet I have also failed to achieve as much as I had hoped. But I have learned a lot from my own mistakes, and this chapter is my effort to share some of my personal improvement efforts to learn from my own mistakes and shortcomings. This chapter could have been its own book or perhaps the size of a small encyclopedia.

Part IV: Compliance, Standards, and Frameworks

The book ends with the issues involved in establishing IT controls, complying with regulations, and the use of industry standards and frameworks. Second only to the people side of CM, understanding industry standards and frameworks is one of the most *powerful* capabilities that you need to master to successfully implement CM best practices. This information will also help you overcome resistance to change because you will rightly be able to explain what thousands (or perhaps hundreds of thousands) of other technology professionals have reviewed, debated and determined to be the official accepted industry best practices.

Chapter 13: Establishing IT Controls and Compliance

Establishing IT controls and compliance is one of my own favorite topics. I like to focus on using these efforts to improve quality and productivity while you are also getting ready to pass your audit. IT controls and compliance is a really critical topic for many organizations, and I expect that if you need to meet industry regulations, you will find this information to be extremely valuable.

Chapter 14: Industry Standards and Frameworks

I strongly advocate the use of industry standards and frameworks, but I also believe that much of what has been previously written is difficult to understand and even more difficult to implement. I believe that those of us involved with creating industry standards and frameworks need to write more practical material on how to actually implement standards and frameworks in a realistic and pragmatic way. My focus, in this chapter, is on describing my own personal journey with implementing process improvement using the guidance described in standards and frameworks along with the essential skills of tailoring, harmonization, and operationalizing the published guidance. This might be the most important chapter in the book, and I hope that you will give me your feedback on your efforts to embrace and implement industry standards and frameworks.

Overall, I think that you want to focus on the first part of this book to understand the core CM best practices and then read the remaining chapters of this book in whatever order you choose to cover the topics that you have an immediate need for implementing within your organization.

Acknowledgments

A lot of people have helped me write this book. First, the Aiello family editing team has been amazing. We are very much like a mom-and-pop candy store except that we write technical journals. My assistant editors have included my sons Shmuel and Dovid (also our webmaster); Massimo, whose ability to see things differently helped me to perceive concepts in new and different ways (not to mention he provided his fresh-baked pizza); my daughter Esther, whose creativity helped us in so many ways; and my youngest princess, Devora, whose hugs and cuddling (not to mention backrubs) always kept me focused on getting the work done. Finally, Leslie, my lifelong partner, proved that we could be colleagues on multiple levels.

There are many colleagues whom I should acknowledge for sharing their expertise and experience. Leading the list would certainly be my colleagues on the IEEE CM Planning working group, starting with our chairperson, Chuck Walrad, and the members of the working group who have taught me so much about CM (and tolerated my diatribes about how we need to write more clearly), including Diego Pamio, Alastair Walker, Darrel Strom, Ranata Johnson, and Mike Smith. I have also learned a great deal about standards from all of my colleagues and mentors on the S2ESC board, including James Moore, Carl Singer, and David Schulz. Equally helpful were my numerous colleagues on CM Crossroads, including Steve Berczuk, Mario Moreira, Ben Weatherall, and of course, Patrick Egan, with whom I have worked on the *CM Journal* and *CM Crossroads* for so many years. The folks at Addison-Wesley were amazing, starting with my development editor, Chris Zahn, along with Chris Guizikowski and Raina Chrobak. Early in my career, I was privileged to work with Dr. Marianne Bays (who believed me when I suggested that software engineering and industrial psychology were a good mix). There are many more colleagues deserving of my appreciation, and I hope that you will come to my website (http://cmbestpractices.com) to enjoy their articles and contributions.

—Bob Aiello
Bob.Aiello@ieee.org
www.linkedin.com/in/BobAiello

About the Authors

Bob Aiello is the editor-in-chief for CM Crossroads and a consultant specializing in software process improvement, including software configuration and release management. Mr. Aiello has more than 25 years of experience as a technical manager in several top NYC financial services firms where he had companywide responsibility for CM, often providing hands-on technical support for enterprise source code management tools, SOX/Cobit compliance, build engineering, continuous integration, and automated application deployment. Bob is the vice chair of the IEEE 828 Standards working group (CM Planning) and is a member of the IEEE Software and Systems Engineering Standards Committee (S2ESC) management board. He is a longstanding member of the steering committee of the NYC Software Process Improvement Network (CitySPIN), where he has served as the chair of the CM SIG. Mr. Aiello holds a master's degree in industrial psychology from NYU and a bachelor's degree in computer science and math from Hofstra University. You may contact Mr. Aiello at Bob.Aiello@ieee.org or link with him at www.linkedin.com/in/bobaiello.

Leslie Sachs is the COO of Yellow Spider, Inc. (http://yellowspiderinc.com) which specializes in providing CM-related consulting services that are aligned with the practices described in this book. Leslie also writes about applying personality to technology endeavors in her column titled *Personality Matters*. A New York State Certified School Psychologist with more than 20 years of experience, Ms. Sachs has worked in a variety of clinical and business settings where she has provided many effective interventions designed to improve the social and educational functioning of both individuals and groups. Ms. Sachs has a Masters of Science degree in school and community psychology from Pace University and interned in Bellevue Hospital's famed Psychiatric Center in NYC. A firm believer in the uniqueness of every individual, she has recently done advanced training with Mel Levine's *All Kinds of Minds* Institute. She may be reached at LeslieASachs@gmail.com, or you can link with her at www.linkedin.com/in/lesliesachs.

Introduction

In this Introduction, I briefly introduce configuration management (CM) and some basic information on how you might approach implementing CM best practices. It is common for organizations to focus on implementing only a very narrow functional area to address a specific goal or problem. In practice, this might be a perfectly fine thing to do, but it is also important to understand how each functional area of CM impacts the other. It has been my personal experience that CM consists of six functional areas, which I will describe below and throughout this book. Implementing good CM is not easy and requires a considerable amount of hard work. This introduction will help us start our journey.

Configuration Management Consists of Six Functional Areas

The six core functional areas of CM are as follows:

1. Source code management

2. Build engineering

3. Environment configuration

4. Change control

5. Release engineering

6. Deployment

Source code management involves the control of every piece of computer code, including source, configuration files, binaries, and all compile and runtime dependencies. We usually refer to all these artifacts as configuration items (CIs).[1]

The main goal of source code management is to effectively safeguard all the project resources. I always called this locking down the code. Source code

---

[1] Please don't be confused by the fact that we will refer to continuous integration (CI) with the same acronym.

management also involves creating a permanent record of specific milestones in the development process. This is known as *baselining* your code, and it is a critical CM function. Source code management also involves creating code variants to successfully manage parallel development, bugfixes, and globally distributed development. We discuss how to assess your source code management requirements and plan interventions to improve your source code management practices. We also look at how source code management is often overengineered, resulting in unnecessary complexity and automation that does not work reliably.

Build engineering involves the selection of a specific variant in the code (e.g., baseline) to reliably compile, link, and package code components. Build engineering adds value by providing a repeatable process and the management of (often complex) compile dependencies. We discuss how to implement effective build engineering to help improve your team's development process. We also discuss the value of continuous integration (CI) versus the (usually) less-rigorous *nightly build*.

Environment configuration involves managing the compile and runtime dependencies that can often change as code is promoted from development to test to production. Environment configuration also involves managing the environments themselves often designated as development, test, integration and production.

There are different types of change control. The most commonly implemented change control practice is essentially a "gatekeeping" function that prevents unauthorized releases from being promoted into production (or QA for that matter). There is also *a priori* change control, whereby intended changes, to the code, are reviewed (before they are made) and permission granted (or denied) to make the proposed changes. We discuss when *a priori change control* is commonly used and when it is instead left to the project or development manager as an implicit task. We also discuss the other types of change control that are commonly seen in organizations. In all, I define seven different types of change control. I also describe how they are commonly used in practice.

Release engineering involves the packaging and identification of all the components built in the build engineering function. This is somewhat different in a corporate IT function versus a software vendor. We initially focus on corporate release management in a corporate IT environment, and then discuss how this differs slightly for a software vendor (e.g., deploying packaged releases to customers). Deployment involves the staging and promotion of packaged releases and, in an IT organization, is usually performed by the operations team. Deployment also involves the monitoring of the production (and QA) environments to confirm that there are no unauthorized changes. Deployment for a software vendor usually refers to delivering the packaged release to a customer along with the requirement to manage updates and patches as needed.

All of these functions are part of a comprehensive discipline that is known as configuration management (CM). Software configuration management is a specialization of CM. Equally important and frequently overlooked is hardware CM, which we discuss in Chapter 8, "Hardware Configuration Management."

Understanding the Linkages

The six functional areas of configuration management impact each other in many ways. Build engineering is almost impossible to do well without effective source code management practices. Release management just won't happen if your releases are not built correctly, especially in terms of identifying all configuration items, as we describe in Chapter 2, "Build Engineering." Environment configuration impacts build engineering, release management, and deployment. Of course, deployment is almost impossible if the releases are not packaged correctly. All of these functional areas are impacted by change control best practices. For example, an effective change control board (CCB) will review the CM plan and release management automation before giving permission for the release to be approved. We discuss change control best practices in Chapter 4, "Change Control," including after-action reviews to ascertain whether mistakes could be avoided by improving any of these configuration management best practices.

The Traditional View of Configuration Management

My colleagues rightly remind me that configuration management is defined as follows:

- Configuration identification

- Change control

- Status accounting

- Configuration audit

They are absolutely correct, and I am not changing the substance of configuration management, but I believe that the terminology used in traditional CM is less than clear and, in this book, I seek to make the terminology that describes configuration management *compelling*. Generally, I jab back by challenging them to give me a clear and sensible definition for *status accounting*. In my opinion, the terms *configuration identification* and *configuration audits* are not much more intuitive. On the other hand, most developers have a basic idea of what's involved with source code management, build engineering, and release management. Let's bridge the gap with the traditional terminology and then dive deeper into CM.

Configuration identification refers to providing a specific and unique identity to each artifact for the purposes of tracking configuration items (e.g., source code, binaries, documents, config files). I have an entire chapter on change control, which I define as being composed of seven functions. *Status accounting* (my least favorite term) refers to tracking the status of a configuration item throughout its lifecycle. *Configuration audits* refer to being able to inspect and identify the exact version of any configuration item. In my opinion, CM experts need to make this terminology easier to understand and use on a day-to-day basis.

For example, configuration identification is actually accomplished by naming the components, streams, and subdirectories (folders) in your source code management tool in a logical and intuitive way. Build engineering best practices enable you to embed version IDs in binary configuration items (it also facilitates configuration audits), and many build tools, such as Maven, help you to organize your code in a logical and sensible way. Release management also involves configuration identification in that you must name your release packages in a clear and consistent way.

Status accounting involves tracking the status of a configuration item throughout its lifecycle. In practice, many source code management solutions are integrated with requirements and defect tracking systems (if not already built in) so that you can easily trace the evolution of a component from its requirement (or perhaps defect record) all the way through to its deployment. Configuration audit mean that you know exactly which version of the code is running in production (or QA). Unfortunately, many technology professionals cannot identify the exact version of a binary configuration item after the code leaves the source code management tool. In my world, you need to be able to tell me the *exact* version of the code that is running in production (or QA) and be able to retrieve the *exact* version of the source code used to build it so that you can also create a sandbox (in a source code management tool) and make a small change to the code—without *any* chance of the code regressing due to the wrong version of a header file or other dependency. If you can't do that today, you have come to the right place!

The first six chapters of the book make up Part I, "The Core CM Best Practices Framework," which describes the core functions in configuration management. I describe how the six core functions relate to the traditional view of CM. I also cover a number of other essential topics in Chapters 7 through 14, which are presented in Parts II through IV. Here is a description of these sections.

The second part of the book, Part II, "Architecture and Hardware CM," deals with understanding the impact of architecture on CM best practices and the impact of CM on architecture itself. In Chapter 8, we discuss hardware CM, which should really be a book on its own.

Part III, "The People Side of CM," covers the essential "people" issues that you need to understand to be effective in implementing CM best practices. Many process improvement efforts fail because these issues are often overlooked. The chapters in this section are as follows:

- Chapter 9, "Rightsizing Your Processes"

- Chapter 10, "Overcoming Resistance to Change"

- Chapter 11, "Personality and CM: A Psychologist Looks at the Workplace"

- Chapter 12, "Learning From Mistakes That I Have Made"

Part IV, "Compliance, Standards, and Frameworks," is the last section of this book and covers establishing IT controls and issues related to compliance, with Chapter 14 explaining the standards and frameworks that are essential for you to know to establish CM best practices:

- Chapter 13, "Establishing IT Controls and Compliance"

- Chapter 14, "Industry Standards and Frameworks"

The Goals of Good CM

I believe that there are three basic goals that any CM effort must accomplish. The first is that all code that has been deployed to production (or QA) must be easily identifiable. In CM terminology, we call this a *configuration audit*. That means that you can *easily* confirm that you know the exact versions of all configuration items in production (with absolute certainty). The second goal is that you can retrieve the exact version of all source code (and other configuration items) used to create that release (without having to resort to "heroic" efforts). Finally, you must be able to create a workspace (often called a sandbox) to make a small "bugfix" without *any* chance of the code regressing due to the wrong version of a header file (or other dependency). If you can't do these three things, your CM practices need some improvement. The good news is that we describe exactly how to accomplish these goals in practical and realistic terms.

PART I

The Core CM Best Practices Framework

Chapter 1

Source Code Management

Chapter Overview

1.1 Why Is Source Code Management Important?   6

1.2 Where Do I Start?   7

1.3 Source Code Management Core Concepts   9

1.4 Defect and Requirements Tracking   16

1.5 Managing the Globally Distributed Development Team   17

1.6 Tools Selection   19

1.7 Recognizing the Cost of Quality (and Total Cost of
    Ownership)   23

1.8 Training   24

1.9 Defining the Usage Model   25

1.10 Time to Implement and Risks to Success   26

1.11 Establishing Your Support Process   26

1.12 Advanced Features and Empowering Your Users   27

Source code management is the discipline of safeguarding all the artifacts that are created to develop your system. Source code management is a key function in configuration management (CM) and directly impacts the productivity of your team and the quality of the product being developed. Unfortunately, many organizations overlook the importance of establishing an effective source code management function to implement and support source code management

3

tools and processes. You do not want to make this mistake, and in this chapter, I help you get started in the right direction with source code management. I have enjoyed having companywide responsibility for source code management in several large globally distributed organizations. This meant that I had to guarantee that the firm never lost any source code once it was part of a release to production (or even QA). Source code management needs to be approached in a flexible and creative way. One size does *not* necessarily fit all, and I have often implemented source code management differently for some development teams than others. But I always focused on meeting the same essential goals as discussed below. I would also say that source code management provides the foundation for the other disciplines of configuration management, especially build engineering, release management, and deployment.

This chapter provides an overview of the many aspects of source code management, including goals, principles, and essential concepts that you need to understand. It will serve to give you a framework from which to understand the rest of the chapters, because, most of the other CM-related functions, including build engineering, release management, and deployment, use the source code repository as a basis for their work. I provide a number of examples from my own experience (and the experiences of my colleagues), and then I discuss where to start with implementing source code management, including winning support from senior management. Next, we focus on the core concepts necessary to understand source code management, starting with baselines and creating your own CM "time machine." Tightly coupled with source code management is defect and requirements tracking, which usually needs to be integrated with the source code management tools and processes. Next, we discuss globally distributed development, which is made possible by source code management. Whether you have a large or small team, you need to consider which tools are appropriate to support your organization. I give you some general guidelines on how to pick the right source code management tool along with guidance on extending your tools through APIs, along with a word of caution about over-engineering your source code management solution. You also need to recognize that quality may be "free," but you still have to fund it, and you must especially consider your training needs. Closely related is defining a usage model that fits your requirements. Next, we discuss how to evaluate risks to the successful implementation of source code management and how to establish a source code management support process. Finally, I share some thoughts on handling your power users. (Hint: Deputize them and cheer them on!)

Terminology and Source Code Management

In an early draft of this book, I used the acronym SCM to refer to source code management and, alternatively, software configuration management.[1]

The terms *source code management* and *software configuration management* (SCM) are obviously not the same because the latter includes much more than the management of source code. Nonetheless, I need to be able to write about source code management in a clear and consistent way without making the material overly dry and boring. Some of my real-life stories about stopping the world economy (with the wrong version of a shell script) and release management for life support systems should help. But for the sake of readability, I refer to source code management as the management of source code or just code management. I hesitate to use the term *version control* in this context because version control has traditionally been used to describe source code repositories that had limited functionality. I usually think of the older CVS, RCS, and SCCS when discussing version control. Today's robust source code management solutions have full process automation, extensive metadata, and powerful variant management using complex branching/streams. So, I refer to source code management as management of source code or just simply code management in an effort to make this essential material as readable as possible.

Goals of Source Code Management

Good source code management starts with making certain that all of your source code is safely locked down and no important source code (or any other configuration item) is lost. That sounds fairly simple, but many of us recall the massive Y2K efforts that uncovered a remarkable number of critical systems that had been running in production for years without anyone knowing where the source code was located. In some cases, we went searching for the correct version of Cobol copybooks; in other cases, we had to rewrite the entire system from scratch (which was often the right choice anyway). My goal in implementing good source code management is to absolutely guarantee that source code can *never* be lost.

Another important goal of effective code management is to help improve the productivity of your entire team. Effective source code management means that you can manage more than one line of code development at the same time. It also means that you can improve the quality of your code in many ways, including helping to implement automated testing on both a unit and systems level. This may include building variants of the code to support the use of test tools and instrumenting the code for performance testing, code analysis (e.g. static, dynamic, etc.) or automated regression testing. One of the most important goals

---

[1] When I teach configuration management, I often call source code management "little SCM" and software configuration management "big SCM." I have similar descriptions for CM and RM.

of code management is to provide complete traceability so that you know exactly who changed your code and are able to, if necessary, back out the change.

Principles of Source Code Management

The principles of source code management can be summarized as follows:

- Code is locked down and can never be lost.

- Code is baselined, marking a specific milestone or other point in time.

- Managing variants in the code should be easy with proper branching.

- Code changed on a branch (variant) can be merged back onto the main trunk (or another variant).

- Source code management processes are repeatable, agile and lean.

- Source code management provides traceability and tracking of all changes.

- Source code management best practices help improve productivity and quality.

1.1 Why Is Source Code Management Important?

Source code management is important because you need to have all of your assets secured and available in a controlled and reliable repository. Code management gives you the tools and processes to manage your source code and all the resulting artifacts that make up your system. In CM terminology, we call these things configuration items (CIs). All development teams need to be able to identify and control configuration items or you just won't get the work done. Source code management is usually the place where organizations begin their journey to implement configuration management. Good source code management allows you to handle long-term development along with quick emergency fixes. Agile and Lean source code management is important because it will lay the foundation for many other related activities that rely upon effective source code management practices. Another matter to consider is that, if you don't have effective (repeatable) source code management processes in place, bad things can happen, including major outages, unnecessary defects, and lots of wasted time doing the same work over again.

When Bad Things Happen

My phone rings when bad things happen. I've realized that people don't call when everything is working fine. I am called when people need help because they have a problem. I also frequently get called right after a huge incident resulting in source code being lost or some other major problem. This might just be the *best* part of my job, because I get to see my efforts result in a significant positive impact on the software development effort. The first step is to understand why bad things can happen. Source code is often lost because of any of the following reasons:

- Nonexistent source code management tools and process.

- Unreliable tools have been implemented.

- Users are not trained, so even the best tools can't help them.

- Poor to nonexistent release and deployment process.

- Complex branching leads to user error.

- Poor communication and poor teamwork.

- Too many moving parts and complexity.

- Source code management tools are not supported by effective administrative procedures.

I have dealt with each of these problems in large-scale (global) environments. I have worked in environments where source code management problems could result in losing millions of dollars or even catastrophic incidents, like planes flying into each other. Although many of my colleagues appreciate the value of good source code management, it is also true that some do not. It's common for even seasoned technology professionals to be completely ignorant of source code management best practices. I have worked in a number of large financial services firms where I had company-wide responsibility for implementing source code management. Although it's my job to promote best practices as the CM evangelist, it is often a challenge to get senior management to recognize and support my efforts.

1.2 Where Do I Start?

The best place to get started with implementing the management of source code is to identify your own goals and requirements for a source code management function. I have worked in organizations where this really had to be a major companywide effort and other places where it was a part of their culture and source code management pretty much ran itself. Most organizations begin this journey by assessing their existing practices for securing their code and managing changes, baselines, and releases, including bugfixes. When you conduct your own assessment, make sure that you ask for both the existing practices that work well along with areas that might be improved. Taking a balanced approach will help you avoid resistance and help your team feel comfortable examining their own strengths and weaknesses. I also recommend starting with an approach that is both agile and lean. For example, only implement just enough process for you to get the job done without any extra steps and build in the ability (perhaps requiring approval from an SEPG as discussed in Chapter 4, "Change Control") to change your processes as needed to support both quality and productivity. Verbose rigid source code management processes may sound nice on paper, but it has been my experience that they do not work in the real world and everyone (including me) will do anything to get around them. Start with only the minimum steps necessary to get the job done. You can always add another control (such as a process step) if necessary. Whatever you identify as an opportunity for improvement, make sure that you gain support from senior management before you start. It has been my experience that lasting change occurs both from the bottom up as well as from the top down. The first thing that you need to know about the management of source code is how to create and manage a baseline of your code.

Winning Support from Senior Management

I recall initiating a meeting with my firm's CIO to ask for his support in implementing a source code management support function. Many of his direct reports were already extremely supportive of my efforts, but I wanted to gain his explicit and open support for improving the firm's source code management processes. This CIO called in one of his direct reports (a senior vice president [SVP]) and asked him to describe his division's current source code management practices. The SVP admitted that his team just stored their code in networked drives (some of which turned out to not even be regularly backed up). The SVP was the least CM savvy manager in the firm (which I realized later was exactly why the CIO had called him in). The SVP was then assigned to be my new manager and given the direction that "all the firm's assets had to be safeguarded." It was funny watching my new boss transform into a strong advocate for CM best practices. He was soon walking around the office saying, "Don't even think of telling me that you did not check in your code!" He also interfaced with other senior technology managers to make sure that I had their full cooperation.

Without support from senior management, your journey will be very difficult and most likely derailed before you even get started.

We describe strategies for winning support from the top down and the bottom up in Chapter 10, "Overcoming Resistance to Change."

1.3 Source Code Management Core Concepts

Source code management has its own terminology just like any other discipline. If you have been baffled by the techno-babble coming from your CM gurus, you have come to the right place, because we will get you up to speed with the core concepts required to understand today's source code management best practices.

1.3.1 Creating Baselines and Time Machines

Many developers think source code management just means you "check in" and "check out" your code using a source code management tool (a repository) that acts like a virtual library. That indeed is what most people think with some of the older version control systems (VCS) that were commonly used years ago. Today, most CM repositories do safeguard all of your changes with varying levels of reliability and functionality. Although simply checking your code into a source code management tool is indeed *necessary,* it would certainly not be *sufficient* as a CM process. The whole point of implementing effective source code management is to provide a virtual time machine that can always bring you back to a specific point in time when a particular slice of the code was a stable release. Identifying the exact versions of the code for a specific release is known as creating a **baseline** of the code. I have seen some authoritative resources that call this a *configuration of the code*. I respectfully disagree with using this particular term because it is misleading and, moreover, there is a much better usage of the term *configuration*, which we discuss in Chapter 3, "Environment Configuration."

Many CM tools call the operation of creating a baseline *tagging* or *labeling* the code. I have also seen some tools that used the term *snapshotting* the code when referring to multiple components that are interdependent. Baselines need to be **immutable**. That means you must have the capability to lock your tag or label down so it cannot be altered. This is important because you must always have a permanent record of the versions of the code that you used to build the release deployed to production (or QA). In addition to the tag (or label) for creating baselines, many people use an additional tag (often just called "PRODUCTION") to indicate the current release in production or perhaps the last good build. This tag is said to "float" with the current baseline of the code that is in production. This is a common (and convenient) practice, but it should never take the place of creating an immutable baseline to identify the code that has been released to production (or QA). Most good source code management tools implement tagging or labeling as *metadata*. **Metadata** is data about data. That means the source code management repository keeps a separate database of information about the code that you have checked into the repository. Metadata can include check-in comments, references to related defects (that triggered change to the code), and links documenting code merges. In fact, all changes to code should be tracked to a change request (CR) so that you know exactly why a particular change was made. Many source code management tools using metadata provide a rich set of features that provide the user with the history of all the changes to the code since the repository was created (often many years later). It is common to handle tracking changes with a "light" (and informal) process in the beginning of the development effort and then get increasingly strict as the application becomes ready for release, and of course, has to be maintained. This is a good example of applying Agile and Lean principles to CM. We discuss right sizing your processes in Chapter 9, "Rightsizing Your Processes." Some source code management tools use branches to create baselines, but that may not be the most optimal approach because code on branches is usually modifiable (unless you have some mechanism to "lock" the branch). The tools that use branches for baselining code usually do so because of performance limitations in the tool (branches take less time than tagging or labeling in these tools). Although some CM tools do try to use branches for baselining, that is not the most common usage of branches, which we discuss later in this chapter. First, we need to understand the "check-in"/"check-out" paradigm in source code management.

1.3.2 Reserved Versus Unreserved Checkouts

Some source code management solutions are based on a *reserved* checkout model. By default, the repository places a lock on the version of the file in the repository when the developer *checks out* the file for modification. Other source code management tools work based on an *unreserved* checkout model (sometimes called an *optimistic* checkout model). This means no lock is placed on the file, regardless of how many developers simultaneously check out and modify the code. I prefer using reserved checkout models because they proactively let me know whether I am trying to work on the same file as someone else. Optimistic checkout models might result in extra work in the form of merges that would have been avoided if the developers knew they were trying to change the same file at the same time. (Some newer source code management tools give you other ways to avoid this problem by providing more visibility into who else might be trying to change the same piece of code as you.) Another use of an unreserved checkout is to simply get a writeable copy of the file (that might never be checked back into the repository).

1.3.3 Sandboxes and Workspaces

Most source code management tools have a concept of a private sandbox or workspace. With a private sandbox, you can work in isolation and then check in your changes and, if necessary, merge your changes back onto a branch (often used just for code integration). It is a common practice for developers to have more than one workspace (or sandbox) to facilitate organizing work. Branching provides an effective way to organize work and improve programmer productivity.

> #### My First Sandbox
>
> When I am teaching CM and how to use source code management tools, I usually mention my first experiences playing in a sandbox as a child. Like lots of other boys, I liked to play with cowboys, army soldiers, and other action figures. My next-door neighbor was a young girl who would sometimes come over and play with her dolls in my sandbox. Inevitably, one of my cowboys would throw some sand around, and Suzy would run home complaining about the sand that I got on her doll (and of course, I would get into real trouble after that). I relate this humorous (and true) anecdote to illustrate that you should never let anyone else into your private sandbox—or else you will run into problems. Working in controlled isolation is one of the key features that helps improve productivity in software development. Another thing that improves productivity is well defined methods for handling variants in your code (such as bugfixes).

1.3.4 Variant Management (Branching)

One of the most important features of good source code management is the ability to make it easy to support multiple variants of the same codebase. You can easily support the same source code with a subset of the code being changed for a particular purpose. Creating variants in the code is often done through creating parallel lines of development, usually called *branches*. There can be many reasons for creating branches.

For example, you might have written some software to display an international clock. The basic functions of the clock are the same regardless of whether you are running the product on a Windows, Mac, Linux, or UNIX machine. But, for the clock to work, there might be a function that reads the (low-level) operating system clock. Therefore, one particular module is coded with operating systems calls that are customized for each operating system.

In practice, most of your common code would be on the main branch (often called the trunk/main), which, for this example, we will assume is on Linux. Then, you would create variants in the code (for example, Windows, Mac, and UNIX branches) that all include the same code (that is on the main branch) plus just the changes (for example, an operating system call to the system clock) needed for that variant. In this example, illustrated in Figure 1.1, the only code on each branch that is different is the system clock lookup function. In this way, you can effectively manage different variants in the code.

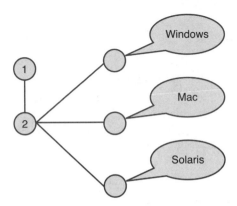

Figure 1.1 *The hello.c program is initially written for Linux. The program is then modified on OS-specific branches. Each is called a variant in the code (from the original Linux version).*

1.3.5 Copybranches Versus Deltas

Some source code management tools require all branches have a duplicate copy of every piece of code that was on the main branch (for example, trunk). This is known as creating a *copybranch*, as illustrated in Figure 1.2. Other tools use a sub-branch that holds only the code that has changed (usually called a *delta*). The sub-branch sits in front of the main branch. Branching can get a bit complicated, especially when people start using branches to manage every aspect of the development effort. One common practice is to use a sub-branch just to hold the changes related to fixing a bug. This is sometimes called *feature branching*.

1.3.6 How to Handle Bugfixes

Supporting bugfixes is also a common reason for branching. For example, suppose you are working on my favorite "Hello World" program, and you decide to also display a nice clock on the screen. (Think of this as including an extra feature that was not required for this release.) A few days after your code is sent to customers, you discover a bug whereby the time is wrong every third Tuesday of the month. We illustrate this scenario in Figure 1.3. Although a clock was never a requirement for this release, you cannot have a clock on the screen that is wrong!

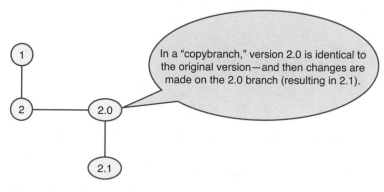

Figure 1.2 *Copybranches are a common way to organize variants in the code.*

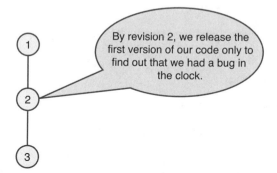

Figure 1.3 *In version 3, we started new work that won't be ready for months. So, how do we fix the bug?*

The rest of the program works just fine, so we have been asked to simply hide the clock so that customers never see the wrong time. (In the next major release of the product, we will have a completely different console that will include a brand new digital clock, so we just need a quick bugfix to hide the defective clock.) The problem is that we have already made more changes (in version 3) as part of the next release that is due in two months. In the meantime, we need to create a bugfix, as illustrated in Figure 1.4, that just includes the code for this temporary fix.

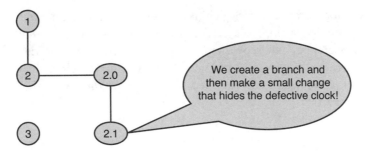

Figure 1.4 *The bugfix on 2.1 provides a quick patch (hiding the defective clock) to solve the immediate problem.*

1.3.7 Streams

Streams are another powerful way to manage variants in the code. Although similar to branches, streams often have powerful features that help to organize variants in the code. Here is a list of some of these features:

- Clear usage paradigm to model software and system architecture
- Hierarchical organization that is clear and intuitive
- Ability to control and flow changesets between streams (sometimes via the workspace)
- Snapshots create baseline of the code
- Ability to load a particular baseline of a component
- Ability to load a particular snapshot (such as baselines of one or more components)
- Strong security authorization and entitlements
- Visual diagram of stream topology helps with design and usage
- Complete history to facilitate traceability

For example, some source code management tools enable streams to be organized in a hierarchical way, which means you can have a parent stream (often used for integration) and child development streams. I know of one source code management tool that allows you to dynamically "reparent" a child stream. This useful feature allows you to work on components that are intended to interface with other components (that are not yet complete). You would create some code stubs (sometimes called "mocks") and put them into a temporary stream and then reparent your stream once the code has actually been implemented. Changes are promoted (sometimes called *delivered*) from the child stream to its parent. It is common for the child stream to first be refreshed (sometimes called *rebasing*) with the latest changes from the parent, before delivering a specific set of changes (sometimes called a *changeset*) up to the parent stream. It is a common best practice to rebase your private workspace, test to make sure that you can successfully build, and then deliver your changes to the parent stream. Streams usually have the concept of flow targets so that changesets can be copied (often promoted) from one stream to another. This is common when you have development streams that then feed an integration stream. It is common for the release management (RM) team to have its own streams that are secured so that the RMs can independently build, package, and release the code for deployment (often by the operations team). Without streams, you would typically have the extra work of integrating your source code management tool with a defect or change request tracking system to organize your branches, especially if you are trying to implement one feature per branch. In practice, streams offer a lot more functionality than branching. Streams can be complicated, but they are powerful and well worth the effort to learn and understand their usage.

1.3.8 Merging

Branching is a powerful feature that many developers find helps them do their work more efficiently. The problem that I have often seen is that developers forget that code that has been branched often needs to be merged back onto the main branch. For example, if you fix a bug on a branch, you probably also want that fix back on the main trunk (assuming it is relevant). Merging from a branch back to the main trunk is usually called an *inner* merge, as illustrated in Figure 1.5.

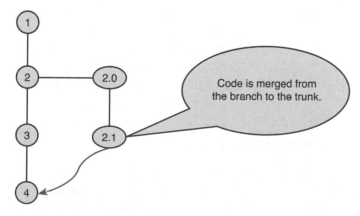

Figure 1.5 *Example of an inner merge.*

There are times when you want to merge code from the trunk back out to the bugfix branch. This is usually called an *outer* merge, and is illustrated in Figure 1.6.

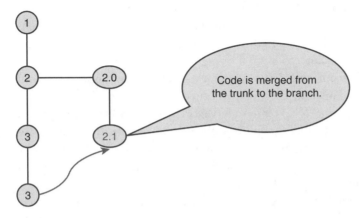

Figure 1.6 *Example of an outer merge.*

1.3.9 Changesets

Changesets are a convenient way to group one or more modifications to the codebase. Most source code management tools that support changesets enable you to apply or back out changesets as needed. Checking in a changeset (usually called *committing)* is usually an atomic transaction, which means that the entire set of changes gets successfully committed (or completely backed out if something goes wrong). I appreciate the value of changesets because I remember long evenings when trying to check in a thousand files that stopped halfway through the check-in. It was very painful and error prone to track down which files had been successfully checked in and which ones had to be reattempted again. Some source code management tools also provide the capability to manage the entire repository itself in terms of changesets, which makes it much easier to handle backing out a mistake if it happens. It's common to associate a changeset with either a defect or requirement, and we discuss how to do that in the next section.

1.4 Defect and Requirements Tracking

Tracking defects and requirements to changesets is a key feature that provides *traceability* into why a specific change was made (or to ascertain that a desired change was inadvertently missed). We discuss the importance of traceability in Chapter 13, "Establishing IT Controls and Compliance." Some CM tools have integrated defect or requirements tracking. Others require some additional programming to integrate with external tools via an application programming interface (API). Interfacing via an API should be a last resort because it can be a lot of work and it can also get very complicated. In practice, I have seen scripts and extensions written in APIs have many unexpected (and painful) problems, including timing issues and unexplained side effects. Overall, you never want to overengineer your source code management solution or process.

> ### Training Is the Hill to Die On
>
> Training is critical and, unfortunately, often forgotten or abbreviated. That is a huge mistake. You need to have training that explains not only how the tools work, but also presents the process and usage model that you want your team to adopt. That means that you not only want vendor training, but someone on your team should have the responsibility for designing and documenting the process for using the tool (often called a *usage model*) in your organization. Expect that this will be an iterative process and that you will not have a perfect solution when you first get started. Even if you don't pick the best tool on the market, training will make the difference between success and failure.

1.5 Managing the Globally Distributed Development Team

Source code management helps to coordinate the work being done by teams that are globally distributed. If you have teams in London, New York City, and Mumbai (see Figure 1.7), source code management best practices will help you coordinate everyone's work in a meaningful and logical way.

The challenge of global software development is that work has to be coordinated and changes controlled across geographically distributed work environments. Although this is not easy when developers sit across from one another in the same room, it is even more difficult when the team is separated in different countries, working in different time zones, each with their own respective languages, cultures, and expectations. Source code management can help by organizing the work on separate branches so that the work in one location can be reviewed and then merged onto the trunk in a controlled and traceable way. I have implemented this by having an offshore branch that was reviewed by onshore resources and then merged to the trunk (with the results replicated back out to the offshore team). Another approach is to allow offshore resources to have equal repository access, as if they were working in the onshore location. It is a common best practice to communicate and track changes through the use of change requests (CRs), which I have seen called workitems, tasks, enhancements, or defects (as in a bugfix). Each of these may have their own lifecycle to establish and enforce effective code control processes. Good source code management practices allow you to establish the right controls and process for your team and reliably control offshore development. I recommend piloting and trying one or more approaches to see what best fits your organization. You should expect them to change and mature over time as you calibrate your source code management so that you have *just enough* process to get the job done effectively.

Figure 1.7 *Source code management helps to coordinate the efforts of a team literally spread all over the world.*

The right strategy includes good coordination, traceability, and visibility.

1.6 Tools Selection

Tools selection is a critical task in the implementation of any source code management solution. Numerous factors need to be considered when selecting a source code management tool. I decided to cover this topic only in general terms in this chapter and, instead, include a tools selection section on the website that supports this book (www.cmbestpractices.com/tools). This way, I can keep the material up-to-date and allow my colleagues to give their input regarding what often turns into a heated "religious" debate.

Let's start with the observation that there are an amazing number of excellent source code management tools on the market. We all owe a huge debt of gratitude to the many vendors who have developed excellent source code management solutions in both the commercial and open source world. It has been my experience that tools vendors deserve credit for developing and spreading effective best practices that go beyond just the short-term goal of selling their own products. I would also say that even the "bad" tools have their place in specific circumstances. The important thing is to start by assessing your own requirements for a source code management solution and then evaluate which solutions would best match the work being done by your team in an open and pragmatic way. All source code management tools are not the same, and there are good reasons why some tools may be better or worse for a particular project. Some have limited features and integrations. Others have a steep learning curve but tremendous power once the users are fully trained and supported.

The biggest problem is that many commonly used source code management tools lack the capability to test and control the *internal integrity* of the repository itself. For example, I have seen code literally disappear from some (well-known) source code management tools without any trace of how and when the revisions were lost. I have had personal experience in dealing with this problem in large-scale financial services environments where code loss could literally result in a material loss to the firm. I have seen both open source tools and some commercial tools (from large well-known vendors) have these and similar problems. Therefore, keeping your trading system code in one of these tools may not be an adequate way to lock down your source. (At best, you need to keep extra backups of the source used to build the release.)

Here are some of the features that you should consider when selecting a source code management solution:

- Ease of use (versus learning curve)

- Branching capabilities

- Merging (graphical and command line)

- History of changes

- Baselining (such as tagging/labeling)

- Changesets

- Administration tools (such as checking for repository integrity)

- Costs (including total cost of ownership)

- Available training and support

- Integration with common IDEs

- Defect and requirements tracking

- Full ALM solution (versus integration with third-party tools)

- Well-defined usage model

- Open source versus commercial

- Product maturity

- Vendor commitment

- Extensibility and open API

- Time to implement and risks to success

It is important to start by defining your goals for selecting an effective CM solution. Then, you can evaluate these and other criteria for selecting the right source code management solution for your efforts. Sometimes, you can rule out a particular tool based on one or more criteria.

For example, many firms have large development teams (say, hundreds to thousands) globally distributed throughout the United States, Europe, and Asia. Source code management tools really show their value in these situations because they help safeguard the code, organize the development effort, and provide visibility into what the team is doing on a daily basis. There are times when teams really want the advanced features offered by the more powerful tools, and then they must also plan on providing training and support. In some organizations, there is an absolute requirement to support multiple variants of the same codebase, which means that the tool must have the capability to support complex branching (and merging).

Most organizations really need to be able to easily view the history of all changes (which can quickly become complicated). All development teams must have the ability to baseline their code (which is a basic requirement) in any organization that must maintain proper IT controls and compliance. I would have a hard time finding any environment more complicated than doing my homework for a graduate class in computer science that does not require reliable baselining. (Actually, I used a source code management tool for that, too.) For example, changesets are very useful if you want to be able to have a defined set of changes that can be easily applied or rolled back as desired, even if this just impacts your ability to get your homework assignments completed on time. Many organizations also have a strong view on whether the tool is supported by a reliable vendor or supported by the community as part of open source.

1.6.1 Open Source Versus Commercial

You should consider whether your organization has a strong preference for open source or commercial CM tools. There are pros and cons to each type. Some developers believe that open source tools are better because the source code is readily available and extended by an active user community. Advocates of commercial tools usually indicate that the support and features are better when there is a large development team getting paid to develop the tool (often with support from a world-class technology organization). A new hybrid approach is emerging with commercial tools vendors that are willing to post their source code for anyone to see and even extend with contributed code (along with well-defined APIs). Yet another popular approach is to provide a free (or unlimited evaluation) copy of the product that may be limited in terms of features and/or the number of licenses. Choosing between commercial and open source source code management solutions is an interesting (and active) discussion with many valid points on both sides of the argument. Again, I defer giving my own opinion here, and continue the dialogue on the website that supports this book (www.cmbestpractices.com/tools). Nonetheless, consider whether your organization has a strong preference for open source or commercial tools and whether this issue should be part of your sales selection criteria.

1.6.2 Product Maturity and Vendor Commitment

I have worked with very mature products that were not likely to get much in the way of improvements anytime soon (both open source and commercial). I have also worked with bleeding-edge technologies that were too new to even have a well-defined checklist for installing them. This latter case meant that I had to work with the senior engineers to install and configure the tools. Mature products may have fewer problems and issues, but they also often have fewer advanced features that can dramatically improve programmer productivity. You need to consider your tolerance (and desire) for living life on the wild side versus keeping your source code management adventures down to a reasonable level.

If you are going to go with the latest and greatest source code management tool-set, you must confirm that the vendor is ready, able, and willing to give you the support that you need to maintain your leading edge source code management solution.

1.6.3 Extensibility and Open API

I always warn my colleagues to go slowly when deciding to extend or modify a source code management tool (usually through an open API or shell scripting). Although scripting (such as triggers) may help you reinforce process, you must also consider the time and effort necessary to adequately support your customized version of the tool. I have seen many efforts to write scripts and wrappers around source code management tools fail miserably. It is usually better to work with the vendor to come up with a solution and then share it with the entire user community. You may not recognize your script when it finally comes back to you, but it will likely be a lot more reliable after others have given their input and suggestions. If you are the only person who knows how your scripts work, that is bad for both you and your company.

1.6.4 Don't Overengineer Your Source Code Management

One of the biggest mistakes that I have seen made by well-intentioned developers is overengineering the source code management tool. Source code management tools have a lot of cool features, and I have seen many technology professionals get excited once things started working, and then they tried to automate everything possible. Sometimes, this resulted in a source code management solution that actually had too many "bells and whistles," which frequently broke (usually when my colleague was on vacation). Adding process automation to a source code management tool is an excellent idea, but this is definitely one case where you want to have "*just enough*" automation to get the job done and nothing more. Your source code management solution should embody both the principles of Agile and Lean in order to achieve the best results.

For example, creating a branch to support a bugfix is a great idea, but requiring a separate branch for every single bug may turn out to add just too much complexity. There are no hard-and-fast rules in this space, but I recommend that you try to keep your processes lean and only automate what is absolutely necessary.

Another mistake that I have frequently seen is people writing scripts to sit in front of the source code management tool's own command language. The problem with this approach is that users typically do not know what the tool is doing because the scripts are hiding the functionality and often substituted for actual training and clear procedures. If you choose to write a script to automate the source code management tool, I strongly recommend that your script clearly show each command that is being executed so that you do not hide the actual operations of the source code management tool. This makes the script transparent and facilitates training. I believe that training is the most critical success factor for any successful source code management tools implementation and that scripts should only automate repetitive tasks. Make sure that you provide enough training for your team to understand how to make the best use of your CM tools. Scripts should not be a substitute for training, and they should not hide the functionality of the tool. When scripts hide the functionality of the tool, developers do not learn how to use the basic functions of the source code management tool, and that always leads to mistakes and loss of productivity. It is also bad because someone has to maintain and upgrade the scripts, which can be time consuming and error prone. Picking the right tools, usage model, and process is important. Training is even more important. It is also important to consider all aspects of delivering quality products, including the cost of quality.

1.7 Recognizing the Cost of Quality (and Total Cost of Ownership)

I have administrated source code management tools for a living, and it has often been the case that senior management failed to recognize the cost of taking care of these tools on a daily basis. Such costs include staff and resources to administer (such as backup), implement, train, and support users.

In one company, I was asked to get everyone onboard using an industry-strength source code management tool (that the company had largely already paid for, but which had fallen out of use). Over time, I was very successful, to the point where I was supporting more than 700 developers using 1,500 repositories worldwide. At that time, I had only two people on my team providing fulltime support (myself and one other person). It really became impossible to do a good job supporting the entire organization. Other managers actually told me that we should "go on strike" and stop trying to take care of everyone in what was truly an impossible situation. This Wall Street financial services firm is no longer in existence today. I believe that one of the reasons that it went out of business was that it began focusing on short-term profits rather than long-term goals. My point is that providing source code management tools and process is a long-term strategic asset, and you need to consider the total cost of ownership (cost of quality), including the cost to administer and support the tool. As far as I am concerned, failing to fund the source code management effort is much like deciding that you don't have time to stop for gas on your drive from New York to Los Angeles. (Sooner or later, you will realize that this short-sightedness was a huge—read: time-consuming and inconvenient—mistake.)

1.7.1 Building Your Source Code Management Budget

Make sure that you consider the cost of everything that you will need to run a successful source code management function, including servers, disks, and peripherals to host your source code management tools, licenses for all required products, maintenance (of the CM tools and other required products), support, backup, and disaster recovery products and services. One area that is constantly overlooked and underfunded is training.

1.8 Training

In selecting your source code management tool, consider whether there is structured training available from the vendor and third parties. I sometimes prefer training that is not from the vendor because I need an unbiased approach to understanding how to use the tool effectively (especially with regard to working around bugs and limitations). Vendors sometimes have a tendency to teach the classes as if they are an extension of the sales process. I was in one class where the instructor had previously worked for the vendor and had actually written some of the same code himself. This gentleman openly talked about mistakes that he made when writing the code (really due to the fact that they did not give him enough time since the priority was to be able to claim that they simply had a certain feature available). He also said publicly that the vendor had never allowed him to take the time to go back and improve the product once it was being sold and in use. Vendor-provided training can be excellent. Sometimes, third-party training is a little more objective and useful.

1.8.1 The "Bob Method" for Training

My own preferred approach is to have someone in your organization start with vendor-provided training and then write a company-specific training program that includes the desired process and preferred usage model. This approach significantly lowers your cost of supporting users on a long-term basis. My way of dealing with this issue is that I offer to give out my home phone number to anyone who successfully takes (and completes) my class. I always offer my colleagues the following deal: "If I don't do a good job of teaching you, then you get to wake me up in the middle of the night when you can't get your code out of the source code management tool!" Ease of use is very close to training in terms of its importance and impact. The good news is that many tools have features that make them much easier to learn and use, including a powerful and intuitive user interface.

It has become popular to use integrated development environments (IDEs) in many aspects of software development. Most CM tools now provide a powerful integration with popular IDEs so that you can check out/in code from within the IDE itself. I have seen this approach not work at all with some technologies and, occasionally, you might find that the integration is so buggy that it is not worth trying to use. Before you buy any source code management tool, make sure that you try out your required IDEs to confirm that you will be able to work effectively from within the interface that you prefer. Another important requirement is to be able to go back and see exactly what changes occurred at any particular time. This is a feature that I have personally needed constantly as part of my role as a person supporting and promoting CM best practices. Along with training and ease of use, you want your source code management tools to be rich in features that facilitate traceability through requirements and defect tracking.

1.9 Defining the Usage Model

It is really important to get someone in your organization dedicated to defining how your entire team will use the source code management tool. Ideally, this person gets input from the entire team. Clearly defining the usage model is a critical part of deciding which tool you should select. You can expect that this will be an iterative process, and you can expect that there will be many differing opinions. You might like a particular tool, but its usage model may prove to be much too complicated (or perhaps not complicated enough in terms of desired features). One example of a common usage paradigm is integrating the source code management tool with a defect or requirements tracking tool to provide traceability.

Traceability Through Requirements and Defect Tracking

I worked on an international banking system that occasionally had a silly little problem where it would incorrectly round off by 1 Japanese yen. This was not a lot of money and would have been merely a nuisance if not for the fact that the Japanese Ministry of Finance would shut this bank down if it learned of this error (because it was a violation of industry regulations). So, every time the 1 yen rounding problem popped up, there was a mad rush to immediately get this bugfix out the door. The change was always the same, but it seemed that no one ever remembered how we fixed it "last time." If you have a requirements or defects tracking system integrated with your source code management tool, all changes are associated with a particular requirement or defect ID (also referred to as a *change request* [CR]). That means that you can search your defect tracking system for "one yen rounding" and see the exact changes that were done to fix this problem six months ago when we last engaged in a fire drill to keep our Japan-based office in business. Some source code management solutions are part of a comprehensive application lifecycle management (ALM) package, and others are just specific source code management tools (usually with integrations with other tools on the market). You need to decide whether you want a complete ALM solution to support your entire SDLC or a specific (sometimes called a *vertical*) solution to meet a particular requirement. Picking the right tool is important, but defining a clear way to use the tool is even more important.

1.10 Time to Implement and Risks to Success

Before you begin any source code management tools effort, consider whether you have accurately considered the time and effort that it will take to implement, train, and support your team. You should also consider any possible risks that may impede your progress toward success. For example, developers refusing to participate in training is a serious risk factor that should be highlighted before you attempt any CM tools implementation effort. You may even decide to select an inferior tool because the better approach is riskier or requires a commitment that your organization just refuses to accept and support.

1.11 Establishing Your Support Process

An essential aspect of implementing CM best practices is establishing a team to help implement, support, and administrate the source code management function and the other five functional areas that I describe in this book. I have found that it is important to market a team's services as a shared resource that adds value to the entire development organization. I usually call this group "release management services" (RMS), which, initially, puts the spotlight on releasing the code. This is often the phase when some developers realize that they can no longer avoid getting involved with configuration management. Truthfully, CM is involved with the entire application (and product) lifecycle. I have learned to focus on running this group as a service and support function that is involved with every phase of the application lifecycle. My team regards the developers as "customers" and endeavors to provide effective support. The only catch here is that we also escalate to senior management if developers are not following the RMS team's guidelines for required configuration management best practices. Source code management is certainly a critical function that is part of the overall CM lifecycle.

1.12 Advanced Features and Empowering Users

I have seen many technology professionals truly take source code management tools and processes to very high levels. Others are satisfied with just doing the bare minimum necessary to get the job done. I am not suggesting that everyone on your team needs to become a source code management tools guru, but you should also recognize and empower those users who want to raise the bar. I have learned a lot from my colleagues, and I encourage you to empower those technology professionals who want to take CM best practices seriously and help share what they have learned. For these colleagues, I have often offered to give them tools admin training and encourage them to share the role of providing support to the rest of the team. Good CM is contagious, and this is one special contagion that you should try hard to spread and promote.

Conclusion

Source code management is a key function within CM best practices. Remember to safeguard your code and expect that your CM tools and process will help to improve productivity and quality. Exercise all due care when selecting your source code management tools and recognize that the source code management function needs to be funded. Training and a well-defined usage model will help ensure that your CM function is effective and well received. Consider your unique requirements and risks to success along with the support process that you will need to implement for success. I also encourage you to share your own experiences as to what works well and any challenges that you find in implementing source code management. I always tell people that source code management is a team sport, and your source code management processes will be more effective if you have had the opportunity to learn and share CM best practices!

Chapter 2

Build Engineering

Chapter Overview

2.1 Why Is Build Engineering Important?   31

2.2 Where Do I Start?   32

2.3 Build Engineering Core Concepts   32

2.4 Core Considerations for Scaling the Build Function   34

2.5 Build Tools Evaluation and Selection   38

2.6 Cost of Quality and Training   42

2.7 Making a Good Build Better   42

2.8 The Role of the Build Engineer   44

2.9 Architecture Is Fundamental   46

2.10 Establishing a Build Process   47

2.11 Continuous Integration Versus the Nightly Build   47

2.12 The Future of Build Engineering   48

Build engineering is the discipline of efficiently turning source code into binary executables. Build engineering can be as simple as running a Makefile or Ant script and as complicated as writing a full-build framework to support the underlying technology architecture. In this chapter, we discuss tactics for dealing with the challenges of build engineering, core skills in build engineering, and some general approaches to selecting the right build tools. We also discuss how to select and train people to be successful build engineers and what you need to know if this is your job. I will suggest a strategy for using existing resources when you just can't find a qualified build engineer. I love build engineering and have always found it to be among the most challenging and rewarding roles within configuration management.

This chapter provides a broad overview of the many aspects of build engineering, including goals, principles, and the essential concepts that you need to understand to establish your build engineering function. We discuss how to get started along with the core concepts that are essential for establishing build engineering best practices, including version IDs, understanding dependencies, and establishing the all-critical independent build. We discuss the broad range of tools available today, along with the cost of quality and considerations for establishing required training. We look at the role of the build engineer and the importance of considering the application architecture along with guidance for establishing a build process that produces accurate results on a repeatable basis. We also cover the all-important topic of continuous integration and the future of build engineering. Build engineering is a core CM function, and this chapter steers you in the right direction.

Goals of Build Engineering

The goal of build engineering is to be able to reliably compile and link your source code into a binary executable in the shortest possible time. Build engineering includes identifying the exact compile and runtime dependencies and any other specific technical requirements, including compiler (linker and managed environment) switches and dependencies. Build engineering improves both quality and productivity for the entire team. I believe that the build engineering team should consider themselves to be a service function with the development team as their primary *customers*. However, build engineering must also sometimes have the authority to enforce organizational policies. As build engineers, we provide a service to support the development effort, but our primary goal is to help secure the assets of the firm that are built and released through the build engineering function.

Principles of Build Engineering

The principles of build engineering include the following:

- Builds are understood and repeatable.

- Builds are fast and reliable.

- Every configuration item is identifiable.

- The source and compile dependencies can be easily determined.

- Code should be built once and deployed anywhere.

- Build anomalies are identified and managed in an acceptable way.

- The cause of broken builds is quickly and easily identified (and fixed).

2.1 Why Is Build Engineering Important?

Build engineering helps the development team by providing an accurate and repeatable way to compile and link the code in the fastest possible way. Being able to rapidly rebuild a release enhances productivity by facilitating software development. Although fast builds are important for any software development methodology, Agile and Iterative development have highlighted this issue for some time now. Getting the build right also avoids serious problems that can have catastrophic impacts on the development team and the entire organization. I have personally seen a release and deployment issue actually impact the entire world economy (which I describe in Chapter 6, "Deployment"). Build engineering problems can have the same impact. Build engineering is important because it can improve both the quality of the application that you are developing and the productivity of the entire organization involved.

Why Do Bad Builds Happen to Good Developers?

Build engineering can be very painful. I have seen environments where the development team could not reliably get the same executable built from one hour to the next. There were several reasons for this situation. The first was that they did not have reliable source code management practices in place (which resulted in them not being able to retrieve the exact same version of the source code from one hour to the next). The second reason was that the build procedures themselves were convoluted and unreliable. The third reason was that any new build requirements could not be supported without a considerable effort to tame the existing automated build procedures into submission. The best approach we could find was to start over rather than continue struggling with a homegrown solution that was only understood by the consultant who wrote it (who had also gone on to his next contract). I have seen this exact situation many times at a number of large firms, including banks and hedge funds.

2.2 Where Do I Start?

You should always start by looking at the existing development build procedures. Sometimes, you will find that the development team already has existing build scripts perhaps using Ant, Maven, or Make. Often, the existing build procedures will only handle deployment to the existing development test environment. It is common for a build engineer to be required to take an existing build script and modify it to support QA and production environments. Existing build scripts may also fail frequently and require developer expertise to support them. Your job will be to make these scripts more reliable and supportable. I have often found that I have to start by understanding the application so that I understand what I am trying to build. Sometimes, the architecture will be complicated enough that you might need to partner with the developer to write a suitable build system. Make sure that you start by evaluating the existing build tools and processes before you start to improve them, implementing build engineering best practices.

2.3 Build Engineering Core Concepts

A few responsibilities must be part of any successful build engineering effort. The first is that builds must be established that are repeatable, based on an identifiable baseline and that all dependencies are well understood and controlled. Every build consists of and creates configuration items (CIs). Almost anything in the build can be considered a CI. The first task of a build engineer is to verify that all executables and essential scripts, documents, and text files are clearly identified.

2.3.1 Version IDs or Branding Your Executables

Just as you need to be able to readily identify a baseline of your source code, you also need to be able to easily identify the exact version of anything that gets created by the build process. That includes all binaries (intermediate code and runtime modules) along with all configuration files. As was mentioned in Chapter 1, "Source Code Management," in CM terminology, we call these artifacts configuration items (CIs), whether they are source, binary, or configuration files. In an ideal world, everything should be identifiable with an immutable version ID. In practice, we are used to looking at the About box in a desktop GUI to see the version of the product that we are using. All documentation, including release notes, tutorials, and tech notes, must include version identification so that we know which version of the code they pertain to.

2.3.2 Immutable Version IDs

The most basic form of this requirement is to stamp an executable with an immutable version ID (and provide an easy procedure to retrieve the version ID). I have set up build systems using a C++ static char variable with the version ID stamped into the executable. I have also created JAVA classes to retrieve the version ID and stamp the version ID into the manifest of the JAR, WAR, or EAR file created by the build. The key is to make sure that the version ID can be easily traced back to the exact version of the source used to build that executable.

2.3.3 Stamping In a Version Label or Tag

In some cases, we actually stamped the executable with the source code management tool's version label or tag used to build the release. Because we created the build sandbox using this label or tag (and we locked it in the repository), we were reasonably certain that we had all the information that we needed to be able to reliably rebuild the baselined release as required. In some cases, we also needed to capture and record the revision of the repository itself (because tags could not be easily locked and developers could conceivably remove the tag and attach it to another version of the code)—after the release was already on its way to QA.

> ### The Two-Line Fix Without the Code Regressing
>
> Good build engineering practices mean that you will always be able to easily verify the exact version of the code that went into building a particular release. They also mean that you can look at an executable running in production and easily ascertain the exact version of the code used to build that release. If you adhere to these best practices, you will be able to create a new sandbox, retrieve the correct code baseline, and then make a two-line change to the code (for a bugfix) and be absolutely certain that your code will not regress because of the wrong version of a header file or some other compile dependency.

2.3.4 Managing Compile Dependencies

I have seen many builds break because an environment variable was set in the developer's own user account and then completely forgotten two months later when the code was being built for the release to production, most likely using another user account. It's not just about source code; all compile (and runtime) dependencies must be understood and controlled. That means that your build scripts should set all required environment variables and confirm that all build dependencies are correctly in place each and every time the build is executed.

2.3.5 The Independent Build

One of the best ways to avoid costly mistakes is to have every release built independently and from the very top of the build structure so that all configuration items are completely rebuilt. This is often done by a separate release management team or by an automated build process as in continuous integration (CI). Many regulatory frameworks that establish the requirements for proper IT controls do explicitly require not only a separation of duties but an independent build, packaging, and release controls process, too. This might seem like a lot of work, but from a compliance perspective, it is a basic requirement and expected in most financial services, defense, medical, and government agencies. This is an example of a regulatory requirement that makes complete sense and enhances productivity and quality. I still remember the smiling face of a development manager who had just implemented my procedures and was able to respond quickly to a major software problem by quickly creating his sandbox, retrieving a baseline, and rapidly deploying his fix into production. He was excited that putting in proper IT controls had helped him rapidly respond to a problem that previously would have taken much more time to address. We discuss the requirement to restrict access to production in Chapter 13, "Establishing IT Controls and Compliance." There are other best practices that can help improve productivity and quality, too.

2.4 Core Considerations for Scaling the Build Function

It has been my experience that a number of essential considerations must be addressed to establish the build engineering best practices for a particular development group. Sometimes, these considerations relate to the cognitive complexity of the existing build processes, which may be resulting in human error, code defects, and loss of productivity due to constant rework. Part of this effort is technical, but part of it is also working with the team to convince them that it is *possible* to simplify the build process. I have seen situations where the technology was hopelessly complex and others where the root cause of the problem was that technology professionals were mired in making things a lot more complicated than they needed to be. Obviously, we want to make things as simple as possible and completely foolproof. You can expect some resistance as many technology professionals focus on showing their prowess at handling complex structures.

2.4.1 Selling the Independent Build

Independent builds are supposed to be a verification that all the required CIs have been baselined (and secured in the source code management repository). The independent build is often required by regulatory requirements to reduce the risk of any possible mistake. That said, it can be a tough sell for you to convince the development team that you need to change the build procedures just to prevent any possible mistake. Developers often see the build engineer as wasting time by rebuilding an application from the beginning. The team may be aware that there is a regulatory requirement to independently build an application before it is promoted to QA or production, but many will still snicker and view this task as a waste of time. Being a member of the development team may help you understand the technical issues involved with the build, but it also may result in the build engineer being put in a compromising position. Ultimately, management needs to create an environment for the build engineer to get the information that he or she needs to be effective and still follow all required corporate standards and procedures. I usually sell this verification step as being a good way to guarantee (and literally test) that we did not overlook a compile dependency. I also try to get the build process to be fast and automated so that it does not require an excessive amount of time. You need to keep these considerations in mind as you dive in and fix the technical problems with the build.

Fixing the build process may require that you address a situation where the build has just been *overengineered,* resulting in too much complexity. There may be some existing automation in place, but frequently, there are just too many moving parts and no one really understands how the existing build works. I have seen complex build systems that no one in the organization could support or modify. Usually, this is a direct result of overengineering the build process. In the next section, I share some thoughts on how to fix this situation.

2.4.2 Overengineering the Build

I have been called into a number of organizations that had unreliable and convoluted build engineering practices that interfered with the development effort. Sometimes, the project and the organization were put at risk due to repeated bad builds that demonstrated that the team could not successfully get a release out the door. Sometimes, this occurred because of poor or nonexistent software configuration management (SCM) practices. But frequently, it was because the build scripts themselves were overly complex and nearly impossible to support. It's been my experience that this problem usually occurred when one very smart person created a build process that was so complex that no one else on the team could possibly understand the procedures and automation to support the build. In one classic situation, the build engineer learned how to use a build feature where he could pass in the environment (for example, development, QA, or production) and then generate the required configuration files to support that environment. (We talk more about the best practices for creating configuration files in Chapter 3, "Environment Configuration.") One part of the problem was that this developer decided to design the build tool so that the same code had to be rebuilt for each environment (such as development, QA, or production). He basically did not understand the QA process and the need to build the code once (but deploy and configure it as needed.) So, QA tested one version of the build, but we promoted another version of the build when the code went to production. We had controls in place to make certain that the same version of the source code was used (e.g., baselined release), but rebuilding the code for each environment was certainly not my idea of a "best practice" that would pass any reasonable IT controls and compliance assessment. Another anomaly that I found was that there were libraries with the same name, but different sizes in several places throughout the build. Again, this was a direct result of a poorly understood, overly complex build created by smart (hardworking) engineers who did not really understand the requirements from a QA perspective or even the tools that they were working with.

2.4.3 Testing Your Own Integrity

On a few occasions, I was pressured by management to do things that I believed to be less than completely ethical. In one situation, I was asked to certify that all the development teams in a large bank were compliant with the IT controls required for section 404 of the Sarbanes-Oxley Act of 2002. In this situation, I was given the responsibility to review the practices of all the development teams to confirm that they had proper change and configuration management controls in place as defined by the ISACA Cobit model. This is the kind of job that is pure delight for a CM evangelist, because I can help the team meet compliance regulations and also improve their quality and productivity at the same time. However, the organization was on a tight schedule to finish the IT controls part of their SOX compliance, and I was actually brought in at the very tail end of the project. My boss sat with me during the meeting in which the SOX compliance officer was surprised to hear that I wanted to actually do a CM assessment for each group before testifying that all the controls were being properly enforced. This time, I was successful, because I actually knew that three quarters of the teams were using the right software configuration management (SCM) processes because I had set them up. So, I begged for the time to just assess the remaining groups, and then I attested that they were in compliance. Six months later, however, I was asked to attest again, and this time, I found some groups had regressed and were not in compliance. It was a political nightmare to deal with this problem, and I eventually left the company. This happened at a large financial services firm that soon went out of business. I believe that its demise was in no small part due to a shift to short-term thinking that resulted in cutting corners and eventually disaster for the firm. I have always viewed this as my personal "Enron," and I am glad that I did my best to get the firm to do the right thing and comply with all industry regulations.

2.4.4 Reporting to Development Can Be a Conflict of Interest

In another incident, I reported to the head of the development team and I helped to build and deploy a large international trading system. Being part of the development team helped me understand the system a lot faster, and this was essential because the technology was pretty complex. I built literally hundreds of releases and deployed this trading system over and over again without a single bad release. However, the deadline was fast approaching, and the head of development had his bonus tied to delivering the application on time. The team fixed bugs, built, and deployed over and over again. Finally, the deadline for going live arrived, and I was ordered to build and deploy a version of the system that had a number of fixes that had not been tested by the QA team. This meant that we had tested one version of the system, which was approved, but we were actually deploying another version of the system instead. I spoke with the head of development and explained that we could not build and deploy a different version of the system than the one that had been approved by QA. This senior manager was not going to risk losing his bonus due to a missed deadline, and he wanted the latest fixes in the release. Eventually, I had to go above his head to his boss who immediately said that he wanted the new release to get the usual testing and approval from the QA team. The project deadline was extended by two weeks, and we followed our process. Unfortunately, the head of development viewed me as no longer being a member of his team, and my job became considerably more difficult at this firm.

2.4.5 Organizational Choices

Ideally, the build engineering team should report at a high enough level to prevent them from being unduly influenced by politics and pressure from managers who are singularly focused on meeting their deadlines. It is common for build engineering to be part of the QA group, but I have found that this usually creates a barrier to really understanding the system in a thorough and effective way. I have also reported to the head of systems administration (because I was deploying applications and my role overlapped with that of the SAs) and the head of data security, because I was enforcing compliance. There are many other ways to structure the organization, but the key goal is to make sure that build engineering gets the information that they need and are allowed to operate with full integrity in protecting the assets of the firm. It is equally important that the head of the build engineering team be someone who is willing to communicate issues and, if necessary, stop the build from being released (pending resolution of important issues). My own personal experience is that this can be a difficult position, and senior management would be wise to provide the necessary support so that the build engineering team can do their job and protect the essential assets of the firm.

2.5 Build Tools Evaluation and Selection

There are a lot of good build tools available and even more best practices to help guide you on your way to establishing a reliable and extensible build process. We'll discuss some of the tools and best practices that you should considering implementing to support your organization. Once again, I will leave the religious debate on which tool is better to the supporting website for this book (http://cmbestpractices.com/tools). There are several types of build tools commonly used in software development. There was a time, not too long ago, where build automation meant using Make (and perhaps some shells scripts) to automate every aspect of the build process. This worked well to support C and C++ builds, although Make often behaved differently depending on the underlying platform. I have worked with Make on HP-UX, Solaris, AIX, and more recently, Linux. Make was originally created by Stuart Feldman in 1977 at Bell Labs. GNU Make certainly took a step forward to solve some of the cross-platform build challenges, and it is worth noting that Make is used not only for C and C++, but in some cases, for Java, too.

2.5.1 Apache Ant Enters the Build Scene

Ant was originally created by James Duncan Davidson as part of the Apache Tomcat project (http://tomcat.apache.org). Ant was originally bundled in with Apache Tomcat, and then Ant version 1.1 was released as a standalone product in July 2000. Ant is very different from Make in that it is implemented using Java classes (instead of writing shell commands).

2.5.2 Of Mavens and Other Experts

Maven began as part of the Jakarta Alexandria project in 2001 and was later released as its own product. Maven tries to be an overall project information source, setting standards for a consistent build framework and boasting that "maven can do the heavy lifting" for you that formally would have required many lines of XML code in Ant. Maven focuses on convention over configuration, in that Maven expects you to stick to its declared and expected conventions. Maven does help to set up your initial project with all the suggested conventions by providing an archetype mechanism whereby Maven can generate the skeleton code to get you started using any one of a number of different Java frameworks. It is also important to understand that Maven has a very specific lifecycle that must be understand to successfully leverage Maven's many features. I will provide more resources for getting started with Maven, along with methods for refactoring the Maven build on the website that accompanies this book (http://cmbestpractices.com).

The Apache website states that a *maven* is a Yiddish word for an "accumulator of knowledge," although I would translate *maven* as being an "expert." I am going to save the religious debate on whether Ant or Maven is better for my website (http://cmbestpractices.com), although I will say that I have used both extensively and definitely consider myself to be a *maven* on whether Ant, Maven, or Make is a better build tool.

2.5.3 Maven Versus Ant

Ant requires a lot of XML code to indicate exactly what you want done. In this sense, Ant is more procedural than Maven. Maven takes a different approach by requiring that the application be structured in a specific and consistent way. This is where Maven focuses on convention over configuration, as mentioned earlier. Maven enthusiasts would note that developers must structure their applications to adhere to Maven's standards and from there, Maven does the *heavy lifting* for you (because it knows where everything is located already and exactly what needs to get built). Maven 2 uses pure Java XML (although Maven 1.1 used jelly scripts). Maven has a well-defined lifecycle that should be understood for optimum performance. In practice, many build engineers use Ant plug-ins to extend Maven's functionality. Maven defines the framework for you upfront, although it can be a bit tricky to follow with complicated builds. It has been my experience that developers can be quite opinionated when it comes to preferring one or the other of these two well-respected tools. I have used Maven version 1.0.2 and 2.0 for some pretty large-scale builds in more than one company. I have also used Ant version 6 and 7. I do believe that there are pros and cons to each of these well-respected tools.

2.5.4 Using Ant for Complex Builds

Ant can be used for complicated builds and can also quickly descend into some pretty obtuse and inconsistent XML. Ant scripts should be structured so that each step can be executed separately with minimal dependencies between each step of the build. For example, I have seen an Ant script that embedded calls to the source code management tool within the code necessary to compile the Java classes. Then, when the team switched from one source code management tool to another, they had to modify all the Ant XML. I have also seen this be a problem where the team could not do a build because the source code management repository was down for maintenance or backup. Good build engineering scripts structure the approach so that you can create the development sandbox, but then run the compile separately. You should never have your build depend on the source code management tool being up and running.

2.5.5 Continuous Integration

Continuous integration (CI) is a popular best practice that refers to attempting a build and deploy of code immediately after a developer commits changes to the source code repository. CI became popular within Agile circles, although today, it is a widely respected best practices in many non-Agile environments, too. CI is usually done using a software package that makes it easier to monitor the source code management repository for changes and immediately start a build. The results of the build are posted on a dashboard, including the most recent changes responsible for any system outages, including a failed build. All CI servers are not alike, and you should evaluate their features for use in your organization. Because these tools change very quickly, I defer this discussion to the Tools section of the website that supports this book (http://cmbestpractices.com/tools).

2.5.6 CI Servers

There are many popular continuous integration servers in use today. The decision on which one is best is a religious discussion that I would be glad to engage in on the website that supports this book (http://cmbestpractices.com). This is an exciting area for CM, with formidable open source solutions and commercial products that boast extended functionality. Leading CI servers all support the capability to automatically start a build when new code has been committed into the source code repository. Alternatively, you can schedule a specific time, each night, for a *nightly* build. CI servers can usually identify the most recent changes, especially the last change that caused the build to break. Most of the CI servers are configured using XML, although some have robust graphical front ends that make administration much easier.

2.5.7 Integrated Development Environments

Integrated development environments (IDEs) are tools that allow developers to improve their productivity and quality by rapidly developing applications in an iterative way. IDEs usually have a compiler (such as C++ or Java) made accessible via a plug-in. Build engineers face extra challenges when developers know how to build only through their IDEs. This can make it difficult to write build scripts (using tools such as Ant or Make) that can execute at the command line. Some IDEs can produce scripts that can be run from the command line. Applications should never be built and deployed to production (or QA) from within an IDE. This approach is inherently not repeatable. One of the biggest problems is that developers often do not understand their own build process that is handled implicitly by the IDE.

2.5.8 Static Code Analysis

Build engineering is sometimes used as a focal point to conduct static code analysis. This makes sense because the build engineer has access to each release of the code and can make a test build of the code, if necessary, to instrument the code. I have worked with static code analysis since the early days of Halstead complexity metrics. A common application of static code analysis is to identify possible security vulnerabilities so that they can be fixed before the code is released. The build engineer is often the only person who can assemble all the code required for a particular release and successfully build the entire system with whatever hooks and modifications are necessary for the static code analysis. Obviously, the build that is done for static code analysis, containing instrumented code, is not normally the version deployed to production.

2.5.9 Build Frameworks

I have worked with many build frameworks that provided a well-considered and well-structured way to develop a complete build solution. Most of these products allowed the user to schedule builds, handle allocation of build machines (usually called *build agents*), and report back the results to a consolidated build dashboard. These products may be part of a full application lifecycle methodology (ALM) solution or just plug-ins to extend the functionality of a specific build tool. You need to spend some time to correctly evaluate the available build solutions, and then select the right build tools for your organization.

2.5.10 Selecting Your Build Tools

Selecting the right tools is always a matter of evaluating your requirements, conducting an evaluation, and leading your team to reach consensus. In practice, many technology professionals find this hard to do effectively. You need to start with identifying the tools available to support the technology that you are using. Here are a few examples:

- GNU make for C/C++

- Ant, Maven, or GNU make for Java

- MS Build or GNU Make for .NET (e.g., C#)

There is a lot more about build tools to discuss, and we will cover that on the accompanying website, http://cmbestpractices.com/tools/.

2.5.11 Conducting the Bakeoff and Reaching Consensus

If at all possible, you want to include all your stakeholders in the tool selection process. Some organizations have a culture in which the decision is made by the development management. Other organizations manage by consensus. Long before anyone was referring to software development as being *agile*, industrial psychologists observed that self-managed teams were more effective, especially in terms of achieved quality and productivity. Self-managed teams, by definition, have the authority to evaluate and select the tools that will be used by their team. Reaching consensus is a core competency of any successful self-managed team. There are pros and cons to each approach, and my view is that organizations need to determine the approach that fits their culture in the best way possible. Overall, conducting a bakeoff between tools, sharing the results and reaching consensus is often the best way to decide on the best direction for choosing a tool or process to use in the software development effort.

2.6 Cost of Quality and Training

Planning a budget to support build engineering needs to include both the hardware and software necessary to provide a fast and reliable build platform. Many firms find it more efficient and cost-effective to use virtualization to provide build and test environments as needed. Make sure that you anticipate the cost of training, along with the resources necessary to support build engineering.

2.7 Making a Good Build Better

I have often found that developers had excellent build procedures already in place, and my role was often to help improve the existing procedures to support additional environments (such as QA and production). There have also been times when I found that the build procedures worked for someone with a strong development background (in the specific technology being built), but were error prone and unreliable—especially for other technology professionals unfamiliar with that particular technology. You want your build procedures to be reliable, fast, and clear enough to be understood by the resources available to support the build and deployment process.

2.7.1 "Bob-Proofing" Your Build

What I am about to describe is my own secret method for creating completely reliable (and repeatable) build procedures. I have applied this method, described in sections 2.7.2 through 2.7.4, in many situations where the development team was struggling to get their builds completed and promoted to QA (and then production) in a reliable and effective way. Often, the team called me in after the project and the organization were already in danger of failure. Using my approach to creating repeatable builds, I was often able to help the team fix their build problems, frequently within just three builds! My technique is based on approaches in other disciplines that I learned about in industrial organizational psychology graduate studies at NYU. While learning about methods practiced in other disciplines helped me develop a creative and unique approach to build engineering, I also learned that there are many reasons why teams fail and only problems related to build engineering can be fixed by improving the build. (We talk about other challenges, including overcoming resistance to change, later in this book.)

2.7.2 Test-Driven Builds

I always capture not only the procedures for creating the build, but any steps that I see developers using to troubleshoot the build, too. In one such instance, I observed that every time the build failed the developers checked to see whether a particular JAR was created and included in the WAR file. I did not fully understand how and why this JAR was sometimes missing, but I captured this troubleshooting step in my scripts, and then always checked for the JAR on each and every build. This gave us an early notification if the build was broken (for this common reason). I call building in these tests and creating scripts to automate and check each step of the build "Bob-proofing" the build. Obviously, this might sometimes seem like overkill, but testing the build proactively will help you create reliable builds and notify you much quicker if something goes wrong. Developers usually like to believe that their builds work and are not likely to go out of their way to proactively test their builds.

2.7.3 Trust, But Verify

As a build engineer, my approach is to "trust, but verify" by testing each and every build. This is particularly important when the results of your work really matter in terms of the health and safety of others. I have worked on build efforts where a mistake could result in planes flying into each other or some other serious incident. In many disciplines, the health and safety of others is very much at stake. For example, aviation engineers spend a great deal of time ensuring that mistakes are avoided through creating controls that are accurate and easy to read.

2.7.4 The Cockpit of a Plane

In some disciplines, extreme efforts are made to avoid any possible mistake. The most obvious reason for this focus on total quality is that a mistake could (and has) resulted in the loss of life. To continue the theme introduced in the preceding section, the cockpit of a plane is designed in such a way as to minimize the likelihood of a mistake. This is done by creating controls that are easy to read and designing the entire interface in a way intended to avoid any possibility of a mistake. I believe that software engineering needs to learn a lesson from our colleagues who design cockpit controls and practice this same approach when designing application build and deployment procedures and automation. I try to create build systems that prevent mistakes and proactively detect problems that might occur during the build process. Build and deployment automation needs to be created in a way that prevents mistakes from occurring. I have done this many times and had the pleasure of leading a team from an unstable and unreliable build approach to a completely foolproof repeatable process. Here are some of the important considerations as you attempt to design your build system as you would the cockpit of a plane.

- Design the build so that each step is easy to understand and follow.

- Anticipate what might go wrong and build in tests to verify that the build is successful.

- Structure the automation so that one step does not break the whole build.

- Use dashboards and reports effectively to communicate build status.

2.8 The Role of the Build Engineer

Build engineers often need to have software development backgrounds and expert knowledge of the technology and the ability to write code, including Perl,

Python, shell scripts, and XML, to create reliable and repeatable builds. (Leaping tall buildings with a single bound could be handy from time to time, too.) Finding a good build engineer is challenging because technology professionals who have strong development backgrounds usually want to develop code rather than write build systems. Being a build engineer is both exciting and very difficult because the other developers frequently adopt new frameworks, which can result in the build engineers being left behind and having to play catch-up. I have also found that it takes considerable creativity to set up good build engineering and still meet the quality and productivity goals.

The build engineer plays a key role in the software development effort. But, it is also true that this role may be very different in one team versus another. I have had the job of being a build engineer in a team where I had to rapidly build and promote hundreds of releases over and over again to assist in supporting the application development effort. Often, build engineers are developers who are assigned the build engineering role for a short time (to write the build infrastructure itself). This requires both an understanding of the application architecture and fluency in the appropriate build tools themselves. We'll examine some of the most common build tools in use today in general terms (and once again leave the specifics and community debates to my supporting website, http://cmbestpractices.com/tools) and consider some of the issues involved with choosing the right build tool.

2.8.1 Know What You Build

Strong build engineers have both an excellent understanding of relevant build tools and a deep understanding of the application architecture. For example, I have worked with J2EE services interface configurations that were handled through specific JMX resources. In other technologies, the same function was handled by using separate configuration files. Developers usually have the expertise to set up these facilities, but the build engineer needs to assist by defining the requirements of the build process itself. As a build engineer, I must often work across many technologies. One day, I may be delving into C#, .NET, and SQL Server while trying to get my arms around all the related platform-specific tools and technologies. The next day, I may be focusing on J2EE SOA with deployment to specific web and application servers. The next assignment might take me into C/C++ using Make to develop embedded software (along with related hardware and firmware components). Build engineers need to have strong skills in the related technologies and also be able to work closely with developers, whenever necessary. This is because build engineers often have to quickly (even suddenly) adapt to working with new and changing technologies.

2.8.2 Partner with Developers

I recall the first time that I had to work with a Java-based object persistence framework (that I had previously never heard of). I quickly tried to get up to speed in this technology, but there was just no way that I could master everything that I needed to know in time to write the build scripts for the upcoming release. In these situations, you must partner with the developers to create a reliable build framework. This can very challenging when developers are only accustomed to using IDEs and, therefore, do not know how to build their applications at the command line. I usually handle this by establishing entry and exit criteria for a build. For example, I usually require that the entry criteria for the build should be a command line procedure to build the release (at least for the development environment). These procedures can usually be modified to support QA and production. The important thing is that the build should be reliable and repeatable.

2.8.3 Drafting a Rookie

One of the best and most successful approaches that I have seen is using a new developer as the build engineer. The new developer won't know a thing about creating repeatable builds, but I can teach them that. Instead, they know the technology (or they are at least extremely motivated to learn it quickly). In fact, it is my view that every developer should spend some time as the build engineer as part of their training and job orientation. This helps to deal with the huge problem of keeping up with the challenging architecture and helps with seeding the development team with technology professionals who really understand build engineering and release management processes.

2.9 Architecture Is Fundamental

Build engineers are often very busy with setting up repeatable processes. Once they are successful, they become even busier and will often find themselves overbooked. The problem is that the development technology is not standing still and other technology professionals are quickly learning and adopting new technology frameworks. I have been on the receiving end of discovering that I suddenly had to adopt and work with a new technology that I had never seen before. In this situation, the build engineer is stuck playing catch-up with the development organization. The first time that I had to work with object persistence using Hibernate, I suddenly learned that there were surprising new build anomalies, including my source management tool behaving differently than the other builds that I had worked with before. I always try to bring this issue to everyone's attention up front and make sure the technology managers know that I have to be kept in the loop as the technology architecture develops.

2.10 Establishing a Build Process

Establishing build engineering best practices can be a difficult task. You may decide which best practices will help your organization achieve success. You may also choose the best tools for creating repeatable builds and setting up continuous integration. However, it has been my experience that the build engineering function must also provide training and support to the development team on an ongoing basis. Some of my successes were in partnering with the development team to fix their build and deploy process and then turning over the day-to-day operations right back to them (with me continuing as backup support). Obviously, this assumes that your compliance department approves this as an adequate IT control. I worked in one organization that complied with SAS-70 and found this to be an acceptable control, and I worked in another organization where this was not considered acceptable. Even in organizations that must maintain a separate build and deploy function to comply with regulatory requirements, there remains a key role to support the developers in establishing repeatable build and deploy processes. If your organization is one of the few who do not need to be concerned with compliance, you should still consider these basic controls to be excellent CM best practices that will help your team improve quality and productivity.

2.10.1 Establishing Organizational Standards

Best practices are also all about establishing a set of organizational standards such as the proper use of build tools, including Ant, Maven, and Make. This may include proper naming conventions and standards for documenting build scripts. For example, in some organizations, all builds are structured using a parent Ant build.xml that is consistent for each team. Establishing organizational standards should be approached in a collaborative way and will likely result in improved quality and productivity.

2.11 Continuous Integration Versus the Nightly Build

Continuous integration (CI) is extremely popular among software development teams. These days, CI is often associated with Agile development. However, this excellent practice has become popular among development teams regardless of the development processes that are being employed. It is also true that many teams do not need nor desire builds to be automatically triggered based on changes being committed to the source code repository as is often associated with CI. Very often, a nightly build is more than sufficient and much easier to set up, too. One reason for this is that CI may trigger many extra builds that will fail, creating unnecessary failed entries on the CI dashboard. In some situations, the build might take a few hours to complete and CI causes builds to be requested even before the previous build has been completed. This can create a backlog of requested builds that are queued up, with specific baselines requested, that may, in fact, be incomplete. I have worked in environments where the better choice was a nightly build. My view is that you should always go for the lightest process possible. I generally call this approach *just-in-time* process improvement, and I believe that it is the most pragmatic and effective approach to establishing an effective development lifecycle.

2.12 The Future of Build Engineering

Build engineering is a critical function that should be developed and supported in your organization. Numerous standards and frameworks highlight the importance of this area, and the industry is developing a number of robust tools to support build engineering, too. We discuss specific standards and frameworks that relate to CM in Chapter 14, "Industry Standards and Frameworks." Build engineering should be understood within the greater context of configuration management, but its growth and well-deserved focus have led to considerable development in recent years. You may have to implement build engineering because it is required by your organizational compliance effort, especially in terms of implementing effective IT controls. But, there is a lot more to consider than just passing an audit. As with any process-improvement initiative, you need to ascertain how build engineering and all of its associated core competencies are required for your technology effort to achieve success in terms of productivity and quality.

Conclusion

Build engineering best practices help your entire development team to be more productive and results in higher-quality code. Your build processes should be automated, traceable, fast, and kept as simple as possible. When the technology is complex, try to break your build into manageable parts. If you "Bob-proof" your build, your team will find that they can develop code in an iterative and efficient way. You also need to carefully select your tools and consider how the build engineering functions fits best in your organization. I hope that you will drop me a line and let me know what you find works and what needs improvement in your own build engineering best practices!

Chapter 3

Environment Configuration

Chapter Overview

3.1 Why Is Environment Configuration Important? 51

3.2 Where Do I Start? 51

3.3 Supporting Code Promotion 52

3.4 Managing the Configuration 52

3.5 Practical Approaches to Establishing a CMDB 55

3.6 Change Control Depends on Environment Configuration 56

3.7 Minimize the Number of Controls Required 57

3.8 Managing Environments 57

3.9 The Future of Environment Configuration 57

Environment configuration refers to identifying, modifying, and managing the interface dependencies required for the system to successfully progress from development to QA to production. Environment configurations are often called *runtime dependencies* because they impact how the code will behave when it is running in a particular environment (such as QA). This is important because the requirements for running a QA environment may be very different from those for a production environment. Even though you want QA to mirror production, in practice, they are often different in many ways. Environment control helps to manage these interface dependencies so that you get to the QA database for testing and you keep the production database safe and secure. When build engineering is done correctly, the code is built only once, and the environment dependencies are configured before the code is deployed to its target environment. Environment configuration is all about controlling the runtime dependencies required for the application to run and behave correctly. Closely related is the function of environment management, which refers to handling the various development, QA, integration, preproduction, and production environments that are needed to handle the effective development, testing, and promotion of applications. Environment configuration impacts all the other CM-related functions. I wrote this chapter largely from the point of view of an IT organization that must promote the code from development to QA to production as part of its software development lifecycle. I have also worked in product development organizations where there was less of a focus on QA versus production environments because all the software was going to be packaged and shipped to an external customer. Still, many development teams must consider environment configuration as an essential practice, and this chapter helps you manage and control your configuration. This chapter also covers the information that you need to manage your environments and their configuration. We discuss how to get started in environment configuration and also the more advanced topics of implementing configuration management databases (CMDBs). There is strong emphasis on supporting the code promotion process and the practical aspects of managing configurations in terms of database selection, protecting production from mistakes, supporting runtime configurations as tokens, and centralizing environment variable assignment as a dynamic environment configuration repository. It is essential to understand that any dependency could impact the application, including the operating system patches and even any supporting hardware interfaces (for example, firmware). We discuss change control as depending on reliable environment configuration and minimizing the number of controls that you really need to operate effectively. We also cover managing the environments and future trends in environment configuration.

Goals of Environment Configuration Control

The goal of environment configuration is to always point to the correct runtime resources, such as the QA or production database. Environment configuration is all about knowing your interface dependencies and controlling their changes accurately. Done well, environment configuration improves quality and productivity. Done poorly, environment configuration will be the cause of defects, wasted time, and other problems. Ultimately, the goal of environment configuration is establishing and maintaining control as your system makes its way from development to QA to production. Environment management also has the goal of providing enough test environments so that development can be done efficiently and with the proper utilization of available resources. Best practices in environment configuration will enable you to develop code faster and with better quality.

Principles of Environment Configuration Control

The principles of environment configuration include the following:

- Environment configuration dependencies are identified and well understood.

- Environments can be interrogated for their current status (for example, ports open).

- Code should be built once with environment configurations changed prior to deployment.

- Environment configurations should be changed in a controlled and predictable way.

- Environment configurations should be documented and understood by all parties.

3.1 Why Is Environment Configuration Important?

Environment configuration helps you to manage both compile and, especially, runtime dependencies. I have viewed this as the Achilles' heal of release management for many organizations. It is a common mistake to accidentally specify the production database (often the default) when you really wanted QA or integration testing. Getting your environment configuration under control will help your release management and deployment. Having the flexibility to manage multiple environments means (obviously) that your team can rapidly deploy and test, which is essential for iterative development. Environment configuration is important because you need to get your runtime (and compile time) dependencies right!

3.2 Where Do I Start?

I prefer to start small with environment configuration control. It can quickly grow into a major project particularly when you start getting into the different types of CMDBs that you could implement. I recommend that you start by getting your key compile and runtime dependencies understood and controlled. Make sure that you eliminate hard coding of all dependencies as soon as possible. The rest of this chapter discusses how to get this done.

3.3 Supporting Code Promotion

Environment configuration control helps support the promotion of code throughout the development lifecycle. Applications are typically developed by technology professionals who iterate through a development effort where they examine requirements specifications (and sometimes handwritten notes on napkins). These *requirements specifications* are then transformed into working, running systems. We discuss tracking requirements throughout the lifecycle of the release in Chapter 5, "Release Management." The development team usually has a runtime environment that can be used to enter tests and write code that is then released to a dedicated test team, often called *quality assurance* (QA). When the code is promoted to QA, it is reconfigured to use a QA database that typically has more security controls than the corresponding database being used by the developers. After QA tests the system and approves the release, the system is usually promoted to production. The production environment typically has the most security of all the environments, especially because production systems often move real money, whereas the QA and development environments were only handling "make-believe" transactions. Environment configuration control helps to make code promotion predictable and repeatable.

3.4 Managing the Configuration

There is nothing worse for a build engineer than promoting a new release from development to QA and wondering whether every dependency was changed correctly. It is even worse when the release is promoted to production and a mistake could mean a bad trade (and losing a million dollars). Many different types of interfaces are managed through environment configuration. For example, interprocess communication ports (such as TCP) are usually wide open in development and QA but closed only to known ports in production. Your data security department may help you out by closing all the ports without warning, effectively shutting down your application. There are many other types of configuration controls required by applications, including the name and location of the target database.

3.4.1 Which Database Are You Using?

Most development environments have copies of databases that roughly match the production database. Development and QA databases are usually smaller and contain fictitious information when there is a business requirement to keep the data confidential. These databases are used by the developers during the application development process and QA during the testing process. Your environment configuration should point to the correct database for the work that you are doing. I have had some amusing experiences with setting up test databases for development purposes. (See the sidebar, "My Own Mickey Mouse Operation.")

My Own Mickey Mouse Operation

Years ago, I wrote a personnel system for a major insurance firm that helped senior managers decide and award raises and bonuses to their staff. To do this efficiently, I created a dummy test database with employees named Donald Duck and Mickey Mouse. One of the senior vice presidents of the firm walked by my computer and observed what appeared to be actual salary data on the screen. She sternly rebuked my carelessness in front of a number of other people and stormed away. I went to my manager and explained what had happened. If the senior vice president (who actually was a delight to work for in every other way) had actually looked closely at the screen, she would have seen that I was awarding Mickey Mouse a 7% annual increase with a merit bonus of $4,000. I had pointed my development code to a test database that did not have any real data in it. It is not always that easy, and there have been many incidents where serious mistakes were made because of an environment configuration error that resulted in significant loss to the firm.

3.4.2 Did That Trade Go Through?

Technology professionals don't like to discuss these incidents, but there have been numerous times when a transaction was supposed to be just a test; however, a mistake resulted in a bad trade or other serious mistake. I have known of incidents where a significant amount of money was lost because a trade executed by mistake. (Imagine buying 10,000 shares of a stock that you did not really want.) Sometimes, the root cause was human (operational) error, but sometimes, the environment configuration was set incorrectly, resulting in what was supposed to be a test that actually resulted in a real transaction (possibly losing a lot of money). Most companies put in controls to prevent this event from ever occurring, but the main point is to configure the application to point to the correct environment. This is not always an easy task and there are a number of tools and processes commonly used for ensuring that the environment is properly configured that have become popular in the last few years. For example, it is always best to avoid hard coding the names of environment resources that may require a lot of changes every time you move the application from one environment (such as QA) to another (such as production). I worked in one place where they had a complicated (actually, convoluted) Maven build that created the environment specific values during the build. The problem was that you had to rebuild the entire application every time that it was promoted from one environment to another. This was definitely not a good way to handle environment dependencies. A much better approach is to centralize the management of this information in one centralized repository using a technique that is sometimes called *token substitution*.

3.4.3 How About a Few Tokens?

One best practice is to use tokens to refer to a specific database. For example, $DBPROD1 would refer to the production database. $DBDEV1 would be a development database, and similarly, $DBQA1 could be the corresponding QA database. At runtime, the token is substituted for the actual database reference. That means that the code would not contain hard-coded values. This approach makes it much easier to manage these references. So far, this is all basic coding strategy, but what is less common is using a centralized database to manage the configurations. I have seen a number of organizations create a centralized repository to store all compile and runtime dependencies that are accessed during the compile phase of the build and the environment configuration phase of the system deployment. It is worth noting that this is a special type of CMDB that has been in practice in many organizations for a long time. Using a repository to manage your tokens means that you have a single location to change, and then all of your applications can pick up the correct environment configuration (for both compile and runtime dependencies). For example, the port required for interprocess communications might be 9099 in QA, but for any number of reasons, 9089 in production. Your application refers to $PortA, and the desired value is substituted for $PortA at compile (or runtime). Similarly, the database holding your trades can be coded using a token that is then instantiated at the right time. This is a common best practice that works much better than hard coding values in your code or even config files that can also prove to be difficult to manage. This approach often becomes so popular that many organizations will centralize their CMDBs as a shared resource. Here's how to do that.

3.4.4 Centralizing the Environment Variable Assignment

One approach that can be used is to create a centralized environment CMDB that holds all of your environment configurations. This database needs to be controlled so that only authorized resources make changes and all changes are accurately tracked. Your build process then looks up the environment configuration values during the build. The substitution of tokens for explicit values should be set up in a way that is traceable so that you can always verify that the correct configurations were created. When the application is configured for deployment, the runtime configuration values should again be substituted for the tokens used in the code. This should all be worked out before the release is actually deployed. The application should not depend on the configuration database while it is actually running in production; otherwise, the CMDB could potentially be a single point of failure. The best practice is to instantiate all runtime dependencies during the release packaging (or possibly the deployment) step, so that all substitutions are completed when the release is packaged for deployment. I have mentioned a common best practice of centralizing environment configurations in what is considered by many to be a configuration management database. But there is a more common application of a CMDB, which we discuss in the next section.

3.5 Practical Approaches to Establishing a CMDB

The configuration management database is a specialized information repository that contains details about the environment configuration. Most CMDBs are specialized devices that examine the runtime environment and report back the status of environment configuration values so that the correct values can be verified and serious mistakes prevented. In this approach, the CMDB performs the function of discovery and reporting back to a centralized configuration management information system. In some environments, the centralized database containing the predefined environment configurations is also called a CMDB. I have seen many organizations implement a number of different specialized CMDBs. In practice, CMDBs often fall short of their intended goals. That does not mean that you should not bother implementing a CMDB. Instead, I suggest that you want to define the goals of the CMDB—whether they be storing configuration details or discovering the current status of a runtime environment. The contents of a CMDB are typically loaded up to a centralized configuration management database. In the ITIL framework, this is called a configuration management system (CMS). We discuss CMDBs further and the Information Technology Infrastructure Library (ITIL) in Chapter 14, "Industry Standards and Frameworks."

3.5.1 Identify and Then Control

The first step is always to identify the environment configuration dependencies. The next step is to control changes to these configurations. Environments should then be verified to confirm that they have the correct values. I have mentioned the selection of the correct database and communication ports. Many other runtime dependencies should be identified and controlled, too. For example, some systems can spawn additional processes to improve performance. This configuration change only makes sense if the selected environment can support the configuration selected. Identifying and controlling your environment configuration will make your application development effort much more successful.

3.5.2 Understanding the Environment Configuration

Application development can be complex and difficult to understand. I have had assignments where there were just so many moving parts that it was almost impossible to promote a release without making a mistake. Most technology professionals won't admit it, but I have seen many projects where mistakes were made and time wasted due to the environment being overly complex. It can be hard to see this unless you actually examine the details of the environment. In my work, I always insist on getting into the trenches and getting my hands dirty doing the builds and deployments myself. For this reason, my processes always work and make sense in a practical way. Getting your arms around the environment configuration will help you achieve success—especially when the environment is complex and prone to mistakes.

3.6 Change Control Depends on Environment Configuration

I discuss best practices for implementing change control in Chapter 4, "Change Control," but for now, it is important to understand that changes to the environment configuration can have major impacts and therefore need to be controlled. Normally, a configuration control board (CCB) is responsible for reviewing requests for changes (RFCs) that may impact the runtime environment. This group is sometimes called a change control board instead, which we discuss further in Chapter 4. The configuration management system and specialized configuration management databases, whether used for managing environment configurations or discovering the current state of runtime environments, will help manage your environment configuration. Whatever controls you choose to put in place, all environment changes need to identified, understood, and controlled. You need to find the right balance between too many (burdensome) controls and just enough to get the job done.

3.7 Minimize the Number of Controls Required

It is common to keep environment control process very light in the beginning of a project. Agile enthusiasts aptly call this "minimizing the amount of *ceremony* required." I support taking a minimalist approach because too many unnecessary controls just motivates people to get clever at bypassing the process and does not really help avoid mistakes. It is much better to take a pragmatic approach and have just enough controls to avoid mistakes. After the code is in production (or even QA), controls need to be much tighter with no room for error. You need to establish an approach to handle environment configuration, such as using tokens and a centralized environment configuration database, as previously described. Using a CMDB is also a recommended best practice and can help you understand and manage a complex environment. It is always best to establish these controls up front, but it is also common to phase them in as needed. This is a good example where I have seen that mistakes and errors can provide the motivation for improving your process through establishing tighter controls. Establishing environment configuration best practices will save you a lot of time and effort, improving both productivity and quality.

3.8 Managing Environments

In source code management, you need a sandbox to be able to write your code. After it is written and ready to be tested (itself an iterative process), you need an environment to host the release of the code. Continuous integration experts always recommend that you automatically deploy a release to a test environment. You also want to know that you can test the code without accidentally dropping a trade into production (by mistake). Make sure that you not only have enough build and test resources, but an infrastructure to manage and maintain them on an ongoing basis. It is usually a good idea to have an established procedure to drop and re-create a test environment from scratch along with test databases and any other required resources. Don't skimp on your environments!

3.9 The Future of Environment Configuration

I have seen a number of interesting tools and frameworks that helped manage environment configuration. Most organizations have homegrown solutions, but I believe we will see more effective tools and frameworks in the not too distant future. I caution, though, that tools and frameworks still require that you do all the real work; they just provide a structure and some best practices to help you get the job done better and faster. I have also seen that virtualization has impacted the management of environments significantly by providing a cost-effective (often green) approach to dynamically building machines as virtual machines (VMs) for use as build and test machines. This is particularly effective when your system needs a large environment for only a short time. I have also seen some approaches using software as a service (SaaS) and cloud computing. All the emerging technologies are good news for people responsible for managing environments and their configuration. You should always pilot these approaches before signing on to confirm that you will get the services that you need to get the job done.

Conclusion

Environment configuration is an important function in configuration management. Done well, it will help your team be more productive and avoid a lot of painful mistakes. This best practice will also help you develop higher-quality applications by facilitating rapid iterative development. Make sure that you share your own environment configuration best practices with me via the supporting website (http://cmbestpractices.com).

Chapter 4

================

Change Control

Chapter Overview

4.1 Why Is Change Control Important?   61

4.2 Where Do I Start?   61

4.3 The Seven Types of Change Control   61

4.4 Creating a Change Control Function   65

4.5 Examples of Change Control in Action   65

4.6 Don't Forget the Risk   69

4.7 Driving the CM Process Through Change Control   69

4.8 Entry/Exit Criteria   70

4.9 After-Action Review   71

4.10 Make Sure That You Evaluate Yourself   71

Change control is the most central function in configuration management. It is also one of the most underutilized and often misunderstood functions. Large organizations always have a change control board to act as a gatekeeper to control changes to the production environment. This is obviously important, but there is a lot more to change control than just gatekeeping. Some organizations have change control processes to govern requests for change. I call this *a priori* change control. Environment configuration is also commonly controlled by change control. I have seen organizations where there was a robust change control structure arranged in a hierarchy from senior management to the technicians making configuration changes and other organizations where the project managers and development team leads handled change control as an implicit project management task. In my own experience, I have identified seven types of change control. In this chapter, I discuss each of these change control functions that I have personally been involved with in large and medium-size international banks, government agencies, defense contractors, and various financial services firms. Sometimes the change control processes were extremely detailed and often they were very light in terms of process. You need to understand which change control processes make sense for your organization and exactly how to implement them.

This chapter gives you a broad overview of the many aspects of change control, including the seven different types of change control and how to create an effective change control function. I provide some examples of change control that I have implemented or seen implemented by others. It is important to realize that change control needs to have a strong focus on evaluating and mitigating risk (as do all IT controls). I suggest that you consider driving your entire change control process through change control with well-defined entry/exit criteria and after-action reviews to discuss how each release was handled and whether there are any areas for improvement. Whether your environment requires very light change control processes or more robust and formal controls, you will want to implement change control best practices as part of your CM efforts.

Goals of Change Control

The goal of change control is to carefully manage all changes to the production (and usually QA) environments. Part of this effort is just coordination, and that is very important. But part of this is also managing changes to the environment that will impact all the systems in the environment. It is also essential to control which releases are promoted to QA and production. Change control can act as the stimulus to all other configuration management-related functions, too. This chapter explains how to use change control to manage your configuration management efforts.

Principles of Change Control

The principles of change control include the following:

- Changes should be planned and not just last-minute events.
- Changes should be understandable, including their downstream impacts.

- Authority and approvals for changes should be established and obtained as appropriate.

- Procedures for emergency changes should be established to cover emergency incidents.

- Change control should assess and confirm that all configuration management processes are being followed.

4.1 Why Is Change Control Important?

Change control is important because it can help you to prevent problems that can be costly. Without change control, changes to your production environment will likely result in serious mistakes that can impact your business in a significant way. A number of different types of change control can add value and help your organization run more efficiently. Change control can also drive your entire configuration management process. From guarding changes to your production environment to controlling changes to your processes, change control is important to your entire application lifecycle.

4.2 Where Do I Start?

Most people get started with change control by establishing a change control board (CCB) to review and approve all changes to production (or QA). This may include releases, patches, and runtime configuration changes. It has been my experience that it is best to start small and then add additional controls as needed based on risk (for example, potential for mistakes). Change control typically starts small and then grows as needed. As always, start by considering your own goals and priorities. There are seven types of change control that you need to consider implementing.

4.3 The Seven Types of Change Control

There are many different types of change control, and you will likely need to have two or more different CCBs with each handling one or more of the following seven types of change control. I am not suggesting that you need to implement all these change control functions. In my experience, change control is usually a mix of these functions.

4.3.1 *A Priori*

Some organizations have a disciplined process whereby permission for a change is requested before any actual change to the code is made. I have seen defense contractors that had to describe the changes that they want to make and then await approval from a government agency before actually writing the code that implemented the change. In this process, requests for change (RFCs) are usually created and reviewed by the respective CCB. *A priori* change control usually refers to changes in the code and most often consists of defining requirements and then the actual design of the system. The role of configuration management in this case is to track requirements throughout the lifecycle and confirm that all requirements were included in a specific release. Many organizations have a regulatory requirement for tracking requirements, and that often includes a change control function. Tracking source code changes to requirements is important, but controlling changes to production are essential, too.

4.3.2 Gatekeeping

The most common type of change control, and usually the first to be implemented, is "gatekeeping" change control where the CCB reviews RFCs that will impact production (or QA). This usually involves giving authority to promote a new release of the code into production (or QA). Similarly, patches to existing releases are also reviewed by the CCB. This function generally evaluates whether there is a risk that the RFC could potentially impact the production (or QA) environments. The CCB is responsible for reviewing the RFC and approving or rejecting the RFC. It is common for the members of the CCB to have questions about whether the change requested could impact the production (or QA) environment. Traditionally, the CCB will require that all necessary technical experts be present at the CCB meeting—although, in practice, this is often not practical. The ITIL framework has made popular the use of a change advisory board (CAB) that consists of experts who can advise on the downstream impact of a particular change. I discuss how to set up a CAB and why it might need to be separate from the CCB later in this chapter. Closely related are configuration changes, as discussed in the next section.

4.3.3 Configuration Control

When the RFC involves a configuration change, the CCB reviews and considers the downstream impact of the configuration change required. Configuration changes can have the same impact as a new release. In practice, understanding the interface dependencies often requires specialized expertise and should be reviewed by a board that contains members who possess this expertise. In this case, I believe that the governing body should be called a configuration control board. However, there is some confusion in the terminology commonly used today. Many of the industry standards describe the configuration control board as governing the configuration of a system in terms of the configuration of the source code itself instead of environment configuration. In these standards, a configuration of the code refers to a specific *set of versions of the source code*. I believe that this usage is confusing and a relic of days past when configuration control referred to controlling the version of a Cobol program that was being promoted on a large IBM mainframe computer. Today, we promote a packaged release that may contain thousands of configuration Items, including binaries, XML, and many other artifacts. I believe that it makes more sense to use configuration to refer to environment configuration and to use terms such as *baseline* or *release* to refer to a specific set of code versions that are promoted as a release. There are many reasons for this. Most releases are packaged, and the entire release package is deployed as a complete package. The last thing that the administrator deploying the release wants to know about is the specific versions of each of the configuration items that make up the packaged release. However, in these same situations, environment configurations such as interprocess communication ports are still managed through the change control process, as they should be. So, if you want port 9444 opened on an application server, you need to complete a change request and, once approved by the configuration control board, the data security team will modify the iptables to allow interprocess communication on port 9444. In my opinion, true configuration control should refer to interface (runtime) dependencies only.

4.3.4 Change Advisory Board

I have been very impressed by the itSMF's ITIL framework that places a strong focus on configuration management in the ITIL section on transition. I discuss this further in Chapter 14, "Industry Standards and Frameworks." ITIL describes a change advisory board (CAB) that acts as an expert resource to the change management function. This is the best description that I have seen that solves the common problem that the folks involved with the *process* of change control might not be the most knowledgeable in terms of all the required technical details. It is appropriate that the CCB have access to all required experts to effectively review requests for change and identify any possible downstream impacts. Without the services of a group similar to the ITIL CAB, changes could be made that are not understood, resulting in mistakes and system outages.

4.3.5 Emergency Change Control

There are always times when emergencies require immediate changes. It is likely that the CCB cannot meet at any hour of the day or night to authorize emergency changes, and focusing on strict adherence to the regular process may result in the company production system being down for an extended period of time. Any successful change control function must include a well-defined process for managing emergency changes. I recommend that a very senior manager's approval be required for emergency changes and that there be discussion after the event to understand why an emergency change was required in the first place. I have seen situations in which technology professionals abused the emergency change control process to bypass the regular change control process. In this case, you will be successful if you have the support of senior management to ensure that everyone follows the process in the best way possible.

4.3.6 Process Engineering

Organizations establish processes to run their businesses on a day-to-day basis. These processes are established, and then the teams affected are expected to comply with the process. The processes will sometimes need to be adjusted, and this can have wide-ranging impacts on the entire organization. In this case, the process engineering should be placed under control of a change control board that is responsible for reviewing requests for changes to the process. The CCB for process is also tasked with communicating process changes to all affected parties and stakeholders. I believe that the best response to a mistake is to reexamine existing processes and ascertain whether additional process steps are warranted. Process improvement is an organized continuing effort, and the process CCB can help to manage the process engineering effort on an ongoing basis.

4.3.7 Senior Management Oversight

The change control function should provide visibility to senior management and other stakeholders so that everyone knows the status of upcoming changes and also changes that have been completed (whether successfully or not). The best way to do this is with a dashboard that lists the upcoming RFCs, including their status, pending approvals, and other relevant information. You should also coordinate these efforts with the project management team, especially if your organization has a formal project management office (PMO). Some of my colleagues have pointed out that this function might seem different from the others, and I agree that it is indeed unique. Many organizations arrange their CCBs in a hierarchical fashion to ensure that change control has the proper oversight and control. This function maintains the topmost organizational oversight from a process and change control perspective and is normally only used in larger organizations.

4.4 Creating a Change Control Function

Change control involves establishing procedures to review all requests for changes and ascertain whether there are downstream potential impacts that might or might not cause a problem. Change control includes acting as a gatekeeper. In this regard, the change control function reviews requests for change and grants permission or rejects the request for change. Most organizations establish a CCB to review and evaluate all requests for changes. We discuss the role of the CCB as is commonly described in many industry standards, including those approved by ISO, IEEE, and frameworks, including Cobit, ITIL, and the CMMI. I also suggest that many organizations often handle configuration change control separately from other change control functions.

4.5 Examples of Change Control in Action

Change control takes many forms, and I have seen effective CCBs and quite a few CCBs that just wasted people's time. I am a process-improvement professional with a background in industrial psychology. I love process and process engineering, but I do not enjoy verbose processes that leave everyone wishing that there was a way to avoid wasting an hour in a pointless meeting. Here are a few examples of useless CCBs and a few excellent CCB best practices.

Conflict Between Teams

I once worked in an organization where the head of data security did not get along well with the head of the UNIX systems administration group. As a result, each group started its own change control function and somehow managed to be able to not attend each other's meetings. This breakdown in communication directly resulted in production system outages because the security team would decide to close a port and the systems team would not find out until the production system stopped working. This happened at a government agency, which had already been cited by the GAO, for failing to have proper IT controls in place. However, the organization continued to be mired in politics, and its change control wasted countless hours in addition to being ineffective.

4.5.1 The 29-Minute Change Control Meeting

I love implementing process improvement when it is specifically intended to solve a particular problem. This usually takes some marketing of my services and convincing colleagues that better process can mean better results. But, addressing specific problems and showing results is probably one of the most enjoyable aspects of being a configuration management evangelist. I worked in the NYC office of a large international bank that had a recurring problem in which changes in one part of the code would almost always break another part of the code. The software was designed to serve offices in major financial cities throughout the world. The problem was that a change for the Zurich office would often break the code impacting the Tokyo office. After this happened a few times, I offered to create a CCB that focused on the common body of code that was often the cause of these problems. Twice a week, we had a meeting that I personally guaranteed would never run longer than 29 minutes. I picked 29 minutes as a target for two reasons. The first was that everyone was extremely busy and already working long hours. I could not successfully implement a process that took very much of their time or else people would just find excuses to not participate. The second was that I spent a fair amount of time working in broadcast radio (starting when I was in college) and learned that it was indeed possible to run programs that started on time and finished exactly at 29 minutes and 29 seconds. Running meetings efficiently is essential for implementing process improvement effectively. I also established the best practice of requiring explicit entry criteria for starting the meeting and also explicit exit criteria for ending the meeting. This helped overcome resistance to change because everyone agreed that we managed the time required for the CCB in an efficient way.

4.5.2 Change Control at the Investment Bank

I worked at another company where change control was a loosely controlled weekly meeting during which the team reviewed open tickets to discuss new requests and completed tasks. Change control in this context ran the full gamut of gatekeeping for new releases being promoted to production and QA to minor changes such as downtime to install a disk drive. The division was relatively small, and this meeting was sometimes effective. The record keeping was not perfect, however, and the division often got into trouble with the audit department because it could not account for every production change that was made to the systems. It also had a recurring problem that developers could get access to the production machines and frequently made *emergency* changes that were not tracked effectively. This team also suffered from busy managers often skipping the change control meeting and then being surprised when they were unaware of pending changes. This was a tough environment to work in, and managers often resisted new ideas and process improvement. They also had frequent production outages, which they would try to explain away as being caused by some *external* factor that was *beyond the control of the team*. In truth, the culture of the organization did not lend itself to improving the process and I had to accept the tough lesson that I would not always be completely successful. There were other times when I felt that the CCB was not operating as effectively as it should be.

4.5.3 Change Control at the Trading Firm

I worked at another company where change control was a simple gatekeeping function. A senior manager from the systems group chaired the CCB and reviewed all the RFCs on a weekly basis. If the RFC was incomplete, the change request was abruptly denied. In some ways, this CCB was rather "effective" in that the decisions were made quickly and approval or rejection communicated effectively. However, important subject matter experts were often not invited to the meeting, and sometimes, the CCB lacked the technical expertise needed to make the right decision. In fact, this CCB often operated based upon political influence instead of technical expertise. This resulted in a number of mistakes and resulting system outages. It also had to rely too much on an emergency change control process when a request was rejected in the regular change control process. In this case, the group was less than effective because one manager exercised too much positional power as the leader of the CCB, and the organization often suffered as a result. I was sometimes surprised at how harsh and abrupt his comments were to our colleagues who were just trying to get their change requests approved.

When Every Day Was My Birthday

I recall one organization where the developers were accustomed to getting access to production and doing their release management and deployment. There was a lot of instability, so management brought me in to establish a repeatable and reliable release management process. The problem was that the development team really didn't want me around because they preferred to be able to have the control to do their own releases. During this time, I noticed that they often left out important details that I needed to know to do the release successfully. I am not suggesting that this was an intentional and calculated omission. But, it was true that every day seemed like it was my birthday because there were always surprises coming my way!

Hierarchy of Change Control

Some organizations have a hierarchy of CCBs that organize and oversee the change control process. The high-level CCB is usually staffed by senior managers who confirm that the change control process is being followed. The next level down is usually a divisional CCB that is responsible for coordinating changes that might affect more than one group. This continues all the way down to a project specific change control group that focuses on changes that impact a particular project. There also are specialized change control groups that serve a very particular purpose.

Specialized Change Control

The data security group might run a specialized change control function that focuses primarily on security-related changes. For example, changes to firewall rules might need to be coordinated by a specialized change control function. Authentication and entitlements are also often handled by the data security group and might be handled by a specialized change control group. This approach works if there are lots of requests that are specific in nature and need to be handled by a centralized resource. Handling firewall rules is probably the best example of this requirement.

e-Change Control

Change control does not always require an in-person meeting. One best practice is to implement the entire change control process through a process automation tool. I have seen this done successfully with just an email list, although that approach is certainly not optimal. Using an automated workflow solution can support both in-person meetings and online meetings, too. In this approach, the RFC is completed online and often categorized depending on the type of change requested and the resources needed to evaluate and approve (or reject) the change. Using an automated tool can also help to track all change requests, including who authorized the change and whether the change was completed successfully. I have seen tools like this provide electronic signatures using cryptographic keys. The e-change solution should include a dashboard to help communicate the status of all changes and provide visibility to all affected parties and stakeholders.

4.5.4 Forging Approvals

It seems hard to believe, but I worked at one international bank where the project managers would actually walk over to someone's desk when they were at lunch and use their computer (and account) to forge an electronic approval. Aside from the lesson learned that you should always lock your computer when you are away from your desk, this environment really shocked me with just how far they would go in bypassing the approval process. This company had a lot of outages and other incidents, and it was no surprise that they often had problems that could be traced to their lack of discipline and repeatable processes. I learned a lot at this company, but most of it was what you should not do! Their practices resulted in a material risk to the firm and that certainly showed up on a day-to-day basis. Risk is something that you always need to consider.

4.6 Don't Forget the Risk

Risks are inherent in any major IT effort. The change control process should always consider risk in terms of what might be impacted by a particular change. This might mean that you will need to escalate a particular request for change to advise others of a problem that could possibly occur. It also might mean that you must take additional steps to mitigate risks. It should always mean that you communicate risk to all the stakeholders involved with this effort. In particular, significant risk is one of the items that should be communicated to senior management. It is common for senior management to be interested in change control, and you should consider driving the entire process through change control, too.

4.7 Driving the CM Process Through Change Control

The change control process can drive the entire configuration management effort by requiring that all requests for change come with all related entry criteria completed. For example, the RFC to promote the release to QA should also include reviewing the CM plan to make certain that all the configuration management functions are completed correctly. Using change control to drive the CM process requires considerable commitment and support from senior management. There needs to be a well-defined CM policy that spells out the need for compliance with all related configuration management directives. Another example of how change control can drive the release process is reviewing all the steps required for the release in detail. The CCB can recommend that the release process be automated and get release managers to work together better to compare and share release management best practices, including script automation. This can and should include all aspects of configuration management, including source code management, build engineering, environment configuration, release packaging, and deployment.

4.8 Entry/Exit Criteria

The entry criteria for the change control meeting should be a concise description of the requested changes. I always require that project managers and development leads provide enough technical details about the change in advance of the meeting that other managers can review the request and ascertain whether there might be some impact on their own systems. The meeting itself is a discussion of possible downstream impacts and whether the change is actually required. The important information is provided for review before the meeting, and the other managers know that they have to participate or else be prepared to handle the consequences of an unexpected change. The exit criteria are descriptions of the required tests to verify that the changes are successfully implemented without impacting the other systems. I liberally use peer pressure to make this effort a success.

Implementing a process can sometimes be a tug-of-war between the project managers and the change management group. The PMs and development managers will insist that they are too busy with *real work* to be bothered with filling out forms and attending meetings. It works a lot better if you can get the PMs and development managers to view their efforts as being a service to their peers instead. I discuss this further in Chapter 10, "Overcoming Resistance to Change."

Impacts on Other Systems

The change control function should be integrated with other process automation systems, too. For example, help desk systems often track events, incidents, and problems that may impact the delivery of a particular service or technology resource. This is well explained in the itSMF ITIL framework. Approved RFCs should always be communicated to the professionals on the help desk who will be getting the call if a problem occurs. The change control system should be integrated with other workflow and process automation systems, too. This will help with the planning of changes and the evaluation of changes after they occur, too.

4.9 After-Action Review

Change control should always be reviewed after the change has been completed. This is important regardless of whether the change was successful. When RFCs are completed successfully, the CCB simply reviews the completed change and advises that the change is completed. When problems occur, the after-action review should facilitate an open and honest discussion of what went wrong, and the CCB should make plans to avoid problems in the future. W. Edwards Deming, widely regarded as the one of the great leaders of process and quality improvement, noted that it is essential for organizations to *drive out fear*. This is especially true when conducting an after-action review. The team needs to feel safe that mistakes and problems can always be discussed in an open and honest way. The focus should be on how to prevent the mistake from occurring again. The after-action review is sometimes called a post-mortem or, in Agile, a retrospective. Regardless of the name, it is essential for the organization to discuss what went well and what needs to be improved. Mistakes are often the best catalyst for enhancing organizational processes to prevent mistakes from reoccurring.

4.10 Make Sure That You Evaluate Yourself

Change control is one of the most important functions in configuration management. It also should be continuously evaluated and improved. The CCB should be open to input from all stakeholders in the organization. This might mean that some people advocate that the CCB lighten up controls a little bit so as to not impact productivity. More often than not, it will actually mean that the CCB is asked to widen its role and actually strengthen its controls. This is particularly true after a mistake has occurred. You might even find that change control is held responsible for failing to prevent a mistake from occurring. The phrase that you will sometimes hear is this: "Gee that should have been caught in the change control meeting." Once change control is considered an essential function that cannot be bypassed, you will really know that you have been successful.

Conclusion

There is a lot to change control, but it is often the most overlooked (and avoided) CM-related function. This is paradoxical because you can drive all of your CM best practices from within change control. I encourage you to start small and implement each of the change control functions as needed. Change control, along with all the other CM functions, needs to be constantly monitored and improved. Please share your change control-related best practices with me, including challenges that you have encountered and your own successes!

Chapter 5

Release Management

5, 6

Chapter Overview

5.1 Why Is Release Management Important?   75

5.2 Where Do I Start?   75

5.3 Release Management Concepts and Practices   76

5.4 The Ergonomics of Release Management   77

5.5 Release Management as Coordination   80

5.6 Requirements Tracking   81

5.7 Taking Release Management to the Next Level   81

Release management is a core function in configuration management that focuses on packaging a system for promotion from development to QA to production. If you are supporting a software production company, "production," for you, may be shipping the product to the customer, instead of releasing the code to the production (or QA) environment. Whereas release management should focus on packaging the code created during the build process, release management is, in practice, often viewed as being a broad function that may encompass both source code management and build engineering. Release management in a corporate IT environment is slightly different from release management for a software product company—although I have worked in software product companies that still maintained separate QA, integration, and production environments as if they were a corporate IT environment even while shipping the finished product to an end user (or pushing changes via an automated installation process). In this chapter, we focus on defining release management as a function that takes over after the build has been completed and prepares the release for

73

deployment into the desired environment. After a release has been created, it should conform to all the standards set by the release management team. In this chapter, we examine these and other best practices related to release management.

This chapter covers the release management functions that include packaging and configuration identification procedures such as creating immutable version IDs and shipping release maps (that can be verified in production). I view the basic ergonomics of release management as essential, and yet they are rarely, if ever, discussed as part of configuration management. This includes avoiding human error and dealing with too many moving parts. Release management should also be viewed as coordination and communication, and needs to consider the links to requirements tracking and traceability. The future of release management will include the use of cryptographic keys to verify that that the entire release is intact. This chapter is packed with essential information on the release management function.

Goals of Release Management

The goal of release management is to create and maintain a repeatable process for packaging a release that includes a clear way to identify every component of the release. Release management must be clearly defined with little or no chance of errors occurring. Generally, release packaging is an automated function that includes creating an immutable ID that is embedded into the release package itself. Release management should also coordinate any dependencies that might be required for the release to successfully deploy. Finally, release management should be completely traceable with a clearly defined procedure to verify that the correct components have been deployed into a runtime environment.

Principles of Release Management

The principles of release management include the following:

- Releases should be readily identifiable with an immutable version ID.

- Releases should be packaged with all the dependencies included.

- Release packaging should be automated and designed to avoid human error.

- Release management should be fast and reliable to facilitate iterative development.

- There should be a mechanism to conduct an audit of a release package to verify all of its configuration items.

- The contents of a release should be well understood, including the tracking of requirements.

- Release management should be a source of information on the status of all releases, ideally though a release management dashboard.

5.1 Why Is Release Management Important?

Release management (RM) provides order to the development process, which is often in a constant state of creative chaos. It is common for all the configuration management functions to be grouped under release management, although I believe that to be misleading. Release management is, above all else, the first line of defense in making sure that the release is ready to go. There is a lot more, though, because release management often plays the key role in packaging, coordinating, and communicating the status of the release. In my world, RM interfaces with the project management function, development, QA, and operations support. In many ways, RM is the glue that keeps the development process on track.

5.2 Where Do I Start?

There are several places where you could start with implementing an RM function. Sometimes, you need to focus on creating a release calendar and communicating status and, in this context, RM is a communications and coordination function. I usually start by making certain that releases are always packaged in a reliable way that eliminates any chance of mistakes. You might find that you have specific goals and priorities that will drive where you start with RM. I usually get called into an organization to solve a specific RM-related problem. In this context, my performance is judged based on whether I can solve the specific problem that is adversely impacting the organization. If you have the luxury of starting up an RM function without a specific fire to extinguish, I would say that you should start by ensuring that you have a reliable way to identify all configuration items (also known as configuration identification) and then proceed to automate your release packaging process.

5.3 Release Management Concepts and Practices

A variety of RM concepts and practices are discussed in the following subsections. The focus of release management should be on ensuring that every configuration item (CI) has a unique version ID. This means that every binary has a unique internal stamp that can tell you the version ID of the CI. It is common for developers to proudly point out that the code in the source code management tool has been baselined using a unique version label, tag, or other identifier. But in release management, we have to ensure that all CIs can be identified when they are no longer solely in the version control repository and are also running in a production (or QA) environment.

5.3.1 Packaging Strategies That Work

In an ideal world, every configuration item should have an embedded immutable version ID that correctly identifies the exact version of the configuration item deployed. Release packages typically consist of one or more complete components that can run as a unit. It is true that there may be other dependencies required for the release, but one of the roles of RM is to identify these dependencies and provide a reliable way to manage them. Of course, you want to make sure that the embedded version IDs can be traced back to the version labels or tags used to baseline your source code in the source code repository. I should also point out that configuration items include all binaries, configuration files, and documentation—essentially every single piece of code or binary that goes into a release. Obviously, you need to take a reasonable and practical approach to this effort. You might not be able to imprint immutable version IDs in every CI. You should always take a "risk"-based approach to this effort, which means that you consider what bad thing might happen if you have the wrong version of a CI running in production. After identifying all of your CIs, the next step is to package and prepare the release for deployment. Remember that the packages themselves also need to be identifiable.

5.3.2 Package Version Identification

Every release should be delivered as a complete package with a unique and verifiable version ID embedded in the release package itself. The release package should be able to tell you exactly what version has been deployed. It is not enough to just have a record of what was deployed at a particular time. I have seen incidents where the release was deployed correctly and then through human error some part of the production release was inadvertently replaced with the wrong version of a runtime component. This should never happen, but in the real world, it does happen. The RM function should create release packages that have an embedded and immutable version ID that can be easily retrieved with established auditing practices. In Chapter 6, "Deployment," I describe an incident that occurred when I was the release manager at a large stock exchange where my techniques for creating package IDs helped to triage a situation where the world economy was impacted by a change that was made to production after my release was successfully deployed.

5.3.3 Sending a Release Map with the Release

The packaged release should always contain a list of all the configuration items that were delivered as part of a release and developer release notes, product documentation, and updated help files explaining what is included in the release. I sometimes call the list of what is included in the release my *release map,* because it shows everything that was deployed, including the size in bytes of all configuration items along with their respective date stamps. Some people call this a *bill of materials.* We should also note that date stamps and sizes can actually be impacted by minor changes or environment issues that do not actually threaten the integrity of the release. There are more reliable methods that we discuss, including the use of cryptographic keys. But still the release package itself should always ship with an immutable version ID that can used to trace back to the exact version of the source used to build that particular release.

5.3.4 What Does Immutable Mean?

An immutable version ID means that the package can be identified with an ID that cannot be overwritten either intentionally or by accident. One way to do this is to embed the version ID into the binary executable at build time. Embedding version IDs into executables was covered in Chapter 2, "Build Engineering." I sometimes call this *branding the executable* because the objective is to stamp the binary once and never allow the version ID to be overwritten. If your release packages and all the configuration items contained in them have version IDs, you are much closer to being able to create reliable RM practices.

5.4 The Ergonomics of Release Management

In ergonomics, we design the job, tools, and workplace to prevent injury and any possible type of mistake. Release management is all about ergonomics in that we try to make it impossible to make a mistake in the RM process which means that we work towards preventing *any* type of human error.

5.4.1 Avoiding Human Error

Good RM puts a strong focus on avoiding the human error that can sometimes occur during the RM process. I have worked on teams that called me in specifically because it seemed that they could not build a release correctly two times in a row. To solve this problem, I always analyze the reasons for the errors and then create controls to prevent mistakes from being made again. There were many reasons for these mistakes that can run the gamut from technical complexity to miscommunication between the people involved with creating the release.

Language Barriers and Ignored Error Messages

I recall one team that missed their deadlines repeatedly over a six-month period largely because of error-prone RM practices. The manager asked me to help review current procedures and help the team change the way that it was working so that it would stop making mistakes. The build used Ant and Maven on a Sun Solaris platform to create Java SOA services through packaging the Java applications into a war file that will be explained further in the next section. I sat with their release manager during the build and deploy process and observed the work as it was being done. During this time, I noticed that the technical resource doing the work did not speak English well. I also noticed that he ignored error messages that flashed across the screen. It turned out that he always ignored them because he really didn't know what they meant. Fixing this problem was as simple as modifying the build scripts to put in a pause and echo out instructions for the build engineer in simple English that he understood. So now, this script popped up a simple message that said, "Please look for any errors on the screen and notify the developer if you see the word *error*." This sounds incredibly simple, but that was all it took for the build engineer to stop making mistakes during the build process that impacted the subsequent release packaging.

5.4.2 Understanding the Technology

Release managers need to understand the technology being used to package their release. In Java, we can have releases packaged as WARs, EARs, and JARs. There are many other ways to package code, and the release manager needs to understand the tools for packaging that are commonly used with a particular technology. For example, packages are often signed with a cryptographic key to insure that they have not been tampered with and contain a complete manifest describing their contents. These packages can be created by hand using tools available at the command line. It is more common to create a WAR file as part of the build engineering process (using Ant, Maven, or Make).

5.4.3 Tools from Build Engineering

During the build, source code is compiled into binary configuration items that may be runtime components. For example, the Java compiler can create classes that can be run by the Java Virtual Machine (JVM). It is more common for the classes to be assembled into a JAR (WAR or EAR) file and then deployed into the runtime environment. Release managers may be lucky enough to get an automated build procedure from the developers, but they still need to understand all the related build engineering tools used to create a runtime package. It has been my experience that the more that a build engineer understands about the technical details of creating these packages, the more likely that he can work successfully with the members of the development team. It is also true that this knowledge helps to prevent human error, which we discuss in the next section.

5.4.4 Avoiding Human Error

The only reasonable way to avoid repeated mistakes in release management is to automate the release packaging effort. I have seen many RM procedures that were followed by whoever was in charge of building and packaging the release. If the procedures were not automated, they were almost always error prone and far from reliable. I like to take this a step further and create procedures that avoid any possible human error.

5.4.5 My Own Three-Step Process

It usually takes me three releases to fix a release management process. The first time, I observe what is being done and I take a few notes, but I always start by trying to understand the current practices in place. The second time, I ask to do the release myself with the developer at my side coaching me through the release process. I always create a checklist and capture screens so that I can do it again in the future without help. Then, I start to write scripts to automate the release process and "Bob-proof" (see Chapter 2 for an explanation of "Bob-proofing") the RM process. By the third release, we should be using my checklist, although I usually still need some support and help from the developers. After the process is documented and automated, I have often given it back to the developers to manage themselves using my procedures, which are ergonomically designed to avoid mistakes and provide complete traceability regardless of who runs them.

5.4.6 Too Many Moving Parts

I have worked in environments where my own procedures still fell short and I was not able to fix the RM process. Usually, this was because there were just too many parts, and it was impossible to tame the environment into a repeatable process. Sometimes, it was due to organizational issues that made it impossible for me to get my job done. This does not happen to me often, but I want to acknowledge that it can happen. I have sometimes felt that I simply became part of the problem and could not fix a truly broken RM process. These tough nuts are not common, and usually, I can fix a bad release process in just three releases. It is also important to fix the communications around the status of a release.

5.5 Release Management as Coordination

Release management is also a coordination function in that it helps to manage all the tasks and requirements for a successful release. This may involve coordinating the release itself and all the items that are required for a successful release. Part of this effort is ensuring that you communicate the status of a release to all affected parties.

5.5.1 Communicating the Status of a Release

I have seen environments where everyone was doing a great job, but just about nobody knew that to be the case. The communication within the team was poor and almost nonexistent to the management above them. Poor communication results in considerable frustration and can undermine the effectiveness of the entire team. The RM process must, at a minimum, provide visibility into the status of a release. I always communicate to all stakeholders that a release is planned, and more important, when it begins to be deployed. Then, I always broadcast the completion of the RM process along with success of the required smoke tests that we describe in more detail in Chapter 6.

5.5.2 Don't Forget the Release Calendar

The RM function should also establish a calendar to maintain and communicate all the pending releases. In practice, I have found that I usually have two calendars. The first is for planned, scheduled releases, and the second for tactical short-term releases that may occur on a pretty frequent basis. It is not easy to establish these calendars and keep them updated, but again, the RM function is essential for the success of any team and you should definitely plan on spending the resources necessary to establish and maintain an accurate release calendar.

In some cases, this can be done by the change control function in support of release management.

5.5.3 RM and Configuration Control

Release management also involves coordinating changes to the configuration that can impact the runtime behavior of a system. Changes to configurations can impact the release just as much as promoting an entirely new release. Coordinating these dependencies can be complex and is discussed further in Chapter 4, "Change Control."

5.6 Requirements Tracking

Many organizations need to be able to track requirements from the very beginning of the lifecycle to the final deployment into production. This is often because these organizations have a compliance requirement to know exactly what is included with a particular release. They also need to be certain that they do not miss a requirement. This is sometimes done in a very formal way. Other times, the project manager or development lead will simply keep a list of requirements and then document them in the release notes that are delivered and packaged with the completed release. As a release manager, I have often had to go to the project managers and tech leads to ask for the release notes. I also often take a few minutes to make sure that QA is kept advised of exactly what will be included in each release. Requirements often trigger test cases, and some requirements tracking tools interface with test case management software to generate test cases from requirements. Developing end-to-end support of the software development process is one of the ways that RM adds value to the organization.

5.7 Taking Release Management to the Next Level

Release management is a function that is continuously growing with continually improving tools and process. Many of the industry standards and frameworks provide guidance on implementing these best practices, and we discuss them further in Chapter 14, "Industry Standards and Frameworks." There are also some major improvements that are becoming increasingly more common.

5.7.1 Using Cryptography to Sign Your Code

Signing a release with a cryptographic key, such as MAC SHA1 or MD5, is becoming increasingly more common. Many software vendors enable you to verify the integrity of a downloaded package or patch to the software by checking the contents of the package against the digital signature used "to sign" the original source when the package was created. I have personally seen this approach save me a considerable amount of time by identifying downloaded packages that were not completely intact and needed to be discarded. Here is how this works. The original vendor creates the package and then signs the package using his private key. The package is shipped along with the known public key (that corresponds to the private key used to sign the package). A utility is provided that regenerates the cryptographic key and verifies that it was signed by the original private key. Using cryptography to sign a release provides a reliable way to verify that the package has not been altered and will improve the integrity of your RM process. I intend to include some examples on how to use cryptography in release management on the supporting website (http://cmbestpractices.com).

5.7.2 Operating Systems Support for Release Management

Many operating systems provide sophisticated mechanisms for verifying update patches to the operating system itself. Two such examples are the Linux RPM and YUM utilities. Linux administrators will tell you that YUM includes dependency tracking that is not usually found with RPM and therefore using YUM is often preferred. You need to be familiar with your operating systems tools and functions to support release and patch management in a reliable way.

5.7.3 Improving Your RM Process

The RM process adds a lot of value to any organization. You need to be familiar with these best practices and integrate them effectively with the rest of your configuration management practices. You also need to be open to continuously improving as needs arise. Release management can help make your team considerably more effective or it can sabotage your entire project. Most groups find it best to start with light processes in the beginning and then become more formal and detailed as needs arise. I believe that the RM process should be reviewed as part of the change control function (for example, SEPG described in Chapter 4) and wherever possible, improved by the team to avoid any possible mistakes. Release management is a powerful function and can help you and your team achieve great success!

Conclusion

Release management is an essential function in configuration management. You need to take a pragmatic and realistic approach to establishing RM best practices that meet the needs of your organization in a flexible and reliable way. These practices may be implemented differently for a corporate IT environment versus a software product vendor. But in either environment, you want to implement a release management process that is fast, efficient, and error free! Make sure that you share your own RM best practices with me on http://cmbestpractices.com.

Chapter 6

Deployment

Chapter Overview

6.1 Why Is Deployment Important?   87

6.2 Where Do I Start?   87

6.3 Practices and Examples   87

6.4 Conducting a Configuration Audit   91

6.5 Don't Forget the Smoke Test   92

6.6 Little Things Matter a Lot   92

6.7 Communications Planning   92

6.8 Deployment Should Be Delegated   93

6.9 Trust But Verify   93

6.10 Improving the Deployment Process   93

Deployment is the final step in the code promotion process. Deployment involves taking the packaged release and promoting it into the target environment, which is likely production or perhaps QA. Deployment is also responsible for rolling back a promotion if something goes wrong. If you can seamlessly deploy and roll back if necessary, you will be able to significantly reduce a common source of risk (and potential outages). Deployment is usually performed by the operations team, which often has a lot of other responsibilities that need to be fulfilled. I like to see deployment be the simplest step in the release process. This means that all the prior steps of the process must have been successfully completed. Deployment usually also means that control shifts from the release management team to the operations team, which is usually pretty busy with just maintaining the current production systems. The operations team is primarily concerned with keeping the systems running and responding to any events that occur. Therefore, deployment procedures should be kept as straightforward as possible. Your release management team needs to create solid deployment procedures that can be gracefully completed by the operations team. Chapter 14, "Industry Standards and Frameworks," discusses the ITIL framework that is commonly used to establish IT service manage (ITSM). It is common for release management and deployment procedures to be required to be consistent with ITIL processes.

In this chapter, we discuss common deployment practices, including staging, avoiding mistakes, establishing a release depot, and auditing a release that has been previously deployed. We discuss how to conduct a configuration audit, smoke testing after the release has been deployed, configuration changes that can impact your release, along with planning for effective communications such as announcing planned outages and completed deployments. We also discuss the fact that ideally deployments should be delegated to the operations team and deployment should always have its own process-improvement feedback process.

Goals of Deployment

The main goal of deployment is to promote a release into production without any possible problem occurring. Promoting a release should be like turning on a light switch. If there is a problem with the release, the operations team follows the deployment procedures to roll back the release so that business can continue while your tech support team figures out how to solve the problem. I believe that the capability to gracefully roll back a release is just as critical a goal as promoting a new release into production. Deployment also has another important goal, and that is to know exactly what is in production at all times and to know immediately whether any unauthorized changes have been made. My primary goal in setting up a deployment process is that all changes are tracked and that promoting a release or rolling back is easy, reliable, and predictable.

Principles of Deployment

The principles of deployment include the following:

- Promoting a release (or backing it out) should be reliable and as simple as possible.

- Promoting a release (or backing it out) should be completely traceable with an audit log of all changes.

- Only authorized personnel should be involved with deployment.

- In most organizations, there needs to be a separation of duties between developers and the team that deploys the release.

- Any unauthorized changes should be detected immediately.

- There should be a well established procedure for checking the versions of a release in production (or QA).

- The deployment process should be continuously reviewed and improved as needed.

6.1 Why Is Deployment Important?

Deployment is important because you want to make certain that you can reliably promote a release forward or take a step back and back out a release that was previously deployed. Done well, deployment should be a "nonevent."

6.2 Where Do I Start?

I usually start by designing my release management automation to stage a release in a shared depot. Then, I create reliable automation to promote the release and back it out if necessary. You want to keep deployment as simple as possible and always ensure that it can be performed by your operations or systems administration team.

6.3 Practices and Examples

The following sections provide practices and examples that illustrate them.

6.3.1 Staging Is Key

I like to *stage* all my releases in a consistent and repeatable way. That means that I do most of the real work up front (in the build and release functions), and then I just load the prepared release package onto the target machine. The release is preconfigured for production and copied to a specific location, on each machine, which I usually call the depot. In today's N-tier technology world, I usually have to stage release packages on a number of machines and promote them all within the same code promotion window scheduled and approved by the change control board (CCB). The key is to make steps to promote the release as simple and fast as possible. There are a number of different ways to set up staging. In Linux and UNIX, I can usually make use of softlinks, which point to a specific directory or file. Below is a simple example, just to illustrate this approach. The important point is that shifting the links takes only a few seconds.

6.3.1.1 *Example of Staging Using UNIX Softlinks*

For example, if I have a system called Equity Trading that is about to be promoted to release 1.2, I might have the directories set up as shown below. In this example, EquityTrading_Production is a softlink that points to the current active release. Right now, it is EquityTrading_Release1.1. Note that we still have the previous release there just in case we had to roll back to EquityTrading_Release1.0.

```
ls -lt

lrwxrwxrwx 1 trad EQY EquityTrading_Production -> EquityTrad-
ing_Release1.1
-rw-r--r-- 1  trad EQY EquityTrading_Release1.1
-rw-r--r-- 1  trad EQY EquityTrading_Release1.0
```

I then stage the release by copying it into the same directory without changing the link:

```
cp EquityTrading_Release1.2 <depot-directory>
```

Then, this directory will look like the following:

```
$ ls -lt
total 1
lrwxrwxrwx 1 trad EQY EquityTrading_Production -> EquityTrad-
ing_Release1.1
-rw-r--r-- 1  trad EQY EquityTrading_Release1.2
-rw-r--r-- 1  trad EQY EquityTrading_Release1.1
-rw-r--r-- 1  trad EQY EquityTrading_Release1.0
```

Then, we remove the old link, as follows:

```
rm EquityTrading_Production
```

And we create a new link pointing to the latest release:

```
ln -s EquityTrading_Release1.2 EquityTrading_Production
```

Now, we have the following:

```
$ ls -lt
total 1
lrwxrwxrwx 1 trad EQY EquityTrading_Production -> EquityTrad-
ing_Release1.2
-rw-r--r-- 1  trad EQY EquityTrading_Release1.2
-rw-r--r-- 1  trad EQY EquityTrading_Release1.1
-rw-r--r-- 1  trad EQY EquityTrading_Release1.0
```

Falling back is as easy as setting the links back.

6.3.2 Scripting the Release Process Itself

When the promotion process is complicated, I usually create scripts to move the links. In practice, I log the current state of the release before I change anything and then snapshot the environment after the promotion is completed. I can always tell when the release was started and when it was completed. The entire process is designed to be fool-proof (or as I have described it before as "Bob-proof") and fully traceable. This is especially important when the release is complicated with a lot of extra steps.

6.3.3 Frameworks for Deployment

A number of deployment frameworks are becoming increasingly popular. Some of them have been around for a long time with varying degrees of success. The key thing to understand about deployment frameworks is that you still need to do all the work. This means you have to write the scripts to automate the steps required for the deployment. The real advantage to using deployment frameworks is that they give you a comprehensive structure to make it easier to write and execute the deployment scripts. Most of them also provide the hooks to update a dashboard so that you always know the status of the deployment. You will be able to find more information on deployment frameworks on my website (http://cmbestpractices.com/tools). Deployment frameworks also help prevent mistakes.

6.3.4 What If Bob Makes a Mistake?

Anyone can make a mistake—even a disciplined and experienced release engineer. I make mistakes all the time (although hopefully not too many during the deployment itself). But one thing that I can always guarantee is that I will know exactly what I did at every step of the process. The reason is that I never do a deployment at the command line. Everything is scripted. I will always know exactly what I did and when I did it. I can also verify that the correct versions have been deployed at any time. I may make a mistake, but I can always tell you exactly what I did and that makes it much easier to make certain that I never make the same mistake twice!

6.3.5 More on the Depot

I usually set up a directory on the production machine called *depot,* which is where I copy the releases to that are about to be deployed. This has the additional advantage of providing one place where you can find all the releases staged for promotion. You need to make sure that you name all the releases in a clear and consistent way. I usually include the project name, version, and target date for deployment. This might seem like a lot of extra work, but the reward will be that your deployment process is completely traceable and reliable.

6.3.6 Auditing Your Release

A configuration audit involves being able to verify that the configuration items (CIs) in production (or QA) are exactly the correct versions that should be there. It is important to have predefined procedures in place to ascertain the exact versions of the CIs in production. When bad things happen, this can make your job a lot easier. I was once told that I had personally stopped the entire world economy.

The Day That I Was (Erroneously) Told That I Had Stopped the World Economy

One day, I was called into the office of a senior executive at a major New York Stock Exchange, where I was working as a release manager. This gentleman told me that he believed that I had made a mistake that had resulted in a major outage that had actually impacted all the systems on the trading floor. The impact of even a one-hour outage in this environment was huge. I had previously been told that outages could actually require that a senior executive would testify before the U.S. Congress. Given the severity of this incident, I felt extremely stressed and worried whether a sloppy mistake on my part had really caused so much damage. This possibility concerned me a great deal, along with the anxiety that soon I might be looking for a new job. I certainly wanted to know *exactly what had happened.*

Reviewing My Own Procedures

I was asked to review my own procedures and make sure that I never made this mistake again. I asked for permission to work with the operations staff to examine the release that was currently in production. Because

I had created an automated script to conduct the configuration audit, this was easy to do. After we examined the production environment, we saw that there were indeed two wrong scripts currently running in production! This meant that the exact same scenario could easily occur again. We checked a little further and determined that operations had an old version of a script being used that was overwriting the scripts that I had originally deployed. The important thing was that we recognized the bug and that it was still in production! We were able to fix the problem and prevent any further incidents from occurring. Our management also saw that our processes worked.

The Job Interview About Life Support Systems

I once had a job interview in which I was asked to consider a situation where a member of my own family needed to use a life-support system. In this scenario, I was asked whether I was confident that my procedures were reliable enough that I would feel confident in doing the release management for this essential medical device. Of course, there are critical systems out there, and they do need to have well-established release management procedures in place. The same is true of missile and aviation systems. There are many technology systems that need configuration management best practices, and there is no room for mistakes. One of the most important key procedures is conducting a configuration audit.

6.4 Conducting a Configuration Audit

"Pre-audits" may be done by the CM team. Official audits must be done by an independent body. That means that the CM team should develop the procedures to verify that the correct versions of the system are in place. The configuration audit should be automated and fully traceable, too. I have worked in places where we set up an automated check of the environment that told me immediately whether any changes occurred. Sometimes, these were authorized changes, sometimes not. I have also worked directly with the audit team to teach them how to request and understand the results of a configuration audit. The CM team partnered with the audit team to review all the systems online to make certain that there were no version control related problems.

6.5 Don't Forget the Smoke Test

After a release is promoted, the release management team (or sometimes the operations team) should be able to execute at least one transaction to verify that the release was successfully completed and the system is up and running. This is not usually an exhaustive test. More testing is better, although frequently it is not feasible. Additional verification could be completed by the QA team or a production support organization. The release management function needs to at least confirm that the release comes up and can function at a basic level. I usually partner with the QA team to ensure that the smoke test is reasonable and a good indication of whether or not the system has come back up after the deployment. I usually ask the QA team to also recommend some specific tests to confirm that the expected changes were successfully deployed (and they actually fix the problem or provide expected enhancements). The best practice here is that CM does indeed include testing to confirm that the deployment was successful.

6.6 Little Things Matter a Lot

It is important to recognize that small changes are just as important as big changes. Some organizations will allow a small configuration change without following all of their release management procedures. This is a bad idea because changing a configuration can result in a system outage, just like any other technical problem. Make sure that you have enough processes in place to prevent any mistake from occurring that might impact your production systems. For example, closing a port in production can shut down a system just like any other change or technical problem. This is sometimes called an interface control, and it is as important as any other change control.

6.7 Communications Planning

You need to create a communications plan that ensures that all stakeholders are kept advised on the release management process. This may include an announcement on when the release is going to be promoted. I usually announce the target date for the release and then give an update just before we bring the systems down. I try to leave enough time for someone to contact me just in case there is a good reason to postpone the release deployment. After the deployment is completed, I send out another notice advising that the release has been completed. I always mention the results of the smoke test and the location of the release notes that explain exactly what changed in the release. Good communications is obviously essential, and you should create a plan for making certain that you have the right communications procedures in place to support the release and deployment effort.

6.7.1 Announcing Outages and Completed Deployments

Make sure that you establish a procedure for announcing upcoming outages so that all of your stakeholders are warned ahead of time when the system will be unavailable. You also don't want to surprise people with unexpected changes. If your communication is good, your team will be much more capable of addressing any potential problems as they occur.

6.8 Deployment Should Be Delegated

Deployment should be the one function that does not stay within the configuration management role. In most environments, it is advisable to get deployment to a point where the operations team can deploy and fall back to a previous release as necessary. Ideally, the release management team should help establish the deployment procedures but then delegate their day-to-day operations to the team that will be monitoring the system on an ongoing basis. It is true that the same procedures (or possibly a subset) can be used by developers to deploy code to development test (sometimes called a test sandbox), QA, or integration test. But, the actual deployment to production in a mission-critical IT environment should be controlled and managed by the operations team using the procedures developed (or at least directed) by the release management function.

6.9 Trust But Verify

It is important to establish procedures that continuously verify that the production (or QA) environments have the correct baselines deployed and that all interface controls are established correctly as well. I recommend that you trust your deployment procedures but also use automation to verify that no changes have taken place. I have found this to be an essential best practice that will save you a lot of time—especially when an unexpected change occurs.

6.10 Improving the Deployment Process

The deployment process should be continuously reviewed and improved as needed. It is important that incidents and problems be reviewed by the operations team to ascertain whether any issues have occurred that were related to the release and deployment process. It is also possible that better deployment procedures can help make the operations and production support teams more effective. I believe that it is important to accept that there may be mistakes from time to time, but process improvement is all about making certain that the same mistake does not happen twice. The ITIL and Cobit frameworks, discussed in Chapter 14, also provide best practices for deployment.

Conclusion

Deployment should be the smallest of the CM-related functions because most of the work should be completed in the other five core CM functions. You want to make sure that you keep your deployment procedures as simple as possible along with being fully traceable. Ideally, deployment is performed by the operations team using procedures and automation developed by the release management team.

PART II

Architecture and Hardware CM

Chapter 7

━━━━━━━

Architecting Your Application for CM

Chapter Overview

7.1 Why Is Architecture Important?   99

7.2 Where Do I Start?   99

7.3 How CM Facilitates Good Architecture   99

7.4 What Architects Can Learn From Testers   99

7.5 Configuration Management–Driven Development (CMDD)   101

7.6 Coping with the Changing Architecture   101

7.7 Using Source Code Management to Facilitate Architecture   102

7.8 Training Is Essential   102

7.9 Source Code Management as a Service   103

7.10 Build Engineering as a Service   103

Configuration management depends on architecture in a number of important ways. Unfortunately, this dependency is often overlooked, and that often results in problems and serious mistakes. I have always believed that architecture was the Achilles' heel of configuration management, especially when the application changes in ways that can adversely impact the established configuration management procedures. I have had source code management, automated builds, and release packaging and deployment mechanisms suddenly stop working because of "surprise" changes in system architecture. The worst part was that no one realized that I needed to be kept advised on these changes, and I usually found out just before the code had to be packaged for a release to production (or QA). CM best practices must be integrated with the architecture of the application. The procedures for building, packaging, and deployment are very much impacted by the platform, technology used, and the architecture of the application being developed. The lesson learned is that CM, in turn, also facilitates good architecture. Most applications benefit from being developed with a well-defined architecture, including component design. Source code management practices, including variant management using streams, helps to design and implement an effective application architecture. This chapter is about the synergistic relationship between configuration management and systems architecture.

In this chapter, we discuss how CM facilitates good architecture and how CM needs to learn the architecture of the application itself. We consider what architects can learn from testers and how testing can be a service to the developers. I suggest a new paradigm called configuration management–driven development (CMDD) and how to cope with a changing architecture. We cover using source code management to facilitate good architecture using components and snapshots and why training is essential. It should come as no surprise that we view source code management and build engineering as a service to the developers and a critical success factor.

Goals of Architecting Your Application for CM

The primary goal of architecting your application for configuration management is to improve quality and productivity by implementing CM best practices that are consistent with the architecture of the application. First, you need to consider the requirements of good configuration management as you design and implement your application so that changes in the architecture are communicated to those responsible for CM as they are being developed. This approach helps to ensure that you can employ CM best practices to support the entire development effort. You also need to embed the version ID into each configuration item and package the application so that these important CM functions can be successfully completed. Another goal is for CM to support rapid and iterative application development and thereby improve both quality and productivity. Developing CM best practices that are consistent with the application architecture will help to improve the application development process. The application should also be architected to support CM.

7.1 Why Is Architecture Important?

Architecture is essential from two different perspectives. First, the CM support team needs to understand the architecture of the application to be effective. I have often found that this is a key risk area that needs to be addressed. If the CM team does not understand the application, it is very difficult for them to be effective. Similarly, CM can provide an essential service to facilitate the development effort by providing tools and process to support source code management and build engineering best practices.

7.2 Where Do I Start?

You need to start by evaluating the complexity of the architecture of the application that you are working with. Ideally, you will have some development experience with the application, but this can be tough when you change platforms as often as I do on a fairly regular basis. Get ready to create example programs in many different languages! You should also start by identifying what the development team can do to help you get up to speed and how you, in turn, can help facilitate the architecture effort.

7.3 How CM Facilitates Good Architecture

Configuration management helps facilitate good architecture by providing a clear and logical structure to help evolve the architecture of the application as it is being developed. Good source code management strategies include procedures for managing baselines and variants to the code, which are essential for supporting the development of a robust application architecture. This comes as no surprise to experienced technology professionals. What is less intuitive is that the architecture itself may need to be designed for configuration management. Too often, development fails to consider CM requirements up front, and then there are no cycles planned or available for considering CM-related requirements when designing or implementing the application architecture.

7.4 What Architects Can Learn From Testers

I remember when the first automated testing tools became available, forever improving the ability of QA teams to check for defects and ensure that the application worked as desired and expected. I recall that there were some technology professionals who felt strongly that the best way to test was to consider the application as a *black box* and execute test cases without impacting the application in any internal way. This approach was considered to be more reliable because it mirrored the way that people would actually use the application in production. However, the use of automated testing tools often failed because of a small cosmetic change to the interface resulting in the QA team having to run all of their tests by hand. In practice, this meant that getting complete code coverage was impractical. Soon, we found that allowing the test team to examine the code and develop test tools that were more reliable resulted in significant improvements in testing effectiveness. I worked on a number of projects where we instrumented the code to help make the test tools more reliable. This bothered the purists a great deal because we had violated their rule that the application should be a "black box." But, in the end, it was a lot more useful to be able to push through a hundred trades in the first hour of testing and then a thousand trades overnight (for full-regression coverage). We were *instrumenting* the code to help make the test tools work and this resulted in a much higher-quality automated regression-testing suite. This was a big improvement, but it was rare for all the tests to succeed, and it seemed to take a lot of time to release code. We needed to think of ways to become more efficient. We then decided to try moving the test process to the beginning of the development lifecycle.

Automated Testing in a Trading System

I worked with one application where we had two separate automated test suites. The first ran for about an hour and quickly gave us an indication whether the application was working. The second battery was a comprehensive set of over a thousand trades that could take almost a day to run. We regularly built the release and ran the one hour automated test immediately. In practice, it was rare for the longer battery to find a problem, if the one-hour test was successful.

7.4.1 Testing as a Service to the Developers

My colleagues in the QA team had long established that the release had to be tested before it was promoted to production. This meant that the developers worked until the application was completed and then turned it over to the QA team for testing. We then documented the defects found and sent the release back to the developers to fix the high-priority issues (known as "blockers"). We decided to try to offer to run the test tools for the developers on unofficial *pre-releases*. The developers found that this helped them code much faster, and because the developers themselves depended on the test tools, they stopped making changes that broke the automated playback. This happened a long time ago, and today, we have Agile methods such as test-driven development (TDD) that put a major focus on testing as being integral to the application development process. I believe that configuration management needs to make a similar paradigm shift.

7.5 Configuration Management–Driven Development (CMDD)

Instrumenting the code to help implement the configuration management functions includes creating a mechanism to embed immutable version IDs in the software being developed. This process is different when you are writing C/C++ code versus Java or some other technology. The team designing the application architecture needs to consider these issues just as it considers any other technology requirement. Packaging the application also depends on the application architecture. You may be using libraries created using GNU Make or JARs (EARs or WARs) to hold Java SOA applications. Regardless of the technology, application architecture can impact the configuration management functions. It is important to get the requirements for configuration management on the table and under consideration by all affected members of the team. Just as many Agile practitioners are finding that TDD can produce better systems, I believe that the development team needs to be trained to consider the architectural requirements for implementing CM best practices.

7.6 Coping with the Changing Architecture

I usually get recruited to work in environments where the CM process is really broken. The technology leaders usually understand that they have a problem because the releases are often late and usually have to be redone several times because of human error. The same leaders often do not understand why there is a problem and what needs to be done to fix it. This type of situation is fun for me because I get a chance to really show that CM best practices can be crucial and really help improve the overall development effort. However, this also means that I have worked in a number of places where the organization had serious problems that led to this situation. One common reason was that the architecture was changing significantly and this resulted in a lack of stability. Poor communication between the groups was often part of the problem. Leslie Sachs discusses communication and personality in Chapter 11, "Personality and CM." There was also pressure to make major technology changes, sometimes because of poor choices that were initially made at the beginning of the project. Now that the team was playing catch-up, there was still poor communication and planning for the changing technology. The first thing that we need to demonstrate is how CM can help solve this problem. One way is to provide a framework for organizing code into components, baselines, and snapshots.

7.7 Using Source Code Management to Facilitate Architecture

Complex technology is often managed better by breaking the problem into smaller self-contained units. In some organizations, it has become popular to break tough technology efforts into smaller, more manageable *components*. Organizing the code into self-contained and well-defined components (each with its own well-defined interface) can help to simplify the work that needs to be done. I have worked with modern source code management tools that enabled me to facilitate the development of application architecture by the efficient use of components, organized in streams. The streams themselves could be organized in a hierarchical fashion and was a very power way to represent the architecture of the system that we were trying to build. We discuss the use of streams in Section 1.3.7. Some of these techniques can get rather complicated. Training developers in how to use the source code management tools effectively can significantly help make the management of components, their interfaces, and baselines much more manageable on an ongoing basis. (In some source code management tools, snapshots are created to create baselines across one or more components.) Establishing change control can further help take a complex technology solution and make it more manageable, thereby improving both quality and productivity. This requires tight collaboration between the SCM team and the development team.

7.8 Training Is Essential

In Chapter 1, "Source Code Management," we discussed the importance of training in source code management. I made the point that training is figuratively the *hill to die on*—meaning that you need to insist that your management support and provide sufficient resources for delivering effective training. That sounds simple enough, but I have found that it can be tough to gain management support for training. It is less important whether the training is formal classroom training or ad hoc briefings on a whiteboard as long as the method provides the necessary content and meets the needs of the organization. Technology professionals taming a complex architecture benefit greatly from the features of a robust source code management system, but they will likely only know how to maximize these features if they receive adequate training. I usually provide a *fasttrack* training approach to getting developers into the source code management tools quickly along with a more formal training offering (such as two days hands-on) and then an advanced workshop that I may give on an as-needed basis. Using source code management to support complex architecture usually involves employing the advanced features of a source code management tool. Advanced training is essential in helping the team to manage the development of a complex architecture.

7.9 Source Code Management as a Service

Source code management is a service function and I always insist that members of my team regard the developers as internal *customers*. (I usually call my team "release management services" to emphasize this focus on service.) This really just means that we provide excellent support by helping developers to use the source code management tools effectively and with facilitating the build process by setting build standards. To do this, my team needs to understand the reciprocal relationship, the technologies involved and the underlying architecture.

7.10 Build Engineering as a Service

Similarly, automating the build means that developers can make small sets of changes and then rapidly build and test the application. This helps improve both quality and productivity. One way to do this is to create a number of build machines that can be used on an "on-demand" basis. The developer may be working from a laptop using an IDE to code, compile, and unit test. But with the right technology and processes, the build can be run from a larger machine and then promoted to the test area as needed.

Conclusion

Configuration management is impacted significantly by the application architecture, and implementing complex architectures is much easier done with CM best practices in place. The CM team needs to communicate its requirements to the development organization and the technology leadership needs to keep in mind the importance of working with the CM team as a full partner. Just as there is test-driven development, today there needs to be configuration management–driven development.

Chapter 8

Hardware Configuration
Management

Chapter Overview

8.1 Why Is Hardware CM Important?   106

8.2 Where Do I Start?   107

8.3 When You Can't Version Control a Circuit Chip   107

8.4 Don't Forget the Interfaces   108

8.5 Understanding Dependencies   108

8.6 Traceability   108

8.7 Deploying Changes to the Firmware   109

8.8 The Future of Hardware CM   109

Hardware configuration management is often overlooked and undervalued. The truth is that hardware components need to be version controlled just like source code. The challenge is that engineers can't easily check a circuit board into a source code management tool, and there is often no easy way to version control changes to a hardware component. Another problem is that engineers may be trying to troubleshoot a problem at a customer site without having an easy way to confirm the version of the hardware component or even the firmware loaded. However, despite these obstacles, proficient hardware configuration management is essential for your team's success. You need to have procedures in place to perform configuration identification, change control, status accounting, and configuration audits on hardware just like software. It is obvious that software loaded onto a hardware chip (such as firmware) needs to be under version control just like any other piece of software. The rest of this chapter focuses on how to address the requirements for hardware CM.

This chapter discusses how to handle configuration management for hardware, including circuit chips and all of their supporting artifacts (such as design specifications and firmware). We discuss handling interfaces, dependencies, and the often-required traceability and the procedures necessary to support deployment. I do not understand why hardware CM is so often overlooked, and I feel strongly that we need to focus more on this essential area of configuration management.

Goals of Hardware CM

The goal of hardware management is to always know which version of the hardware component is in use (or being tested). You also need to be able to track any changes to the hardware and control changes to the interface and external dependencies that might affect the operation of the hardware device. The goal of hardware CM is to version control the hardware just as you would version control software. A closely related goal of hardware CM is to control environmental changes that may impact the release management process. Ultimately, the goal of hardware CM is to help facilitate the development of hardware in a way that enhances productivity and quality.

8.1 Why Is Hardware CM Important?

Many people are alive today because of medical instrumentation, including pacemakers, computer-driven medical test equipment, not to mention the defibrillator that we carry on the ambulance where I volunteer as an emergency medical technician. Getting the wrong version of any circuit chip or the hardware to support it could have disastrous consequences. Yet frankly, hardware CM is routinely overlooked. I don't understand the reason for this omission, as engineering has always led the way in terms of every other aspect of quality management and testing. When I consult with engineers, I often find that they have no procedures in place to track versions of hardware or even the software that is downloaded to make the device function correctly. This is clearly an area that needs a lot more attention in the future.

8.2 Where Do I Start?

For the most part, the procedures used for software CM can be applied to hardware. There are a few differences, starting with the fact that I cannot check a circuit board into a version control system. Generally, I suggest that engineers get started by putting all the design documents under version control, just as if they were source code. But there is much more that is required to just get started. For one thing, all hardware devices need a version ID, just like software and a clearly defined procedure to retrieve the version ID (which is essentially a configuration audit on a circuit chip). I have seen situations where the engineers did not know (and could not ascertain) the exact version of a circuit chip that was on a test device already deployed to a customer site. This complicated troubleshooting the device and adversely impacted both quality and productivity. Make sure that your engineers know up front that you are expecting version IDs to be imprinted in the device. If this is impossible, they need to give you some equivalent way to ascertain exactly which version of the device is used. This is essential and your product will suffer significantly if you cannot definitively ascertain the exact version of the device (and any software loaded onto the device).

8.3 When You Can't Version Control a Circuit Chip

Hardware CM starts with version controlling the design documents used to create the hardware component. The design documents should be version controlled just like any other configuration item, but in this case they represent the hardware device itself. Version controlling the design documents should always be the first step in hardware configuration. These documents need to have unique version IDs and should clearly show the version ID imprinted on the hardware device. In CM terminology, we say that both the hardware device and the design documents are *configuration items*.

8.3.1 A Configuration Item by Any Other Name

In CM, you always version control all the configuration items used to create the release. Typically, CM experts consider a configuration item to be a component that serves an end-user purpose. This is explicitly stated in some of the industry standards that define the Software Configuration Management process, including ISO 10007. For example, documents, code, configuration files, and all resulting packages should be treated as configuration items. Sometimes, it will serve an end user function to consider configuration items at a much finer granularity, including config files, scripts, and documentation.

8.3.2 Version Control for Design Specifications

While the design document needs to be controlled (and linked to the respective hardware device), changes to the document itself also need to be version controlled. That means that there may very well be several versions of the document for one version of the hardware device itself. In some cases, the hardware device may have programmable memory that may be able to run programmable instructions that should be promoted as a release. In fact, all the configuration items should be traced and handled just like any other source code component. Even though the programmable instructions may be running on a programmable device (such as an eprom), they should be version controlled just like any other configuration item.

8.4 Don't Forget the Interfaces

The precise interface of each component must be ascertained and documented. Changes to the interface should be managed through the change control process. This means that requests for changes (RFCs) are created and either approved or rejected by the change control board (CCB). It is common for hardware components to have specific interface dependencies that must be managed and controlled by a well-defined change control process.

8.5 Understanding Dependencies

Changes to one component may have a downstream impact on another configuration item. It is common for changes to one component to require that changes to another component be handled and controlled to account for the dependencies between configuration items. It is also common to have a situation where only some of the dependencies are understood (and of course, controlled). If a change occurs that results in an unexpected impact on another configuration, the dependency should be documented and controlled from that point forward.

8.6 Traceability

Traceability is a key goal of hardware configuration management. You need to be certain that you can account for all changes to configuration items, whether they are documents, source code, or hardware components. This means that all changes should be traced to RFCs or other change requests (CRs) to who authorized the change and exactly when the change was carried out. Every production release must include release notes that indicate exactly what changes are included whether they be hardware or software related.

8.7 Deploying Changes to the Firmware

Changes to firmware should be handled as a packaged release that can be traced just like any other changes to configuration items. It is a best practice to handle the deployment of changes to firmware as if it is a change promoted to a release of code. In this sense, you can think of promoting the changes to firmware to be similar to promoting a release to production (or QA).

8.8 The Future of Hardware CM

Hardware CM has been given short shrift, but really deserves more attention. Future standards should support hardware CM and specify that all hardware configuration items be fully identifiable and traceable, just like software configuration items. Aside from identifying configuration items, hardware CM should also include change control, configuration audits, and tracking the evolution of the hardware CI throughout its lifecycle (known as hardware status accounting). The ITIL framework is also highlighting the importance of asset management, which is indeed an industry best practice. We need to support hardware CM as being just as important as software configuration management.

Conclusion

Hardware configuration management is often overlooked. Even worse, many technology professionals do not know how to handle hardware configuration management. Technology professionals need to control changes to hardware just like they control changes to any other configuration item. Obviously, technical issues and requirements must be addressed to handle promoting firmware changes to hardware. Versions of hardware configuration items must be controlled just like any other configuration item. In addition, you need to analyze and control the interface dependencies for hardware configuration items. Hardware CM is a full lifecycle discipline that enhances quality and productivity just like software configuration management.

PART III

The People Side of CM

Chapter 9

Rightsizing Your Processes

Chapter Overview

9.1 Why Is Rightsizing Your CM Processes Important? 115

9.2 Where Do I Start? 115

9.3 Verbose Processes Just Get in the Way 116

9.4 SPINs and Promoting the CMM 117

9.5 Disappearing Verbose Processes 117

9.6 The Danger of Having Too Little Process 120

9.7 Just-in-Time Process Improvement 120

9.8 Don't Overengineer Your CM 120

9.9 Don't Forget the Technology 121

9.10 Testing Your Own Processes 121

9.11 Process Consultation 122

9.12 Create a Structure for Sustainability 122

Rightsizing your CM processes is all about focusing on exactly what you must accomplish to get the job done. It's also true that lasting process improvement doesn't usually happen unless there is some structure established, including a strong change agent providing leadership and direction. Process improvement can take on many shapes and forms. I have seen very extensive formal process engineering efforts using the SEI's Capability Maturity Model (CMM), spanning years of effort, and I have seen very modest efforts that were coordinated in short cycles, often called *sprints,* with modest improvement milestones set and, often, actually even met. I always try to focus on developing *just enough* process to get the job done without any extra *ceremony.* Some organizations develop a culture for process improvement and begin a journey that becomes a central part of everything that they do. I have seen this especially in organizations that adopted Six Sigma as a process improvement methodology. This business process improvement methodology had its roots in work done at Motorola and used many of the techniques developed by W. Edwards Deming. There are benefits and challenges with each of these approaches and the most important factor is that you need to *rightsize* your processes to meet your goals and priorities. Of course, like many other goals, that is frequently easier said than done. This chapter describes how to navigate through this journey.

This chapter starts by discussing the fact that verbose processes just get in the way, creating a lot of energy (and motivation) to avoid the processes that just don't seem fair and realistic. We take a step back and recall the SEI's Software Process-Improvement Networks (SPINs) that were established to promote the CMM. The verbose process models have lost much of their support in favor of Agile processes and iterative process models, including OpenUP, which is part of the Eclipse Process Framework (EPF). The familiar "Lean" approach has been taking the industry by storm, although I have to also mention that there is obviously a danger in having too little process, which leads us to my own approach, which I call *just-in-time process improvement.* Closely related is the danger of "overengineering" your CM process which means that you have overly complex CM processes that may work, but are not optimal for your entire team. We discuss the importance of testing your own process, old-fashioned process consultation and the need for transparency, and creating a sustainable structure for supporting process improvement.

Goals of Rightsizing Your CM Processes

Whether you embrace an organizational transformation or a limited tactical effort to fix a specific problem, process improvement must be focused on establishing and meeting the right goals. I don't usually get to spend much time on this issue because most organizations call me in when they have a serious CM-related problem that needs to be immediately addressed (or bad things can happen). Sometimes, I have been very successful, and other times, I have felt pulled right into the deep abyss of the problem itself. For example, I may be asked to fix the release management process, but the real problem is that the technology architecture is so brittle (e.g., too many moving parts) that the release process just can't be easily changed, and the organizational culture makes it nearly impossible to achieve any lasting positive results. I have learned to look carefully at the big picture and focus on achieving the goals that make sense from a pragmatic, business, and technical perspective. Your goal should be to realistically evaluate your business priorities and decide just how much process your organization needs and, for that matter, can tolerate. Too much process is just as bad as too little, and you need to take a close look at exactly what the right balance should be.

9.1 Why Is Rightsizing Your Processes Important?

Having too much process is just as bad as not having enough. I have seen many process-improvement efforts fail because the processes just required too many steps to complete. In my experience, the people defining the process had never been in the trenches a day in their lives and often did not understand the "hands-on" practical side of what they were busy defining a process for. Many Agile enthusiasts refer to the process rigor as "ceremony" (which I find quite descriptive). You don't want too much ceremony, but you do want to make sure that you have enough controls in place to avoid costly mistakes. Rightsizing your processes is important because you need to have *just enough process* to get the job done effectively and avoid costly mistakes.

9.2 Where Do I Start?

You need to start by defining your goals and priorities in a clear and pragmatic way. You also want to define the risks involved and set your priorities accordingly. Make sure that you also start by communicating with the key stakeholders in your organizations. Rightsizing your processes is a "team sport," and you need to consider who you want carrying the ball to make the right choices and help you achieve success.

Process Improvement and Being Blind

I have often explained to my colleagues that I discovered the need for process as a teenager trying to travel alone in NYC armed only with my white cane and a good sense of hearing. I was born with a severe visual handicap that could not be corrected with the existing medical procedures of the day, and I had to wait many years for the laser surgery that I needed to be perfected. During my childhood, high school, and years into college, I could see only shapes and shadows, although there were times when I was able to see well enough to read for short periods of time. I did most of my reading using the Library of Congress talking books and tapes. However, my eyes would fatigue quickly, and I would constantly get eye infections (especially during final exams) that would leave me functionally blind. My trip into NYC to see my ophthalmologist was usually exciting. I quickly learned that crossing Fifth Avenue with a white cane and no real usable vision required that I had previously planned out my journey street by street, because some corners were easier to navigate than others. Process improvement for me meant figuring out whether I could master the traffic patterns more easily from the northwest corner or the southwest corner, and making a mistake meant dealing with irate cabbies who never seemed to understand my white cane was a clue that I could not see them.

9.3 Verbose Processes Just Get in the Way

The fastest way that I know of to fail in process improvement is to establish a ridiculously verbose process that introduces layers of required steps that are unnecessary and just can't be defended as adding value. Yet, many organizations suffer from this exact approach. In these environments, the change agent wins a temporary coup of forcing the organization to follow a process that involves many extra steps and documentation that is just not necessary or even advisable. I have seen this happen despite lots of resistance when the project was sponsored by a very senior manager who had considerable positional power. Because there was no one there to oppose, the team scurried to figure out what they had to do to comply with the requirements of the process. Verbose processes waste energy and are simply not sustainable. As soon as that senior manager moves on to his or her next assignment, the organization reverts quickly back to the way of life as it was before the inefficient processes were forced on them. This was exactly the well-deserved criticism with some of the first efforts at implementing the CMM in NYC financial services firms. These efforts rarely lasted beyond the tenure of the senior manager who sponsored them.

My First CMM Experience

The Capability Maturity Model (CMM) framework from the Software Engineering Institute at Carnegie Mellon was one of the first and most comprehensive models for assessing and improving processes. The CMM was followed years later by the Capability Maturity Model Integrated (CMMI). Many organizations have successfully implemented the CMMI (and its predecessor CMM) in a number of its forms (now called constellations). At its core, the CMMI is a tool for assessing an organization's process *maturity*. One problem that I have seen is that many people focus on the maturity model (levels 1–5) instead of the process areas (or what we used to call key process areas or KPAs). The original CMM was also presented in a rigid fashion, with many process gurus insisting that the KPAs at one level had to be completed (which meant that you could not skip levels) before the processes at another level could be started. This was often both unrealistic and unnecessary. For example, the original CMM framework called for subcontract management to be implemented before peer reviews and establishing a training program (both level 3 KPAs). In practice, I often found that peer reviews were a great place to start with process improvement, and training for configuration management was non-negotiable (especially when the source code management tool was hard to use). In practice, I often found that efforts to implement the CMM were at very high risk for failure.

9.4 SPINs and Promoting the CMM

I have been a proud member of the NYC Software Process-Improvement Network (sponsored by the SEI) for many years. The original purpose of the SPINs was to promote the use of the CMM, and in the early years, we had many NYC-based firms working to implement the CMM. Process luminaries, such as Watts Humphrey, were among the excellent speakers at the SPIN meetings, while technology professionals came to network and share best practices for improving their processes—including implementing the CMM. Years later, almost all the members are focused on Agile practices (a few focus on Six Sigma and Lean), and almost none even consider the CMMI. For many organizations, the CMM journey was very painful and left them completely opposed to such efforts. This is unfortunate because the CMM contains a lot of wisdom and excellent best practices. In some ways, the Agile movement has been a *reaction* to what was perceived as verbose ineffective process-improvement efforts.

9.5 Disappearing Verbose Processes

Verbose processes don't add much value, and most organizations have long since abandoned them as an acceptable approach. I have heard senior managers emphatically insist that they would block any process-improvement effort that involved additional red tape. Unless you are contractually required, most companies look for the process-improvement methods that involve minimal *ceremony*. In this spirit, Agile processes have become extremely popular in many circles.

9.5.1 Agile Processes Just Work

The Agile Manifesto (http://agilemanifesto.org) lists the basic Agile values, including the importance of focusing on the following:

- Individuals and interactions over processes and tools

- Working software over comprehensive documentation

- Customer collaboration over contract negotiation

- Responding to change over following a plan

In practice, Agile recognizes that establishing and tracking requirements is extremely difficult. Awareness of these challenges is essential because many development efforts fail as a result of requirements not being well understood. In addition, there is often no practical approach for effectively dealing with requirements ambiguity, not to mention the inevitable problem of requirements changing. However, Agile also has its own challenges, including the difficulty of scaling to large organizations and harmonizing with required non-Agile approaches. Agile practitioners rightly feel that you *become* Agile as opposed to adopting Agile practices. As such, *going Agile* is a journey that changes you and your development team in many important ways. Still many organizations feel strongly (and may have regulatory requirements for) about maintaining a waterfall lifecycle with well-established requirements specifications, functional, and design phases. What's needed is a practical and pragmatic approach that focuses on the appropriate balance. One popular Agile/iterative approach has been the Unified Process.

9.5.2 Open Unified Process

The Open Unified Process (OpenUP) has itself evolved over time. I am resisting going into the history of the Unified Process (and its open source implementation known as OpenUp) in this book, and instead will discuss its evolution on the supporting website. The Unified Process is iterative, but curiously supported by many documents (known as artifacts). Too often, people believe that they are required to include more artifacts than are really necessary (making this approach more verbose than necessary). But the organization and topology of the OpenUP documents is excellent, and many organizations rely heavily on the

Unified Process in one of its many forms. It has often been said that the key to success with the Unified Process is to use only the artifacts that are absolutely necessary and to guide and limit your selection by repeatedly asking yourself this question: What bad thing could happen if we do not include this artifact? Many people implement OpenUP using the Lean principles that are described in the next section.

9.5.3 Getting Lean

Mary and Tom Poppendieck's work on Lean Software Development has felt like coming home for me in a number of important ways. First, it's no surprise that they mention W. Edwards Deming in their work, and his influence is clear. For me personally, there was also a déjà vu experience of feeling like I was listening to my father-in-law, Benjamin K. Sachs, to whom this book is dedicated. My father-in-law worked in engineering and manufacturing throughout his career and put most of these Lean principles into practice as part of both his company and his personal life. Briefly, the Poppendieck's excellent work mentions the principles of

- Eliminate waste

- Amplify learning

- Decide as late as possible

- Deliver as fast as possible

- Empower the team

- Build integrity in

- See the whole

9.5.4 An Extremely Brief Description That I Hope Motivates You to Take a Closer Look at Lean Software Development

In a Lean approach, you want to avoid unnecessary features and avoid specifying requirements prematurely. And, you definitely want to build in testing from the beginning of the effort. Learning is essential and should be coupled with making good use of the scientific method—that is, establishing a hypothesis, testing, and documenting your findings. You then implement the best results based on your scientific study, along with following and improving standards. You also commit to building quality in from the beginning and deferring commitment—that is, you want to make decisions at the *last responsible moment*. Bringing results to market quickly is essential, as are trying to balance rapid delivery, high quality, and low cost. From an interpersonal perspective, Lean encourages you to work as engaged, thinking people who thrive on pride, commitment, trust, and applause, along with effective leadership. Finally, improving the system needs to focus on examining the system as a whole. The Lean approach is popular among both Agile and non-Agile practitioners. Although I have focused on the fact that it is essential to not have too much process, it is also true that too little process usually results in mistakes and problems that can be extremely expensive in terms of both quality and productivity.

9.6 The Danger of Having Too Little Process

Having too little process means that you will probably make the same mistakes over and over again. You also won't have a repeatable and reliable way to achieve the desired results. Taking a risk-based approach is an excellent middle ground, with a strong focus on heavy processes where a mistake could have disastrous and expensive consequences. For example, most people won't object to developing and tracking requirements carefully for missile systems and life-support systems, where a missed requirement could have disastrous consequences. Having too little process means that unnecessary mistakes can happen with, often, unacceptable consequences. So, what exactly is the right balance? I believe that it can be described as *just-in-time process-improvement*.

9.7 Just-in-Time Process Improvement

In just-in-time manufacturing, the processes are established and understood to the point where the factory receives all of its required parts in exactly enough time to be used efficiently without delay or extra costs associated with warehousing an unnecessary depot of materials. Just-in-time process improvement means that you correctly balance your goals and objectives so that you have exactly the amount of process necessary to have efficient, reliable, and repeatable processes without waste due to extra, unnecessary steps. Many Agile practitioners (among others) call this having just enough *ceremony* to have efficient processes.

9.8 Don't Overengineer Your CM

Similarly, you do not want to overengineer your configuration management processes. I have frequently seen development teams that had branching schemes that were impossibly complicated to follow. Sometimes, code was actually "lost" out somewhere in *n*-dimensional branching space, because the code was checked into the source code repository, but no one really knew which branch it was on. Someone on the team had gotten the hang of branching, and then went and overused branching, with the result being that no one else knew how to follow the resulting convoluted branching process. It is usually a lot better to keep things simple. This is a good example where "less is more." You don't want to overengineer your branching strategy. We have already discussed some branching approaches that work well, and my colleague Steve Berczuk (with Brad Appleton) discussed branching patterns in his excellent book *Software Configuration Management Patterns: Effective Teamwork, Practical Integration* (Addison-Wesley, 2003).

9.9 Don't Forget the Technology

Rightsizing the process also needs to be in alignment with the technology involved. Processes for a mainframe may be quite different from those used in the distributed world of UNIX/Linux (and even Windows systems). One reason that many process engineers fail in this respect is that they lack adequate technical expertise to create effective processes. (My comments might ignite a vigorous debate about whether process engineers need to be technical and hands-on. I will be happy to host that debate on the website supporting this book. Be forewarned, though, that I will take the position that process engineers are much more effective when they do know the technology and have the experience of being hands-on and experienced.) I have seen change control and release management processes that were just entirely not realistic. This simply motivated the technology professionals to work around the established processes. I will talk more about this in Chapter 10, "Overcoming Resistance to Change." But, I will make the case that the process needs to be in close alignment with the technology and the technology requirements of the team impacted by these decisions.

9.10 Testing Your Own Processes

Rightsizing your processes also requires that you test your own processes. This means that you not only need to trust but actually verify that your process meets your goals. You also need to reconfirm that you have set the right goals. This is particularly important because it is common for the journey itself to result in you learning more about the effort along the way—the goals and priorities as you first understood them may have evolved into what you now know to be more correct and appropriate for the situation.

9.11 Process Consultation

When I first started learning about industrial psychology, process engineering was called process consultation, and the assumption was that the process guru would collaborate with the people who would actually use the process. These folks were usually business experts who were subject matter experts in their own area of focus. I miss that traditional collaborative nature of process engineering. Today, we look for process x masters and people who have passed certification exams. Although I absolutely value the wisdom of all these frameworks for process improvement, I also believe that we need a fundamental back-to-basics approach. I believe that process improvement must be collaborative and include input from those who are affected by the processes that are implemented. You also need leadership and direction. When I do a configuration management assessment, I always listen to the input from stakeholders on their existing practices. I always learn something new on each engagement—even when the team has bad processes. But, my core approach is to be collaborative and do my best to include the views of the people who will be impacted by the processes that we implement. This has the additional advantage of providing transparency without the appearance of being superficial.

9.11.1 Transparency That Is Genuine

I have been in organizations where senior management announced the new process initiative with much fanfare and excitement. These announcements were not always well received, and many people questioned whether the organization was really being open. Providing transparency is usually a good idea and usually results in better results for the organization.

9.12 Create a Structure for Sustainability

The minute that you have finished, it is usually time to review and revise your processes again! This is because the environment changes, and therefore your requirements will change, too. This is not a bad thing at all. The lesson learned is that you not only need to create effective processes, you also need to establish a mechanism for evaluating and updating the processes themselves. I usually recommend that organizations establish change control for the processes themselves. This group is usually called a software engineering process group (SEPG) and is discussed in Chapter 4, "Change Control." This is important, because without a mechanism for managing change, processes will quickly become obsolete, and then everyone will stop following them. Processes need to be sustainable and continually improved.

Conclusion

Rightsizing your processes is all about choosing the first things first and focusing on your goals and priorities. Too much process is just as bad as too little. In some situations, formal processes with lots of ceremony are entirely appropriate, whereas in other scenarios, the processes really need to be agile and lean. Your approach should be collaborative and sustainable. The key is to rightsize your processes in a pragmatic way that fits your needs precisely.

Chapter 10

Overcoming Resistance to Change

Chapter Overview

10.1 Why Is Overcoming Resistance to Change Important?   127

10.2 Where Do I Start?   127

10.3 Matching Process to Culture   127

10.4 Mixing Psychology and Computer Programming   129

10.5 Process Improvement from Within   129

10.6 Picking Your Battles   131

10.7 Fostering Teamwork   131

10.8 Why Good Developers Oppose Process Improvement   132

10.9 Procedural Justice   132

10.10 Input From Everyone   132

10.11 Showing Leadership   133

10.12 Process Improvement People May Be the Problem   133

10.13 Combining Process and Technology Training   134

10.14 Listening to the Rhythm   135

10.15 Processes Need to Be Tested   136

10.16 Baby Steps and Process Improvement   136

10.17 Selling Process Improvement   137

10.18 What's in It for Me?   137

10.19 Process Improvement as a Service   137

10.20 Guerrilla Tactics for Process Improvement   138

Overcoming resistance to change can be difficult to achieve. Many well-intentioned process-improvement efforts fail simply because there are enough people who fear change of any kind and will work hard to block what they believe might threaten the status quo. Sometimes, implementing a change, such as implementing CM best practices, can feel like trying to move a mountain. There are also times when you are very lucky if your colleagues block change that is ill conceived and unlikely to result in positive improvements. Resistance to change might not seem rational, and it is usually hard to diagnose why you are running into resistance. Sometimes, you might need to engage in guerrilla tactics yourself to bring about lasting change. This chapter is all about how to recognize and address resistance to change.

In this chapter, we discuss tactics for overcoming resistance to change, including matching process to culture. I describe my own efforts to mix psychology and computer programming and starting process improvement from within, picking your battles, and fostering teamwork. Everything that I discuss in this chapter has come from my own experience working to implement process improvement, especially CM best practices. We also consider the valid reasons why good developers oppose process improvement and the essential construct of *procedural justice*. We consider best practices such as incorporating input from everyone while showing leadership, and why process improvement people themselves may be the problem. We also look at combining process and technology training. I describe my own method of "listening to the rhythm," testing your processes and how to achieve process improvement via baby steps. I also describe the importance of selling process improvement and explaining to your colleagues how process improvement will make their jobs easier. This chapter ends with a discussion about process improvement as a shared service and, when all else fails, "guerrilla tactics" for process improvement.

Goals of Overcoming Resistance to Change

The goal of overcoming resistance to change is to identify the forces that are blocking process improvement and, more important, their underlying motivation to block change. Overcoming resistance to change is very much about designing strategies to help the team overcome the forces impeding process improvement. It's also about recognizing legitimate reasons for opposing change and addressing valid concerns where they exist. At times, it's also about forcing the team to embrace change, even though they may be kicking and screaming all the way. Most of all, you need to be careful to pick the right type of intervention to successfully bring about lasting change.

10.1 Why Is Overcoming Resistance to Change Important?

On many occasions, I was able diagnose why a particular team could not function correctly or was making many painful mistakes. Unfortunately, I have not always been able to convince the key players that they needed to change the way that things were being done. There are lots of good reasons for that. This chapter is important because even if you have the best tools and process, you may have to use tactics to overcome resistance to change. Sometimes, this is because some people are just mired in doing things in a particular way or it may be because of organizational or interpersonal dynamics that impede the process-improvement effort. I have seen organizations where process improvement was at a complete stop because warring parties had political motivations that adversely impacted the organization. In these environments, getting started with process-improvement can be very difficult or even impossible. The good news is that this is often when you can make a real difference and demonstrate value. Remember, failure is just not an option!

10.2 Where Do I Start?

I usually start by looking at the goals and priorities of the organization. It is always a good idea to take a risk-based approach and tackle process improvement in the right order. I sometimes find that I have to take a different approach and work on the items that I can change within a short period of time, just to build up some momentum. Generally, we call this going for the *low-hanging fruit,* which is often the only pragmatic approach to getting started.

10.3 Matching Process to Culture

The most basic reason that teams resist change is that it is packaged in a way that is just not consistent with their culture and current modes of operating. In some cases, this might prove to be ultimately fatal for the team because the organization might have to choose between survival and dealing with the reasons that employees are blocking change. I have worked in development teams that consisted of many highly intelligent and very independent software and technology developers. Senior management wanted to improve organizational efficiency and the quality of their products, so they decided to embark on a multiyear process-improvement effort. The CMMI and SCAMPI (CMMI's assessment framework) were picked as the models to be implemented for this effort. Pretty soon, the organization was deeply focused on establishing process controls and assessing their own process maturity. Meanwhile, the developers felt disconnected by this entire effort and simply chose to not be involved. Many told to me privately that they had seen these efforts come and go before. To them, this was just another fad and a waste of time that, if ignored, would simply go away. The fact is, they were right. As soon as the senior manager who had sponsored this effort went on to another opportunity, the entire process-improvement project faded away and things got back to "normal." I personally recall a number of New York City firms that attempted CMMI-based process improvement efforts that did not survive the tenure of their management sponsor.

Why Did So Many Groups Fail with the CMMI?

It would be valid to then ask why it is that so many CMMI-based process-improvement efforts failed. The truth is that CMMI efforts were not the only process-related projects that failed. But, the CMMI also had a well-deserved reputation for providing very little guidance on how to actually start up and implement the functions that were advocated. As such, the CMMI was more useful for assessment than for establishing the processes in the first place. Much has been written about using IEEE standards for the guidance to establish a process and then use the CMMI (or other frameworks) to assess existing process and identify areas for future improvement. In my opinion, the original CMM from the Software Engineering Institute at Carnegie Mellon is an excellent framework for process-improvement, followed by the even more formidable Capability Maturity Model Integrated (CMMI). SEI's models have always has been, and with the evolution of its diverse constellations (to provide different functional views) will continue to be many of the best process-improvement models for many years to come. However, there were obviously many areas where its implementation could be improved. For example, we can certainly improve our ability to address the people issues that are part of any large-scale development effort. The SEI People Maturity Model (PMM) certainly addresses some of these issues, but I also believe that we need to do a better job of blending psychology and software engineering for the best results.

10.4 Mixing Psychology and Computer Programming

Overcoming resistance to change can prove incredibly difficult to achieve. I have spent more than 25 years working on creating repeatable processes to address common technology (and a few nontechnology) problems. In the early years of my career, I focused on gaining technical skills in both software engineering (we called it programming back then) and process engineering. This journey took me deep into the trenches of industrial psychology and quality management. It was quite lonely at times because I was always the only techie in the psychology circles, and I was also the only programmer thinking about psychology in my computer science circles. Back then, I thought that as long as the process was valid, people would follow. Soon, I learned that there were a number of reasons why good processes would often never fly and, to my own surprise, some rather suboptimal approaches would achieve wide acceptance. I also soon realized that something was missing from my own skill set, and so I went back to school (again) to study how other disciplines handled process engineering and quality management. It is worth noting that engineering, medicine, and defense all have long histories of focusing on process improvement. In some organizations, these were large-scale process-improvement initiatives, and sometimes they were more modest efforts started from a particular group that wanted to improve their own processes. I believe that the best process improvement does indeed come from within the organization and those who are most affected.

10.5 Process Improvement from Within

I have participated in process-improvement efforts that focused on getting the members of the organization to identify areas for improvement. That's not to say that they ignored existing process-improvement frameworks, but rather that they began their journey by asking the current employees for their expert advice. We had many sessions where we brainstormed on identifying existing problems and opportunities for improvement. Some of the ideas were far-fetched, but many were also were also right on target. This was no surprise because the people in the trenches were leading the way to identify valid and useful improvements. It was no surprise that this effort was led by industrial psychologists, and with their influence, that employees felt safe to even make their own jobs *obsolete*. The firm, a major insurance company, pledged to be a good corporate citizen by offering good severance packages to those who left and making every effort to find suitable roles for those who really wanted to stay. Some employees took (fair and reasonable) buy-out packages, and others transferred to different roles. One reason that this worked was that the organization had a strong culture that valued training and employee development. Most members of the organization had a reasonable expectation that they would move into a new and better position if they helped to improve organizational effectiveness.

My Transition Out of This Organization

I personally had a life change while employed at this insurance company that required that I move my home to another state. I felt comfortable explaining my situation to my manager and began helping to train my own replacement. My boss began using her contacts, and actually helped me get an offer with another firm. We worked together in two other companies after that, and I am in touch with her to this day. This organization overcame resistance to change by creating an organizational culture where employees felt that they were treated fairly. They also had a learning organization where training was an expected part of working there. That's not to say that things were perfect there, but many of the lessons that I learned about effective process improvement came from that first experience. One of them is to carefully survey the organization and get a good idea of what process improvement should be implemented to solve problems and improve our own effectiveness.

Survey the Scene

I have spent many hours volunteering as a civilian in police and emergency medical services. From these experiences, I have learned more than a few lessons that I employ when implementing process improvement. In emergency services, we talk about surveying the scene. This means that as you approach the scene of a car accident, fire, or other incident, you carefully examine the entire scene and evaluate possible risks and dangers. The scene survey must be done before you start to treat any patient; otherwise, you might try to address one risk when a greater danger is nearby. Process improvement people need to learn to conduct their own scene survey. This means that you evaluate the risks and dangers in the organization. You should do your best to size up your support team. (In police and emergency medical services, we call this *backup*.) Similarly, when you size up the organization where you are trying to work, you need to know whom you can count on for support. The scene survey may uncover that you have little or no support, and that impacts what you can really accomplish and how you should approach process improvement

10.6 Picking Your Battles

I lived in Brooklyn, New York, for 18 years. During that time, I worked with many different cultural communities to develop civilian patrols and auxiliary police. Crime went down significantly during this time, which was a very exciting outcome to be part of. I recall working with one group that operated in the worst neighborhood imaginable (with rampant crime and drug dealing). The head of the civilian patrol there used to approach some of the tough guys in the neighborhood and talk with them about leaving the older people and the children out of the fight. At first I was shocked, but then soon realized that my buddy was picking his battles wisely. I could work in other neighborhoods and stop people from stealing cars (using a trained German shepherd as my own backup). My colleague had to work within the neighborhood where he lived and with the environment that existed. Obviously, I had great admiration for this friend whom I always call "brother." I hope your situation is not that drastic, but picking your battles can make the difference between success and failure.

10.7 Fostering Teamwork

I have worked in organizations that were very challenged in terms of getting the teams to work cooperatively together. It often seemed people were willing to sacrifice the needs of the organization for their own agenda. Getting everyone working toward the same goal can be difficult, indeed. There is also no shortage of conflict within the police and emergency medical services. I have had times when I found myself at odds with my colleagues in the emergency medical services environment, especially other volunteers. Fortunately, we never allowed this to impact our ability to help others. In one such instance, I recall working with a medic whom I found particularly difficult to get along with. His attitude and personality and mine were just not meant to be in the same room. Yet when we were on the emergency scene together, our cooperation, communication, and teamwork were impeccable. No one could have possibly guessed that we crossed swords when chatting at the local coffee spot that was our nightly "base" between ambulance calls. I have seen excellent teamwork result in saving people's lives and poor teamwork result in mistakes that had disastrous consequences. Teamwork on a software development project might not be as dramatic as defibrillating a person who has no pulse, but nonetheless, teamwork is essential if the organization is to survive and thrive. Cooperation is important, but sometimes there are good and valid reasons for the team to push back on process improvement.

10.8 Why Good Developers Oppose Process Improvement

Many developers oppose process improvement because they genuinely believe that these efforts are unlikely to succeed and that they also interfere with them getting the real work accomplished. They may also believe that the organization lacks credibility (perhaps because they have seen efforts fail before). Even worse, the process-improvement effort might have technically succeeded but resulted in making their job more difficult. Good developers oppose process improvement for good reasons, and it is important to solicit input from key stakeholders who can help steer you safely away from the big rocks in the river that may adversely impact your efforts.

10.9 Procedural Justice

Tom R. Tyler and Steven L. Blader's work on cooperation in groups discusses the role of procedural justice and its impact on cooperative behavior. Simply put, when employees feel that the organization is behaving in a way that is fair and reasonable, they may be more likely to cooperate. I usually apply this conceptually to the environments where I work by looking at how employees may react when they do not think that their employer is being fair. For example, when employees think that their employer is not behaving fairly, employees may get very creative in undermining their management. This obviously translates into employees cooperating with process improvement efforts when they think those efforts are *fair and reasonable*. I suggest that the opposite is also true: that people feel justified in not cooperating when they think the organization is being *unfair* and *unreasonable*. Procedural justice is an important consideration in managing organizational behavior, especially when trying to implement process improvement. An important consideration is whether the organization is including input from all stakeholders.

10.10 Input from Everyone

Some organizations do well by focusing on eliciting and receiving input from all stakeholders. In this approach, we elicit input from everyone who will be impacted by the project. This can sometimes be a problem because of the diversity of views and agendas. More important, it can be logistically impossible to include input from everyone. One good approach is to get input from a representative sample from each group the change may affect. I have seen this type of effort get badly bogged down in trying to get input from everyone. Senior management needs to show leadership, in that everyone should have a voice, but there is also someone or a specific group that has to make the final decision. Many frameworks use an approach known as *RACI* (pronounced "racy"), which is an acronym that stands for responsible, accountable, consulted, and informed. In the RACI matrix, you specify the person or people *responsible* for the effort involved. *Accountable* refers to the specific person who is accountable for a particular task, consulted refers to the resources who are asked for input and *informed* refers to the person or people who should be kept informed. Although there can be many approaches to organizing and getting input from everyone, there still needs to be leadership and accountability.

10.11 Showing Leadership

I have seen many process-improvement efforts fail because of a lack of effective leadership. Getting input from everyone is great, but there also needs to be someone steering the ship. Being inclusive should not be a license to derail the process-improvement effort. However, that is precisely what happens in many organizations. Successfully overcoming resistance to change also requires good leadership. This usually comes in the form of a specific change agent who is empowered to establish the processes that will be used to help change the way that people work on a daily basis. Senior management needs to show support for this effort and help drive the effort forward.

10.12 Process Improvement People May Be the Problem

Many process-improvement professionals do an excellent job and really help to improve organizational effectiveness in terms of both productivity and quality. Unfortunately, a lot of other process-improvement folks are really trapped in their ivory towers and do not have a clue about how to actually do the work that their processes will impact on a daily basis. I know that I may ruffle a few feathers with this statement, but I really believe that process improvement is much more *valid* when it is designed and implemented by people who are hands-on and actually know how to do the work. That means that close collaboration needs to occur between process engineering experts and the technology professionals impacted by the change. I have seen process-improvement efforts become a complete waste of time when the processes that were established were completely impractical. In these situations, the process "improvement" just resulted in extra work for everyone involved while failing to address the real requirement. In this regard, the process-improvement "experts" may really be the problem rather than the solution. The best approach is to have technology professionals who have both the process engineering and the hands-on technology expertise.

10.13 Combining Process and Technology Training

I believe that it is important for the technology industry to develop more professionals who are strong in both process engineering and hands-on technology. This can obviously come from two directions. Process engineers can be trained to have more hands-on technology skills, and technology professionals can learn more about the value of process engineering. You certainly see Agile doing this today, with many SCRUM masters being hands-on technology professionals. This might be less common among folks who are expert in the CMMI framework. At least it's been my own experience that CMMI experts are less likely to have hands-on expertise and experience. That's bad, and I have personally worked with CMMI experts who had no clue how to actually conduct a configuration audit or even promote a release of code into production. They knew the concepts on paper, but had no idea of how to actually do the job in the real world. To say the least, their process-improvement recommendations lacked credibility and were often less than helpful. We need a new generation of process-improvement experts who have both the hands-on skills and knowledge of process-improvement best practices. I have personally put this view into practice for more than 25 years.

Tales from the Trenches

Many times, I have gone into a group that was making mistakes (often, they were creating code releases that did not work as expected). Overcoming resistance to change, in this context, meant that we had to implement processes to help the team stop making bad mistakes. Usually, the team believed that bad releases were just a way of life when the technology was complicated. I would come in as a member of the team and take on the role of assessing the current release management process and looking for ways to improve and bulletproof the process. This is a good example of where ivory tower approaches would not have been successful. Instead, I became a part of the team and examined the steps necessary to package and promote the release. In most cases, I was able to create a process that had just enough controls to prevent mistakes. In almost all cases, I was able to significantly speed up the release management process into what I always call the "one-hour" build and deploy. Overcoming resistance to change, in this case, was a matter of gaining the credibility that I could actually do the work and that I would use the same processes that I was advocating. Obviously, I had to try to quickly get up-to-speed in technologies ranging from C#/.NET to Java SOA. I can't say that I have always succeeded, though; sometimes, the technology just had too many moving parts for me to manage learning the release management process while simultaneously writing the release management automation myself. In those cases, I needed to take a step back and let the developers do the hands-on work. But, the more hands-on work that I *could* do, the better and more valid my processes would be. Even if I could not successfully pull off being a code-monkey, I certainly gained the deep trench-level knowledge that I needed to understand and create valid processes that were the right size to accomplish the goals of the team. I have also learned to listen to the rhythm in the trenches.

10.14 Listening to the Rhythm

Getting a feel for the organization is essential if you are to bring about lasting change. I have often found that I had to listen to the *rhythm* of the organization to really understand what was going on. A good part of this is recognizing the quality of the communication and interactions, including both verbal exchanges and nonverbal exchanges. Part of my own training in industrial psychology is to listen to my inner voice and get in contact with how I personally *feel* in any organization (often a good indication of how others feel as well). Every group has a particular way that members interact. Sometimes, these interactions can be subtle and hard to pinpoint. In one organization, there seemed to be constant pressure from senior management that caused many employees to feel stressed. It was no surprise that they had high turnover and lots of mistakes being made on a regular basis. One day, I walked into my boss's office to see him looking pained and stressed. I felt courageous and genuinely liked this leader a great deal. So, I asked him whether everything was okay and whether I could do anything to help. His responded by telling me that he was having one of the worst days that he had in a long time. Not long after that, he announced that he was leaving the company for another firm. After he had gone, I continued to feel the same pressure there, and it was not long before I left the organization, too. What was interesting was that another colleague of mine had reason to visit the same office. This person was also trained in psychology and asked me pointedly about the culture of the organization. With only a short time in that office, this colleague had picked up on the hostile work environment that existed in this organization.

Listening to the rhythm can be difficult when you are in the organization. There are always factors that could be coloring your own perception. But my message in this section is that you really need to listen to your own inner voice and use that information in deciding how to approach the organization and, in particular, how to implement process improvement. Obviously, you also need to be a good scientist and test your own hypothesis and the processes that you implement.

10.15 Processes Need to Be Tested

So, after you have overcome resistance to change and implemented processes, you also need to test to confirm that your processes actually meet the goals of the organization. In this sense, I always try to do test-driven process improvement (TDPI). In TDPI, you design your test cases up front before you implement your process changes. For example, I tell people up front what a good release management process will look like. This is important because it's easy to solve the wrong problem (and thus fail to achieve your goals). Just as test-driven development advocates put the testing process up front (even before you have written a line of code), you should also objectively test your own processes. There are two parts of any test. The first is that your processes will consistently result in the same results. The second is that you achieve the correct results. In testing terminology, this is called *verification* and *validation*. Verification means that your processes have the *intended* results. Validation means that your processes have the *right* results!

10.16 Baby Steps and Process Improvement

You will have to decide whether your changes should be implemented in a big bang approach or in small steps. Generally, I have found baby steps to be much easier to implement, as long as you give some indication of what the end game really looks like. I have found it much easier to overcome resistance to change by compromising and winning small changes than to try to make the teams change the way that they are working in a manner that could really impact their short-term deliverables. For example, helping a team use their existing SCM tool a little better is generally much easier to achieve than to try to implement a new tool altogether. If you attempt a more aggressive approach, it will be much harder to gain support and approval for your intended change. Obviously, sometimes you really need the big bang approach, but more often than not, small and incremental changes make for better overall results.

10.17 Selling Process Improvement

The most important factor in overcoming resistance to change is to learn to market and promote your process improvements in an organized and effective way. I usually focus on marketing my services to the development team (and my senior management sponsors). This is an important distinction, and many technology professionals miss this point entirely. Selling process improvement should be proactively marketed. This is also true for implementing new tools. I have implemented many source code management systems and often found that the team was torn between one approach and another. Marketing process improvement means that you package the process interventions in the best way possible and consider that your team may decide to reject the process and go with a different approach. This means that you need to demonstrate why your approach is better and should be the one adopted. Just like any sales effort, you need to demonstrate exactly how a proposed process can add value to each of the stakeholders involved.

10.18 What's in It for Me?

It might sound simplistic, but most technology professionals want to know how a particular process improvement approach will impact them personally. Will the new process help them do their work better or just add hours of meaningless work onto an already impossible schedule? When I am working with a particular team, I always try to understand their requirements and priorities. In this respect, I am really acting as a salesman, and I try to understand exactly how my processes will impact each team. Generally, I hope that each team will view process-improvement as helping them individually and come to think of process-improvement as a valued service.

10.19 Process Improvement as a Service

The process-improvement team is most appropriately viewed as a shared service. Well-defined processes can impact many groups. I try to promote the services of my team as a shared service. That means providing your colleagues with customer service that is efficient and meets their needs. It also means that I need to be conscious of improving my own processes on an ongoing basis. Taking this approach helps to overcome resistance to change by building credibility with your colleagues. For example, setting a reasonable expectation for providing support is essential. Many companies talk about creating a service level agreement (SLA), which defines and sets expectations for how quickly your colleagues can expect assistance and support.

10.20 Guerrilla Tactics for Process Improvement

I have certainly spent a fair amount of time discussing cooperative and soft skills for overcoming resistance to change, which are my preferred means of operating. But there is another side of this approach that needs to be discussed, too. Sometimes, you just need to take the gloves off and push change through at all costs. In one such instance, the organization that I was part of was simply going to cease to exist if they did not fix their error-prone processes. They were way past the point that we could use "soft" tactics (such as consensus building), and the resistance was high. In this case, I had to put on my "bull in a china shop" act and come in and dictate changes. In this case, there just wasn't going to be a "tomorrow" if I failed. Obviously, this is risky, and you need to try to gain some positional power before trying to do this on your own. Guerrilla tactics, include involving senior management and possibly working to get some members of the team removed or reassigned. When this is necessary, I focus on the goals and communicate as clearly and openly as possible. I also usually point to other organizations and argue that there is no logical reason for us to be different from other organizations. This is not a good place to be and often results in failure, yet sometimes you have no choice and need to resort to guerrilla tactics. In Chapter 14, "Industry Standards and Frameworks," we examine standards and frameworks that you can use to push for change in these situations.

> ### Failure Is Just Not an Option
>
> As I mentioned earlier in this book, I was blind as a child. People with severe handicaps survive by developing a fierce sense that failure is just not an option. I cherish that spirit, and will always identify with the disabled because of that trait. When I was a child, my mother used to take me to meet people with significant challenges to show me that many disabled people were indeed very accomplished. In one such instance, when I was 12 years old, I met and spoke with an activist named Harold Rosenthal, a quadriplegic who suffered from multiple sclerosis. I listened attentively as he discussed his frustration with trying to get elected officials in Nassau County, New York to pass a new law enabling qualified handicapped people to have special parking permits. Back then, many people did not believe that the blind and disabled could live independent lives. Many people did not even believe that the disabled had a *right* to independence

and reasonable accommodation. The parking permits were needed to help many disabled people be able to travel and take care of their day-to-day needs. This was an extreme example of resistance to change.

One evening, I innocently asked Mr. Rosenthal whether getting petitions might help sway the elected officials who seemed to be dragging their heels on what seemed like a simple request. In those days, these special parking permits existed only in California, but this was the first time that a group had petitioned for them anywhere in New York. At the time, Mr. Rosenthal said, "Sure, that would be helpful." I knew, at the time, that he did not believe that I would be able to do anything to help with this effort. Of course, being a little blind kid, I was much more determined than anyone could imagine, and I organized ten of my friends, all under the age of 13, and we stood on street corners getting people to sign our rag-tag handwritten petitions.[1]

Pretty soon, I had a hundred signatures (with local newspapers starting to take notice), and the next thing that I knew we had a court date to petition the Nassau County legislature for the handicapped parking permits. What was personally exciting for me is that I was going to be allowed to hand my petitions to the county executive directly (which was incredibly exciting for a 13 year-old blind kid). Sadly, my mentor passed away a few nights before we were to be allowed to speak in court. Then, I heard that I would be allowed to speak in his place and, at the age of (then)13, I learned firsthand that mountains can be moved with the right amount of effort. Today, we see cars with handicapped parking permits all over, and most people have no idea how the handicapped parking permits were first approved and implemented.

If overcoming resistance to change matters to your organization, you need to adopt the view that failure is just not an option. I can tell you from my own experience that mountains can be moved and miracles can happen through lots of hard work and determination.

Conclusion

Overcoming resistance to change is difficult to achieve, and technology professionals are often unprepared to address the challenges involved. Successful process improvement involves considering the culture of the organization and

---

[1] It is worth noting that the original petitions specifically said that they would never be used to block fire hydrants, bus stops, or crosswalks.

a clear evaluation of the root causes prompting the need for change. In some cases, you need to understand why the group is currently failing in their efforts. We all need to focus on improving our soft skills to complement our technical skills. Approaching this effort involves looking at the entire situation in what I have described as a scene survey. Process improvement should start from within the group and involves carefully picking the right battles, goals, and priorities. Addressing challenges related to poor teamwork, being inclusive, and taking an honest and open look at why you are meeting resistance to change are essential. It is also important to test and verify that the proposed changes are valid and consider whether baby steps are the best strategy or whether extreme measures are necessary. Rightsizing your approach to overcoming resistance to change also means that you need to consider each of these issues as appropriate. Sometimes, you will need to employ guerilla tactics and that may touch your inner "bull in a china shop." (Careful, don't break those nice crystal wine glasses!)

While you are at it, don't underestimate the abilities or especially the *determination* of the blind and disabled. In fact, take a lesson from this "blink" and start moving some mountains around!

Chapter 11

Personality and CM: A Psychologist Looks at the Workplace

By Leslie A. Sachs

Chapter Overview

11.1 Personality Primer for CM Professionals   144

11.2 What Do CM Experts Need to Consider in Terms of Personality?   146

11.3 Applying Psychology to the Workplace   152

11.4 Family Dynamics!   155

11.5 Workplace Culture and Personality   156

Why does personality matter to a CM guru? Implementing CM best practices impacts each member of the team in a number of important ways. Understanding the personalities of other members of your team, and how others experience you, will significantly enhance your ability to succeed in any position that involves cooperation and integration among individuals and groups. Given the reality that the IT profession is becoming a globally interdependent industry at what feels like "warp speed," CM practitioners, in particular, must possess finely honed "people skills" for their complex collaborations to succeed.

This chapter provides you with insights into "what makes people tick" and specific strategies that will enable you to work more effectively with even the most challenging personalities you may encounter. We have already discussed overcoming resistance to change, but there is a lot more to the people side of CM best practices, and this chapter will help you communicate more effectively as it highlights some of the factors that may affect your efforts to implement CM. I suggest that you read this chapter with a view toward increasing your awareness of how these personality issues relate to you personally and toward improving your insight into how others may perceive you. Many of the dynamics presented are common in most organizational environments, and you will probably find that they sound familiar. If you are aware of them and can adjust accordingly, you will be more effective in any environment.

In this chapter, you will find just enough information on personality to help you to more effectively implement CM best practices. You can find more theoretical background material on the website for this book (http://cmbestpractices. com/personality). We start with a helpful personality primer for technology professionals and then discuss what you need to consider in terms of personality. For example, we look at communication styles (including differences in interpreting language) and how to provide effective consultation (especially verifying that your message has been received). We consider the variability in how people process information and discuss how you may experience the effects of birth order at the office (e.g., firstborns). And most importantly, we cover how to apply psychology to the IT workplace, with particular focus on principles of effective teamwork and the group dynamics unique to CM. We also consider the interpersonal dynamics where CM impacts QA and how to tackle indecisiveness. In addition, we examine workplace culture and personality, along with how personalities handle structure and how to deal with those who believe that they have already invented all the good ideas. We close the chapter by considering the loose cannons who just don't want to comply, enforcing process, and some formulas for success. In a nutshell, this chapter focuses on applying psychological insights to more successfully implement CM best practices.

Goals of Understanding Personality: What's in It for Me?

One primary motivator driving most people to learn is the realization that *knowledge is power*. Increasing your understanding of personality enables you to be a much more effective communicator, which usually translates into both improved workplace performance and satisfaction. Individuals who not only understand the various personality types but also know how to work harmoniously with most of them are generally very well regarded by their peers, and their superiors certainly appreciate this hard-to-find sensitivity. Most MBA professors would probably identify this attribute as one of the five most important factors found among successful managers. In the IT workplace, which today requires collaboration of a breadth and depth unimaginable just a generation ago, the ability to identify a colleague's personality style and recognize the most efficient way to work together is crucial to the success of even small projects, which may still involve multiple teams distributed among several physical sites. When a particular team or project includes multiple strong personalities, the resulting dynamics will certainly impact progress. The plethora of managerial support consultancies attests to the need for objective feedback to avoid the common pitfalls that frequently arise when these personality factors are not considered and addressed in a supportive and productive manner.

What Exactly Is Personality, Anyway?

Unfortunately, despite all the hours of scholarly research and the thousands of volumes written, there is still no neat and concise definition for *personality*. The origin of the term comes from the Latin word, *persona*, which is commonly understood to refer to the "mask" that people often present to others as they fulfill the various roles in their life. Yet, despite the flexibility that most humans demonstrate to alter behavior somewhat to meet varying demands, we seem to possess an underlying "core" from which this modifiability flows. Throughout the years, both social and clinical psychologists have focused on specific aspects of this core identity in their studies of human personality. Many questions regarding the origins and permanence of observed personality trends remain the subject of vigorous debate. However, despite the complexity of the human psyche, enough data exists to formulate a consensus definition based on the recognition that personality is determined by studying a broad pattern of a number of human tendencies[1] that give some degree of consistency to human behavior. In a nutshell, however, the key factor that makes understanding personality so crucial to so many situations is that we are usually not so concerned with a unique occurrence of a particular behavior, but rather we try to focus on an individual's consistent pattern of behaviors, cognitions, and emotions. The notion that one's personality is reasonably stable and consistent makes the lure of both analysis and prediction somewhat inevitable. The many systems that have been created to observe, measure, and categorize personality types, several of which are discussed in greater detail later in this chapter, rely on the fact of this relative stability across time and place.

---

[1] Those tendencies include traits, dispositions, unconscious dynamics, learned coping strategies, habitual and spontaneous affective responses, goal-directedness, information-processing style, and genetic and biological factors.

11.1 Personality Primer for CM Professionals

Two main personality-related interactions affect the workplace. The first dynamic, which is usually what comes to mind when people think of this topic, involves the myriad possibilities that occur when various personality types must interact. The second, which is addressed later, concerns the fit between an organization's "culture" and a specific individual's unique personality. There are numerous systems for organizing personality types into subsets of major categories, some more respected/utilized than others, but one essential feature defines all the systems that have withstood the test of time; they enable us to reliably sort others into groups according to observable behaviors so that we may somehow benefit from specifying these criteria. It really doesn't matter whether a personality system names its categories Artists, Judges, and Yodas, or A's, B's, and C's, as long as the terms are delineated clearly enough that different people can consistently agree on who falls within each category (This prior statement presumes, of course, that all the types are given a title that is considered neutral and none carries a negative association.) You can learn more about the theory of personality by visiting this book's website (http://cmbestpractices.com/personality), but in this chapter, we discuss the basics and how you can apply them to situations that may impact you and your efforts to implement CM best practices.

Myers-Briggs

The most widely recognized personality assessment geared to the work environment is the Myers-Briggs Inventory (MBI), which focuses on four distinct functions: social comfort zone, receiving of information, decision-making style, and organizing style. Each of these dimensions is measured in terms of selecting on which end of a continuum an individual falls. By combining each of these four factors, the inventory specifies 16 distinct types. Odds are that most of you have completed an MBI at some point in your professional career and have a fairly accurate idea of how you function in the work setting with regard to these personality traits. But, how well can you assess your colleagues' personalities in a meaningful way? Please come to this book's website if you'd like to brush up on your ability to recognize someone's preferred style in each of the four main dimensions of the Myers-Briggs.

The Big Five

After decades of research into personality factors, many prominent psychologists have developed a view of personality that focuses on five broad personality traits:

1. Openness to experience (culture)

2. Conscientiousness

3. Extroversion

4. Agreeableness

5. Neuroticism

These are commonly referred to by the acronym OCEAN. I will resist the urge to go into the details of the research method (meta-analysis) involved and instead explain that these five personality traits have been studied as predictors for success (or failure) in many different professions. I suggest that of all of these traits, conscientiousness, which has been found in many studies to be helpful in predicting the success of people in certain occupations (e.g., police officer), is the factor most relevant to CM. It is understandable that configuration management professionals often have to perform a type of enforcement, especially in organizations that have compliance requirements, to ensure that everyone follows organizational processes, including safeguarding the assets of the firm (e.g., production releases). Therefore, it should not surprise readers to learn that Bob has been a member of the auxiliary police for more than 15 years. Configuration management experts also need to have a measure of agreeableness and extroversion to work successfully with all members of the team, but their primary goal is to make sure that the code is always built following all corporate standards.

DSM-IV R

Another paradigm for understanding personality comes from the medical establishment and their psychiatric diagnostic manual, known as the *DSM-IV R*. This standard reference provides clinicians with an objective framework for evaluating their clients. Although this volume is used primarily to diagnose major psychiatric disorders, there are also lists of symptom clusters that can be indicative of milder, yet specific defined personality types. These less-severe types are categorized based on the predominant pattern of maladaptive behaviors a sufferer tends to exhibit when stressed. In fact, awareness of mental health issues has increased so much in the past few decades that most people are now somewhat familiar with the characteristics frequently associated with many of the major types and can recognize exaggerated tendencies in their colleagues. The savvy professional can use an informed understanding of personality style according to these labels to swiftly observe when specific personality deficiencies might impair productivity and suggest how the situation might best be addressed.

Erik Erikson

The work of developmental psychologist Erik Erikson provides another popular framework for understanding personality development. He theorized that all people must navigate through a series of eight specific challenges as they mature. During each of these phases, they struggle to find some balance between opposing urges and one's resolution of each stage helps to define their personality with regard to that dimension. For example, Erikson suggested that between the ages of 1 ½ to 3, as children learn to manipulate objects, walk, and control their bodily functions, they are particularly prone to feelings along a continuum from autonomy to shame and doubt. How successful children and adults are at learning to handle these key conflicts will continue to affect their functioning long after they have progressed to the next phase. Insufficient mastery of many of these levels will often result in personality issues (such as lack of initiative, poor self-image, and so forth), which will probably interfere with work performance.

11.2 What Do CM Experts Need to Consider in Terms of Personality?

Experts in the field of human resources frequently rely on one of the major personality categorization hierarchies to understand and enhance workplace dynamics. Several researchers have authored their own to more accurately describe the people they encounter in their daily lives. Although familiarity with the afore-mentioned and other personality systems is certainly an asset, you need not be thoroughly versed in specifics to benefit from the insights such information can offer. A pragmatist by nature, I am a rather eclectic practitioner and usually combine therapy modalities to achieve behavior change more successfully than would be possible with any single methodology. So, too, I take a broad approach when it comes to sharing critical information gleaned from the professional literature. Rather than an in-depth analysis of any particular system, the balance of this chapter is devoted to discussions of the key personality variables likely to affect your daily work experience. For each variable, I also suggest the approaches best suited for addressing that specific issue.

11.2.1 Communication Styles

Communication is both the "glue" that keeps an organization together and the "grease" that keeps the gears in motion. Probably no other single personality factor so directly impacts our ability to function in society, especially on the job. Very often, when people don't seem to click, the friction can be traced back to subtle "misfires" in the way that they are communicating with one another. Such misfires may result from differences in age, gender, education, language, culture, or personality. Language and cultural differences tend to be the easiest to spot and correct. However, just as frequently, subtle nuances fly "under the radar," and one or both of the individuals involved may have no conscious awareness, just a vague sense of not being fully understood.

11.2.2 Do Men and Women Use and Interpret Language Differently?

Deborah Tannen discussed intergender relations with her best-selling book,[2] which detailed what she believed to be evidence that men and women interpret language differently. It seems logical that you could apply her findings to the workplace, and indeed she subsequently wrote another book[3] exploring the implications of language differences for employee communications and dynamics. Co-workers can have vastly different communication styles and unintentionally, yet repeatedly, offend one another by not realizing the negative effects their style has on the other. Whether you accept all of Tannen's conclusions regarding the relationship of gender to communication styles (many of her critics have pointed out that gender differences in communication are more about *what* men and women communicate about than *how* they use language), her research has implications for generational and cross-cultural communication differences, too. Open and frank discussions about this phenomenon simply cannot be avoided if a team truly values constructive communication. Communication styles cover a wide spectrum, and each end of the continuum has something to offer. Management

---

[2] Deborah Tannen. *You Just Don't Understand: Women and Men in Conversation.* New York: Morrow, 1990.

[3] Deborah Tannen. *Talking from 9 to 5: How Women's and Men's Conversational Styles Affect Who Gets Heard, Who Gets Credit, and What Gets Done at Work.* New York: Morrow, 1994.

must establish a work environment that recognizes this reality and that rewards employees' efforts to help bridge the inevitable communication gaps for the benefit of the entire organization. In practical terms, this means that you need to be aware of whether any gender, age, cultural, or other bias impacts your own communication style, and if so, what you need to do to communicate effectively with the other members of your team.

11.2.3 Effective Consultation

In my consultation experiences, Step 1 is to highlight how and why these problems arise, and Step 2 involves clearly identifying the team's primary goal as improving everybody's lines of communication. After these objectives have been accomplished, the final step is to outline those practices that will ensure that all voices are heard and respected. In general, I have found that when no inherent value is associated with either end of the communication spectrum (so that no employee need feel one particular style is wrong or bad), individuals are more likely to make sincere attempts to respect others' styles and accommodate those whose preference might differ from their own. The bottom line is that successful firms foster a climate where people try to really "hear" each other and respond respectfully, even if they have difficulty with the communicator's style or they disagree with the message.

11.2.4 Verifying the Message

"What I hear you saying is ____. Is that correct?" One of the simplest and most effective strategies for enhancing communication is to encourage employees to ask for verification from colleagues that the message they heard is the one that was actually intended. I frequently use a great icebreaker exercise to dramatically illustrate how often people subconsciously ascribe meaning and nuance that was never intended by the speaker. I ask everyone in the circle to turn to the person seated to their right and make a neutral comment. (For example, "I notice you're wearing a blue sweater today.") Then each group member is asked to remark on what he or she thought and felt on hearing the comment. The group is usually amazed to discover that more than 50% of the individuals perceived the comment directed toward them as distinctly positive or negative, rather than neutral. So, it is crucial to have all employees develop the habit of "checking in" with others to minimize the incidence of such inaccurate "reading into" others' statements. During group meetings, those employees who are the most adept at this can take turns summarizing the group process so that all are clear on what is being outlined. An added bonus of this practice, commonly known as *active listening* (and highly valued in the therapeutic community), is that it has been shown to enhance trust and improve both the quality of communication and satisfaction with interpersonal relationships. Verifying the message will help you ascertain and implement CM best practices that actually meet the needs of your team.

11.2.5 Information Processing Preferences

You have probably noticed that everybody has a preferred method for gathering and organizing information. Sometimes, this preference is linked to a person's own communication style, but not necessarily.

11.2.5.1 Sensory Modalities and Sensitivities

Certain individuals learn best from auditory input, others from visual. Some people learn best with verbal material, whereas others perform better with data presented as numbers or pictures. Analogously, individuals often strongly prefer organizing and presenting their results in one format or another. People also vary considerably in their sensitivity to external sensory stimuli, with some requiring total silence to concentrate, while others actually prefer some mild background distraction to maintain optimal focus. The most effective team leaders try to ascertain the personal information processing strengths of each of their group members and allow them to work in ways that maximize the opportunity to utilize their preferred processing modality. Good teams usually have a mixture of all types, with some competent "translators" to smooth out the rough edges and keep the process moving along. Employees are more satisfied and efficient when they are operating within their natural "comfort zone."

11.2.5.2 Processing Style

Processing style is another important factor that impacts both individual and group functioning. Some individuals work best when data is incorporated one piece at a time in a serial fashion. Others like to have all the relevant details presented all at once and organize it simultaneously. Employee A may not be willing to comment until he has "all the facts," whereas another team member might feel more comfortable suggesting options to consider while more data is being collected. None of these approaches is absolutely right or wrong; each has its advantages and disadvantages. The key is that the skillful manager recognizes the various tendencies and takes that information into account both when forming project teams and when evaluating the type of feedback each employee is tasked with providing.

11.2.5.3 Processing Speed

A related, yet distinct, variable concerns the speed with which individuals process new information, integrate that knowledge, and can provide necessary feedback to others. Employees who can perform these functions extremely rapidly may become impatient with colleagues who are not as speedy. Meanwhile, those workers who take a bit longer than the average may become anxious if others appear overtly irritated and might feel pressured to respond without sufficient understanding/consideration of all the factors. Faced with angry foot-tappers, some less-confident personalities might just shut down and fail to give input, thereby depriving the organization of potentially useful ideas. It is the manager's job to be attuned to each of these information processing issues and help the team balance their innate preferences for the benefit of achieving their shared goals and objectives.

11.2.6 Birth Order at Work

Much has been written about what role, if any, birth order has on personality development. Most readers are probably familiar with the most common stereotypes such as *assertive eldest, conciliatory middle, carefree youngest,* and *self-absorbed only.* Just how accurate are these perceptions? Well, it turns out that social researchers have determined that there is more than a "grain of truth" to these labels, although only in the most general terms. The effects of your position in the family may indeed influence your work style and the way you relate to others. As you might have guessed, certain atypical circumstances in a given family may result in individuals who function more like someone with a different birth order. For instance, a child born when the older sibling is mostly grown and fairly independent will frequently act more like an oldest or only. Always bear in mind that social science observations about correlations and data trends should never be confused with inferences of causation. That said, both popular and professional research literature abounds with well-documented reports that outline the characteristics most commonly associated with each birth-order position. However, it is important to remember that insights regarding birth order should be used only for their capability to illuminate employees' potential dynamics rather than to predict probable behaviors.

11.2.7 Firstborns as Leaders

Disproportionately represented among the world's CEOs, firstborns are described as leaders, managers, and organizers par excellence. They like to feel in control and may become quite unsettled if unexpected events transpire or they suddenly feel they are "in over their head." However, their laser-like focus on a goal coupled with their talent for organizing others means firstborns can often achieve what they desire, whereas less-driven personalities might not succeed. What typical firstborns lack in risk taking is positively balanced by the stability they offer as they spur others on to strive for excellence in both quality and productivity. Placing considerable value on the approval of authority figures, they can be usually be relied on to not "shake things up" too dramatically In their zeal to forge full steam ahead, however, these enthusiastic (and frequently perfectionist) employees might sometimes need brakes to avoid steamrolling over others.

11.2.8 The Middle-Born Compromiser

Often described as "people" people, second and middle-borns are usually the most flexible and are regarded as consummate compromisers. Having had to deal with a sibling from day one, this personality is frequently the best at negotiating and balancing competing social needs. They usually enjoy working alongside others and are likely to be motivated by the idea of a team goal. Middle-borns value friendships and a feeling of belonging, so they naturally try to get along, also encouraging harmony among others and helping the team stick together. Relationships are clearly a priority for this personality, and the savvy manager will make certain that the middles in their midst aren't unintentionally offended by being excluded from any major activities. A strong desire to put people first and the ability to work well with many different types makes many middle children the lubricant that keeps a team's gears running when a process is in danger of becoming derailed due to personality conflicts.

11.2.9 The Youngest as Initiator

Not surprisingly, youngests display yet another distinct cluster of characteristics: They tend to be the initiators, idea people, and the challengers of the world. They represent a high preponderance of the creative, spontaneous free spirits who are known for injecting fun into whatever they do. Loose and lighthearted when compared to their more responsible older siblings, later-borns are often requested to "grow up" already and get serious. These inventive types may persevere enough to see their intriguing plans begun, but despite their impatience and initiative, they are not noted for following through until completion and may benefit from clear guidelines or need some gentle prodding to finish assigned tasks. Very proud of their originality, members of this lively group usually like to be noticed, so sharp managers are encouraged to acknowledge the efforts of their youngest-born employees (not a particularly difficult challenge given the noteworthy contributions youngest employees frequently make).

11.2.10 The Only Child

The only child tends to be a unique blend that combines aspects of each of the other three types: They tend to be quiet achievers who reliably finish what they begin while striving to reach the highest level possible. Because they will settle for nothing less than superior results, these individuals also frequently improve the performance of the group as a whole. Having been left to their own devices much more often than others due to their family circumstance, onlys frequently demonstrate a remarkable ability to work for long periods of time in solitude. However, their comfort with solitary endeavors can make them appear secretive to others, and they often don't deal well with interpersonal conflict. Yet, their aptitude for strategic thinking will be appreciated by managers who know how to harness the unique talents of those in his department. Frequently raised as the sole focus of adult attention, onlys expect to be recognized, but this desire is usually tempered by a strong aim to please, too.

11.2.11 Being Yourself

Sometimes, because of specific circumstances (such as parental absence or a large gap between siblings, for example), a person will function according to a type not necessarily associated with their actual position in their family of origin. Although many individuals may recognize isolated traits from each type, your dominant birth order personality can be determined by seeing which overall description best matches your basic daily style. Know yourself, and be aware of your work situation, because sometimes your birth order personality *should* take over, but in other situations, peak performance may dictate that you try to work more like someone in another position. This might make you feel uncomfortable at first, but if you can do it, you are way ahead of the pack!

11.3 Applying Psychology to the Workplace

Many professionals in the behavioral sciences (e.g., industrial/organizational or school psychology) apply their understanding of learning and motivation to work environments to maximize productivity. These practitioners are frequently called on to help solve behavioral problems to optimize the performance of both individuals and teams. Although Deming, the father of quality management, insisted that rallying individual employees with esteem-enhancing slogans is counterproductive (and arouses frustration and resentment in some), other behavior scientists have actually found that combining positive statements with tangible rewards does lead to improved performance. The real fun begins when one has to inspire colleagues to "play nicely" together in situations when the interests and objectives of one person may, at times, conflict with another member of that group or a different group with which they interface regularly. Such scenarios are common in the world of CM as the various development and testing teams continuously interact throughout the software development process.

11.3.1 Effective Teamwork Begins at Home

This dynamic is also common to the one social grouping to which everyone belongs: the family. Every person has had firsthand experience living with others who have very different personalities, tastes, and so on. Many times, the individual group members (especially siblings) may have had conflicting interests/goals regarding resource allocation or other issues. Yet, the managers (a.k.a. the parents) repeat the mantra that "we are a family" to emphasize that *the whole is greater than the sum of the parts*. In families that function well, every child is recognized first for their uniqueness and inherent worth but also for how they utilize their gifts to enhance the family as a distinct entity. By repeatedly reinforcing the message that individual success depends on group synergy and mutual support, parents provide the first example of effective teamwork. This core understanding of the benefits of positive interdependence is a latent, yet very valuable, social skill readily available just beneath the surface for successful managers to promote in their employees, too.

11.3.2 Volleyball or Effective Collaboration

Imagine the two previously mentioned groups as opposing teams playing a game of volleyball. Developers hit the release over the net to QA. Then QA finds bugs and hits it back to the testers. If the product gets past QA and afterward bugs are found, QA is blamed for not finding the bug. So, the developers are subtly motivated to have QA "accidentally" miss some problems until after release, so that they can claim to have done their "piece" of the project on time. (In fact, many discussions usually occur regarding whether a given bug that has been found is serious enough to hold up the release.) The only way out of this dilemma is to consistently and conspicuously reward effective collaboration between the two groups. Ideally, individuals within both teams should be incented only to create successful products, not just to have someone else to blame for failures!

11.3.3 Embedding Build Engineers and Testers in the Development Team

Many Agile practitioners advocate embedding testers directly within the development team. However, having the testers in the development team can create a conflict of interest for the firm (and might not be in compliance with required IT controls or meet governance standards). Developers want to meet their deadlines (and may have significant financial reasons for wanting to do so). If a bug is found in production, the firm may lose a lot of money. Embedded testers might feel pressured to let problems "slide by." If they resist, the developers may consider the tester to no longer qualify as a supportive (and committed) member of the team. This can result in less information being given willingly to the test team, and of course, will result in them being kept in the dark during subsequent releases. Embedded testers are obviously more effective when they do know exactly how the application is supposed to function and exactly what functions have been changed for a particular release. Similarly, embedding build engineers in the development can help to stay on top of changes in development requirements that might impact the application build, release, and deployment. Clearly, open and honest communication is critical for successful Agile and, in fact, for all teamwork.

11.3.4 Blackbox Versus Whitebox Versus Graybox

Blackbox testing means that the testers have no visibility into what has been changed. The testers just follow their regular test plans or some just "bang on the keys" to see what breaks. (Some people actually insist that this is the best testing methodology). *Whitebox testing* means that you know what has changed and can focus testing solely on the changed functionality. This is convenient when testers are embedded with the developers. *Graybox testing* is, not surprisingly, an eclectic compromise between the two approaches: The testers still do some blackbox testing after they use their inside knowledge to specifically test the known functional changes. Agile also strongly advocates robust unit testing (such as JUnit) and continuous integration.

11.3.5 Group Dynamics That Can Damage the Organization

With all that in mind, QA still needs to have visibility into what has changed without having to be pressured into approving a release before it is ready. There has to be a tolerance for missing deadlines or at least some mechanism for communicating the risk of putting a release into production before it has been fully tested. Without these controls, the group dynamics create an adversarial relationship that pits the development team against the test team—all to the detriment of the organization.

11.3.6 Where CM and QA Fit In

CM provides the QA team with visibility into what has changed (e.g., changesets) so that priorities can be managed more effectively. But, the real priority is for management to lead the hardworking members of both teams to realize that each group can truly fulfill its function within the organization only by cooperating completely with the other. Both development and testing professionals must be motivated, by management, to consider their job done only when they have enabled the others to do their best work, too. Technology leadership needs to recognize that neither team alone can produce a working system, but managed as a cooperating team, their efforts complement one another and produce results that win.

11.4 Family Dynamics!

In the fields of both school and community psychology, we sometimes see family dynamics that are also less than desirable. It's important to note that the most common characteristic found in most dysfunctional systems are poor communication systems and lack of respect. Effective interventions are often needed to help the parents understand their own unique contribution to the family system. By empowering each parent to recognize his or her special talents and to communicate more effectively, the parents become more confident and subsequently more accepting of the others' contributions, too. Agile parents, in turn, are more able to support their children as they learn to resolve conflicts that inevitably arise. Developing the ability to appreciate interpersonal differences and derive benefit from this awareness is a life lesson with numerous applications. Parents who effectively manage the conflicts of sibling rivalry also empower their children to live happy and productive lives (not unlike the value added when development and testing enjoy a healthy relationship). When everyone works together, the results are always superior to whatever the individuals could have accomplished independently.

11.4.1 Indecisiveness

Much of this chapter has focused on well-defined personality types. But what of the individual who is not so "visible?" Every organization usually includes some employees whose most obvious personality characteristic is their desire to remain in the background. Many times, this tendency relates to issues of poor self-esteem. The person who is reluctant to "take a strong stand" may lack confidence. However, this behavior might derive from shame suffered at the hands of overly demanding or punitive adults in the past and is not at all a reflection of their actual competence. Sensitive colleagues will encourage such quiet and indecisive employees to speak up more and contribute to the team's planning and project execution. As their contributions increase, so will their awareness and appreciation of their significant and productive role, leading to greater self-confidence, and thus setting in motion a repeating cycle of calculated risk, positive reinforcement, and continued professional growth and improvement.

11.5 Workplace Culture and Personality

Personality type affects one's performance not only in terms of individual productivity and relationships with colleagues, but also with regard to the individuals's "fit" with the organization's "culture." While researching the many variables that impact employee performance, some industrial psychologists have focused on the importance of the role that the work environment plays. For some very autonomous types, a rigid culture might feel stifling and lead to active insubordination or more subtle, but equally sabotaging, passive-aggressive behavior. However, the same highly structured setting may bring out the best in less-decisive, less-organized, or less-motivated employees. Similarly, a laid-back office can elicit great work from certain self-directing personality types, whereas others will not blossom in such ambiguous situations. The stronger and more clearly defined the employee or organizational style, the more likely it is that "fit" will be a significant factor in the success of that particular individual. Some organizations require almost cult-like adherence to their "way," and they limit their hiring to individuals willing to buy in to their vision, even if that means passing up experienced individuals with proven track records. Other, more flexible firms may modify their corporate climate and mores if they detect a large turnover of competent, high-quality employees as a result of overly narrow policies. When productivity conflicts arise, adjustments that address this particular dynamic should be included for consideration. There are many organizational culture issues that you may observe. Here are a few that are especially important and some suggestions on how to work with them effectively.

11.5.1 Personality and Structure

It can be hard to convince certain people that standards and frameworks are important in the first place. Individuals may resist adopting set standards for several reasons. For example, certain very organized personality types prefer their own internally created systems to those suggested by others. You may experience these people as being very difficult to work with (and they often are). For those struggling with OCD (obsessive-compulsive disorder) or Asperger's syndrome (a high-functioning form of autism), the need to follow their own standards is difficult to subordinate to what may "feel" to them like arbitrary constraints. The savvy manager will not fight this issue head on, but should focus instead on pointing out how following the required standards will enable them to meet their own goals more efficiently. Once resistant employees are clear that these standards enhance their own efforts, compliance is usually 100% guaranteed.

> ### Bob's Motorcycle Gang
>
> Bob grew up in the culture of the physically disabled where the only "cool" people were either blind or otherwise challenged in some way. The cultural norm was to accept whatever handicap you were stuck with and then fight ferociously to overcome it. In this context, a person with Asperger's or OCD would have been encouraged to be open about the disability (which does not always work well in the workplace) and battle relentlessly to compensate. Belonging to this community was a little like being part of a motorcycle gang, except everyone had "rides" (e.g., wheelchairs) with four wheels rather than two, and it was a victory when a quadriplegic drank from a cup without assistance. Although there is a lot more acceptance of people with handicaps in the workplace today, there remains much more work still to be done before every able-minded (even if not 100% able-bodied) individual wanting to work finds employment where their unique capabilities and expertise can be utilized in the free market despite the possible need for minor accommodations.

11.5.2 We Already Invented All the Good Ideas

Some people just don't deal well with accepting others' ideas. This particular problem crops up time and time again in many different scenarios. I have found that the most effective way to minimize this distracting behavior is to stress group identity and foster team building at every opportunity. Linking personal recognition to group productivity encourages all personality types to bring out the best in one another. When team members feel a strong allegiance to the group and its mission, satisfaction can derive from the success of others, as well as from one's own actions. Fostering a climate where colleagues regularly compliment the other members for their part in a team effort increases everyone's sense that his or her ideas matter.

11.5.3 Loose Cannons Who Don't Want to Comply

"If it's a rule, then it probably needs to be broken." At one point or another in a professional career, everybody has probably encountered an individual who embodies this philosophy. Whereas you can simply avoid such people in your social life, contact at work might prove unavoidable. Such behavior is usually a combination of both genetics and early childhood experiences and can be difficult to alter after it has become ingrained. Therefore, the most pragmatic resolution is often a two-pronged approach: a combination that involves making it clear what the cost of breaking this rule is, and making sure the individual won't be tempted to chance it while simultaneously providing another "innocuous" rule that this person can violate to obtain that adrenaline rush they experience by beating the system. If you can convince this personality type to view the technical challenge as the "system" that needs to be beat, so much the better!

Embracing Risk and the Upcoming Audit

Bob has worked with a number of people who became extremely successful by embracing and thriving on risk. This is common in trading environments where technology professionals sit next to traders who are very successful at betting on risk in fast-paced, dynamic environments. Such scenarios are typical at large investment banks, and these folks often did not want to hear about process and compliance requirements—that is, until the internal IT auditors came knocking or a serious loss occurred due to a software bug that could have been prevented. In these environments, you need to balance the culture of risk with the protection offered by implementing CM best practices.

11.5.4 Enforcing Process, While Still Keeping the Train Moving

When you have to lay down the law and force technology professionals to follow a standard, you will often hear some grumbling. However, it is helpful to remind the team that these standards and frameworks have developed from real-life experience. Nothing motivates like success, and these "rules" have proven their usefulness time and time again. As your team comes to see that these guidelines actually do improve their efforts, cooperation will increase correspondingly. Your job is to keep them motivated long enough so that they can begin to see the fruits of their labor. (Imagine yourself as the caring parent who daily nags a child to brush his teeth until that youngster learns from personal experience the inherent value of good oral hygiene, whether from a cavity or bad breath, and gradually develops the self-discipline to continue without external prompting.) Once the CM process is implemented enough for the team to appreciate the power and benefits of these safeguards, you can usually count on them to self-monitor.

11.5.5 Formulas for Success

Building consensus and acknowledging every member's ideas are essential building blocks. Even the most resistant individuals become more compliant when recognized by others. In general, when people feel valued for their contributions on a routine basis, there is less need to act out or gain attention in other, and possibly counterproductive, ways. Emphasizing the rewards for compliance and group success is usually more effective than threats or coercion. Knowledge of personality types and excellent interpersonal skills can help the astute IT manager to keep each member of his team "within bounds."

11.5.6 Caveats

Everything we have discussed so far is backed up by both research and experience. That said, however, remember that the information presented is just that, interesting facts, not predictions or prescriptions. I have endeavored to present a rich array of personality matters that have been found to significantly impact an individual's work performance and the group environment. However, each particular situation is unique, and no one-size-fits-all solution exists which is capable of addressing every given issue. The parties involved must review the relevant personality factors and use this awareness to guide their future interactions. There is no denying that personality matters, both at home and at work. So the more we know about ourselves and our colleagues, and the dynamics that result, the more successful we can be.

Conclusion

Everyone, no matter how mellow and/or flexible he or she may appear, has a distinct personality that tends to be fairly stable and consistent. And these personalities result in each of us having certain processing and interaction patterns that are more comfortable for us. We carry these preferences with us at all times and, although at times with focused effort we can override a specific natural tendency, they remain our "set point" and usually determine our automatic first response. Deepening the understanding and awareness of our own and others' personalities is key to maximizing everyone's potential. Although we might only be able to modify our basic nature a given amount, there is no limit to the number of adaptive strategies the motivated individual can dream up to enhance and improve his or her ability to get along better with others. I hope that the information presented in this chapter sparks your curiosity and provides the raw ingredients you need to cook up some novel "tactical recipes" of your own (which effectively address your specific and unique personality challenges, both internal as well as those you encounter as you try to enhance your collaborations with others).

Chapter 12

Learning From Mistakes That I Have Made

Chapter Overview

12.1 Why Is It Important to Learn from Our Mistakes?   162

12.2 Where Do I Get Started?   162

12.3 Understanding Our Mistakes   163

12.4 The Mistakes I Have Made   163

12.5 Turning a Mistake into a Lesson Learned   166

12.6 Common Mistakes That I Have Seen Others Make   167

Mistakes are good, especially when you learn from them. I cannot say that I have always been effective in reaching my goals as a hands-on process-improvement professional. There have definitely been times when I have failed or at least not achieved as much as I had expected of myself. But I do know that I have always tried my best, and I have always thought long and hard about why my performance may have been less than optimum, including how I could improve. With each new assignment, I have tried to reinvent myself, often excelling at the very task that I had previously fallen short on at the previous position. Learning from our mistakes is fundamental. There are also times when we can observe and learn from the mistakes of others. Here is a short description of some of my own *lessons learned* working to implement CM best practices.

This chapter is all about understanding our mistakes and how to learn from them. I describe a few of my many mistakes, including missing the big picture, thinking that a good process will just carry itself, and failing to gain consensus. I have also had times when I failed to show leadership for CM or, even worse, became part of the problem. There were times when I forgot to ask for help when I really needed it, including clarifying what I needed in order to get the job done. I have also seen others who were so ivory tower that they were not effective. Similarly, I have seen others who were afraid to get their hands dirty by getting technical and hands-on along with a fear of being honest and open.

Goals of Learning from Mistakes

The first goal of learning from mistakes is to be the best that we can be in terms of designing and implementing process-improvement interventions that are practical and effective. In my work, this specifically means that I want to define CM best practices that support the application and systems development process. There is obviously also a self-improvement goal here, too. We all want to be the best that we can be. Taking a hard look at how we did and how we can improve is essential.

12.1 Why Is It Important to Learn from Our Mistakes?

Learning from our mistakes is as important as breathing the air around us. If you don't learn from your mistakes, you are doomed to make the same mistakes over and over again. Worse yet, you will never grow and improve. W. Edwards Deming, regarded by many as the father of quality management, said it best with his view that we have to "drive out fear," and nowhere is that more important than in honestly and accurately evaluating our own mistakes.

12.2 Where Do I Get Started?

It's been my experience that this is one situation where it is easy to get started because lots of people are willing to point out others' mistakes. If you let people know that you are open and willing to improve, then you have already started this journey, which is essential on both a personal and professional level. Start with being honest and candid and then hold on as the roller coaster to self-improvement takes over!

12.3 Understanding Our Mistakes

Mistakes are not bad, although the consequences of our mistakes can certainly be very bad indeed. When a release manager makes a mistake, large computer systems can fail with significant impact, including the loss of millions of dollars. Mistakes are good if we learn from them and improve. The first step is to rationally and coldly examine what we did and how our actions impacted the results. The fact is that your team needs to know that it is okay to make mistakes. They also need to know that it is *only* okay if they admit the mistake so that the team can work together to make things better. I have seen situations where the fear of admitting a mistake adversely impacted the team's ability to improve their processes, including release management. Deming had as one of his legendary 14 points, "Drive Out Fear." I believe that the reason this was one of his 14 points is that fear within the workplace adversely impacts quality because members of your team will be afraid to speak up and give their input. Obviously, admitting our mistakes is an essential aspect of a well-functioning team. I admit some of mine in the next section.

12.4 The Mistakes I Have Made

I recount my sins here not to get them off my chest but so that you can learn from them. Although it is okay to make mistakes, it is always better to learn the easy way than the hard way. Just like lifting weights is a journey to gaining strength and physical fitness, learning from mistakes is a journey to self-improvement on many levels. I recall having a discussion with a couple of my colleagues in which I began to calmly and coldly start discussing the mistakes we had made. No one disagreed that we had made some mistakes and that the firm (and each of us personally) suffered as a result. The mistakes cost us money and missed opportunities. It was also unclear that any of us were really "to blame" for the mistakes. I was not looking to blame anyone, but I wanted to understand what we had done and work on solving the problems. What did interest me was that my colleagues were extremely uncomfortable discussing mistakes. Don't be. If you can take this walk with me, you can truly achieve excellence. Let's relax and take an honest look at some of these common mistakes.

12.4.1 Missing the Big Picture

One mistake that I have found myself making, from time to time, is missing the big picture. I have always focused on getting into the trenches and doing the day-to-day hands-on work that is needed for all aspects of configuration management. I like to build the release, understand all the requirements to support the environment, and especially dig deep into all the detailed technical steps needed to automate the release management process. I usually find that digging into the details and coming up to speed is an all-consuming task that can be challenging. I have sometimes found myself so focused on handling the details that I forgot to come up for air and look around me. I think that a lot of people make this mistake, and it is almost inevitable. When you are knee deep in a task and making progress, it can often be hard to recognize that you missed the larger perspective, and that is a bad mistake to make. An example of this problem is trying to handle all the automation tasks myself when I should have asked for help sooner. Deep down, I know that I was trying to prove that I could do the work and solve the technical challenge myself. The larger goal was to fix the release management process and not make Bob a champion Perl scripter. This is a tough challenge for me because I really love writing the automation myself, and yet sometimes, it is better to handle this task as a team sport.

12.4.2 Writing Release Automation Can Be Challenging

As a release engineer, I often work on many different platforms. One week, I might be deep in releasing Java Web Services on UNIX (or Linux), and two days later, I will be working with C# and .NET on a high-end Wintel platform. In the same month, I might work with the mainframe guys who are deploying Cobol copybooks on an IBM mainframe using ISPF. Release automation can be challenging, especially when you are working across many platforms. The developers usually have considerably more to time to learn a platform and often specialize on a particular technology. Good release engineers can work on any required platform. Writing the automation to handle the release management process requires some knowledge of the platform and the technology. Creating release management automation adds value by improving both quality and productivity by allowing developers to rapidly build, package, and deploy applications. This is the very best part of being a release engineer. But, it is also the most challenging part, too. The first time that I tackled Java SOA using Hybernate was indeed challenging for me. I recall being so consumed with coming up to speed that, at times, I forgot to ask for help. I really wanted to understand it all, although my job was to create a fool-proof release management process (and not to become a Java architect). That said, there was often no one else available to help me, so often, I was on my own. Nonetheless, don't forget to focus on the big picture of what you are trying to accomplish and identify any possible risks that might impact your success.

12.4.3 Thinking That a Good Process Will Carry Itself

Early in my career, I focused on learning to define good processes that were as clear and as comprehensive as possible. My processes were great because they were repeatable and covered all the necessary steps, but I often forgot to effectively market my ideas and approaches to others. Release management is a service and support function that requires effective skills in communication to achieve success. A good process will not just carry itself automatically. You need to effectively market and promote your ideas to others.

12.4.4 Failing to Gain Consensus

Years ago, the process-improvement mantra was focused on the importance of gaining senior management buy-in for the process-improvement effort. That is certainly a necessary step, but it is also not sufficient. It is often essential for you to also work from the bottom up at the same time, and especially work toward gaining consensus among all the stakeholders. I recall times when I felt armed and validated by gaining senior management support, only to discover just how clever my colleagues could be in working around the processes that I was trying to establish. If you review your processes with all the stakeholders and then gain their consensus, you will be more effective in achieving your goals. Failing to gain consensus is a mistake that you should not make!

12.4.5 Failing to Show Leadership for CM

Gaining consensus is great, but CM also requires leadership. You should not fall into the trap of analyzing too long when your best approach would be to put forth a first draft of our recommended process. As a CM guru, you are expected to provide leadership and demonstrate how and why CM best practices add value. Make sure that you step up to plate and lead the way! I always enjoy becoming entrenched and a member of the development team. Software development is certainly a team sport, but there is also a danger in becoming an embedded member of the development team.

12.4.6 Becoming Part of the Problem

I am usually called into a group when there is a problem. The group often knows that it is in trouble, and it is not uncommon for some people to feel defensive and concerned about their jobs. When trying to understand why there are problems, I listen and observe the group dynamics. When I diagnose the problems and start to recommend interventions, I try to become part of the solution by actively getting involved with building, packaging, and deploying the releases.

There have been times when I found myself becoming part of the problem. This is often diagnostic, but there is also a danger of getting sucked right into the abyss of the problem that caused the organization to solicit my services in the first place. For example, there have been times when I found that the technology just had too many moving parts and was too complex for anyone to tame the release management process. At times like these, I often dived deep into the technology and was no more successful at solving the release management problems than anyone else. If you discover that you have become part of the problem, take a step back and reevaluate your recommended interventions. This is not a bad thing, though, because after you have seen the problem at this level of detail, you will have a much more credible idea of how to solve the issues that need to be addressed. Watch out for becoming part of the problem and, when appropriate, make sure that you define and communicate the risks that confront the organization. You also should communicate whether help from other members of the team can help you get your job done better.

12.4.7 Forgetting to Ask for Help

Don't forget to ask for help when you need it. Release engineers are responsible for creating automated and repeatable processes. You may have a good development background, but as the technology changes (and it changes fast), you might need some help to stay on top of what the development team is doing. The best way to handle this is to define the risks and tasks that need to be accomplished. Then, you should communicate how help from the rest of the team will help you be more productive or effective. Remember that you are a member of the team and the important thing is that the team needs to be successful. Make sure that you pragmatically define what you need to get done to be successful.

12.5 Turning a Mistake into a Lesson Learned

So, how exactly do you turn a mistake into a lesson learned? The most basic approach is to honestly and fairly evaluate the action without regard for who is involved. If you can be honest with yourself, you are already halfway there. Here are a few that I have personally experienced.

12.5.1 Clarifying What I Need to Get the Job Done

It is common for you to initially not really know what you need to get the job done. There are often many unknowns, and the situation may change faster than you can adjust to. Make sure that you proactively communicate what you really need to get the job done. This may seem obvious, but those around you may not have a clear idea of how they can help you. More important, your management also needs to know what you need to get the job done. One important area to consider is to clarify the training that you need to be effective.

12.5.2 Getting the Training That I Need

Training is essential. If you do not know how to work with the technology, you will just not be successful. It is common for release engineers to have frequent steep learning curves. Make sure that you communicate your training needs and how that will help you do your job more effectively. I have occasionally made the mistake of trying to learn everything on my own. I can recall times when I saw my productivity improve dramatically after I received the training that I needed.

12.6 Common Mistakes That I Have Seen Others Make

There are a few mistakes that I have seen other folks make often, although I can't claim that these have been my issues. In the interest of clarity, I present them here and invite you to evaluate whether they fit you yourself.

12.6.1 Ivory Tower

Too many process-improvement practitioners are lost in their ivory towers. I have worked with many people who knew process models well, but had never actually done any of the day-to-day work, such as building, packaging, and deploying a release. I may upset a few people with my opinion on this issue, but I believe that process-improvement experts are more effective if they have some hands-on experience. If that's not possible (and obviously, that is often the case), make sure that you sit next to us and get a realistic feel for the trench-level view of the work that we do! Ideally, getting some technical knowledge and expertise will help you be more effective at implementing CM best practices.

12.6.2 Failing to Get Technical and Hands-On

This is one mistake that I just don't ever make. I am always working to be hands-on and technical. But many of my colleagues, in the process-improvement field, fail to get their hands dirty with learning the technology at a deep and meaningful way. You don't have to be a Java architect, but getting technical knowledge and hands-on experience will certainly enable you to be more effective. It will especially make you more *believable*.

12.6.3 Not Being Honest and Open

Some people are too busy worrying about whether they look like they know what they are doing. Personally, I believe that this is real waste of time and effort. It is much better to be honest and open in everything that we do. Again, I would be on the other side of the continuum for being *too* honest and open. In fact, I have occasionally gotten into trouble for openly admitting that I did not know something (instead of just trying to bluff my way through). I must admit that sometimes people don't know how to process this information, and they may even lose confidence in my abilities. I find it much more comfortable to be completely open with what I know and don't know even if this sometimes results in people losing some confidence. Don't worry when you get in my ambulance; I show complete confidence because that is what you need to hear at that time to feel comfortable. There is a time to show confidence because it is in the best interest of your patient. The rest of the time, you can expect me to be open and candid about what I know and don't know, and I encourage you to be the same!

Conclusion

Mistakes are not bad. Learning from our mistakes is essential and effectively part of any CM guru's own internal process-improvement effort. It is important to make learning from your mistakes a key part of your process-improvement efforts.

PART IV

Compliance, Standards, and Frameworks

Chapter 13

Establishing IT Controls and Compliance

Chapter Overview

13.1 Why Are IT Controls and Compliance Important? 173

13.2 How Do I Get Started? 173

13.3 Understanding IT Controls and Compliance 174

13.4 Essential Compliance Requirements 181

13.5 The Moral Argument for Supporting CM Best Practices 182

13.6 Improving Quality and Productivity Through Compliance 183

13.7 Conducting a CM Assessment 183

Configuration management plays an essential role in establishing IT controls and compliance by implementing the best practices required to pass an audit and establish IT governance. The most common IT controls include the ability to track and control changes to production systems and the prevention, detection, and remediation of any unauthorized changes. IT controls also include security and a central goal of providing accurate reports (used by senior management to govern the organization). Compliance refers to meeting the requirements of a particular standard or framework mandated by an outside regulatory authority, the company itself, or contractual obligation. At the center of this topic is IT governance, which means that senior management has visibility into the organization and can make accurate decisions based on the information available. I always define IT governance as providing visibility to senior management so that they can make the right decisions based on accurate and up-to-date information.

In this chapter, I quote specific laws and compliance requirements that I have found helpful in demonstrating that CM best practices are often required by federal law. What is also interesting is that there have been a number of high-profile incidents where corporations and government agencies failed to establish acceptable controls and were then cited in a public forum that you can easily read about today. Configuration management experts are often required to conduct an assessment of the existing practices. We should always promote compliance with all legal requirements and realize that the effort to comply itself is usually an opportunity to improve quality and productivity, too. In this chapter, we examine how to meet compliance requirements through CM best practices. I also describe how to conduct an assessment of configuration management practices.

This chapter focuses on understanding IT controls and compliance, including section 404 of the Sarbanes-Oxley Act of 2002 and the management assessment of internal controls. It also covers the Committee of Sponsoring Organizations (COSO) and the use of Cobit as a framework for IT controls and what it means to attest to and report on the assessment made by the configuration management team. Other compliance requirements, such as the Health Insurance Portability and Accountability Act of 1996 (HIPAA), are described and what happens when the Government Accountability Office (GAO) or the Office of the Comptroller of the Currency (OCC) comes knocking on your door. Understanding the results of the audit is explained with examples, including GAO reports on National Archive and Records Administration (NARA) configuration management practices and the Electronic Records Archive (ERA) configuration management plan, along with areas for improvement. Then, this chapter describes the related role of Office of the Comptroller of the Currency (OCC) and some of the essential compliance requirements, including providing traceability of requirements to releases, production separation of controls, and I suggest a moral argument for supporting CM best practices and how to improve quality and productivity through compliance. Finally, this chapter provides some guidance on conducting a CM assessment, including how to get started and a reminder to always listen first regardless of how bad the situation initially appears.

Goals of Establishing IT Controls and Compliance

The goal of establishing IT controls and compliance is to implement procedures that bring IT governance into alignment with corporate governance. The most classic case is to establish controls that ensure that financial reports are accurate. Compliance is usually implemented based on an established standard or framework. This means that the IT controls established conform to the recommendations specified in the framework mandated by a regulatory agency or adopted by the organization. For example, most financial services firms are required to have a separation of duties between the physical control of assets, such as a payroll or banking system, and those who have responsibility for developing and maintaining these systems. They should also have appropriate security measures in place that prevent unauthorized access and, of course, modification (for example, fixing a release in production). In the event of unauthorized access, detection and audit controls should make remediation possible, if necessary, by rolling back and reinstalling a release as described in Chapter 6, "Deployment." In this chapter, we also have a goal of examining regulations that may be useful when you need to overcome resistance to change. Used sparingly, I have found it effective to mention that CM is often required by federal law and the absence of CM best practices will often trigger a report by the audit team if appropriate IT controls are not in place. I also want to note that although I have worked in government agencies, engineering, defense contractors, and financial services firms, and have personal knowledge of compliance violations related to poor CM practices, I have been careful to provide only information that is publicly available. No doubt, many senior managers have compliance and governance very high on their priority list and are proactive in addressing these issues. When most professionals think of IT controls and governance, they generally think of Sarbanes-Oxley (SOX) compliance.

13.1 Why Are IT Controls and Compliance Important?

IT controls are essential for a number of reasons. The most obvious is that many organizations have to comply with federal laws. I believe that good corporate citizenship should be an even more compelling reason to make sure you are in compliance. The rules that we discuss just make sense, and organizations should comply regardless of whether their lawyers have found some way to avoid compliance (as a regulatory requirement). One serious area of concern is that many hedge funds today do not have to comply with establishing IT controls and compliance. Sometimes, this results in organizations where production passwords are openly shared and there is no separation of controls. I believe that this is a huge mistake and that the compliance laws should apply equally to all financial services firms. The same is true for firms in the pharmaceutical and medical industries. I also strongly advocate that the journey to implement these IT controls should be focused on improving quality and productivity and not just simply passing an audit. Implementing these controls just makes sense, and their successful implementation is essential for any organization.

13.2 How Do I Get Started?

You should get started by evaluating your own risk profile. What are the things that go wrong with your systems? Could you accidentally make a million-dollar trade resulting in significant losses for your firm and your shareholders or expose confidential employee information? Could you accidentally expose confidential patient information in violation of HIPAA regulations? Obviously, the risk of causing a problem in a life-support system is more critical than exposing your favorite social-networking password. But these days, there are many risks and consequences. I recall one recent incident where my own university exposed the social security numbers of thousands of students on a website. You need to start by considering your organization's profiles and priorities. Then focus on making your journey to implement IT controls and compliance an effort that focuses on improving quality and productivity.

13.3 Understanding IT Controls and Compliance

Many of the compliance models are actually well thought out, and you can learn a lot from studying them and the standards and frameworks that have evolved to support them. Make sure that you reach out to other professionals to understand existing best practices. While you are at it, make sure that you come over to my website (http://cmbestpractices.com) to share best practices!

13.3.1 Sarbanes-Oxley Act of 2002

The Sarbanes-Oxley Act of 2002 was originally written by Senator Paul Sarbanes and Representative Michael Oxley as a response to several high-profile corporate scandals, including that of the much publicized Enron Corporation. In the Enron fiasco, shareholders (many of whom were employed by the company) suffered huge losses, and a complete breakdown in corporate governance occurred. The purpose of the SOX legislation was to hold senior management responsible for seeing that financial reports were accurate and that there was full financial disclosure and transparency in corporate governance. In short, SOX requires that companies have accurate financial reports and that they also establish proper IT controls. Section 404 of SOX specifies the requirements for management assessment of internal controls.

13.3.2 Management Assessment of Internal Controls

As specified in the text of the act, section 404 requires internal controls and accurate reporting:[1]

---

[1] Sarbanes Oxley Act of 2002, section 404

a. RULES REQUIRED. The Commission shall prescribe rules requiring each annual report required by section 13(a) or 15(d) of the Securities Exchange Act of 1934 (15 U.S.C. 78m or 78o(d)) to contain an internal control report, which shall—

1. state the *responsibility of management for establishing and maintaining an adequate internal control structure and procedures for financial reporting*; and

2. *contain an assessment, as of the end of the most recent fiscal year of the issuer, of the effectiveness of the internal control structure and procedures of the issuer for financial reporting.*

b. INTERNAL CONTROL EVALUATION AND REPORTING. With respect to the internal control assessment required by subsection (a), *each registered public accounting firm that prepares or issues the audit report for the issuer shall attest to, and report on, the assessment made by the management of the issuer.* An attestation made under this subsection shall be made in accordance with standards for attestation engagements issued or adopted by the Board. Any such attestation shall not be the subject of a separate engagement.

After SOX was passed, a number of organizations began working on establishing an effective control framework so that corporations would have adequate guidance and could comply with the requirements set forth under law. One of the first organizations to work on this effort is known as COSO.

13.3.3 Committee of Sponsoring Organizations

The Committee of Sponsoring Organizations of the Treadway Commission (COSO) is a voluntary private-sector organization comprising a number of well respected industry leaders, including the American Accounting Association (AAA), American Institute of Certified Public Accountants (AICPA), Financial Executives International (fei), The Association for Accountants and Financial Professionals in Business (ima), and the Institute of Internal Auditors (IIA). COSO is dedicated to guiding executive management and governance entities toward the establishment of more effective, efficient, and ethical business operations on a global basis. It sponsors and disseminates frameworks and guidance based on in-depth research, analysis, and best practices. In 1992, the Committee of Sponsoring Organizations outlined five essential components of any internal control system:[2]

---

[2] COSO website (http://coso.org)

1. Control Environment

2. Assessment of Risk

3. Control Activities

4. Accounting, Information, and Communication systems, and

5. Self-Assessment or Monitoring

Most organizations use the ISACA Cobit framework for guidance on implementing IT Controls.

13.3.4 Cobit as a Framework for IT Controls

Although COSO is generally considered a proper starting point for establishing financial controls, Cobit is commonly used to assess IT controls. In the Cobit framework, there are 34 high-level IT processes and 34 control objectives. These control objectives include guidance on establishing change and configuration management. I have been the person responsible for attesting that these two IT controls were in compliance in a large financial services firm.

13.3.5 What Does It Mean to Attest to And Report on the Assessment Made by the Management?

Section 404 (of the Sarbanes Oxley Act of 2002) requires that "with respect to the internal control assessment required by subsection (a), *each registered public accounting firm that prepares or issues the audit report for the issuer shall attest to, and report on, the assessment made by the management of the issuer.*" In practice, this meant that the public accounting firm established a tool for the organizations' subject matter experts (SMEs) to attest to compliance with each of the 34 required Cobit controls. This was supposed to involve assessing current practices and then attesting to compliance. Where noncompliance existed, I proactively worked with the development teams to improve their CM practices so that they could pass their next audit. Even if the teams failed the first time, the important issue, from a compliance perspective, was that we had a short-term plan to help them quickly come into compliance. In most cases, this took less than a month. Unfortunately, I have also seen organizations where this effort was little more than a rubber stamp. In fact, I recall one incident where a senior manager, in charge of compliance, expected that the attestation would happen *before* the groups were reviewed and assessed! I personally felt that this organization obviously did not take SOX compliance seriously, and that was truly a lost opportunity, because these best practices can improve both productivity and quality.

We will examine further how to meet the requirements of these control practices in Chapter 14, "Industry Standards and Frameworks." Cobit is a common framework, but it is not the only source of information on IT governance. Many pharmaceuticals and medical firms need to comply with HIPPA regulations.

13.3.6 Health Insurance Portability and Accountability Act of 1996

The Health Insurance Portability and Accountability Act of 1996 (HIPAA) Privacy Rule protects the privacy of individually identifiable health information. The Patient Safety Rule also has confidentiality provisions that protect identifiable information from being used to analyze patient safety events and improve patient safety. I have had technology professionals from pharmaceutical companies contact me to implement IT controls that were very similar to those required by SOX and Cobit. In both cases, the organization has to comply with regulations that are described in a specific framework. I have been told that pharmaceutical companies may have their IT controls subject to review by agencies such as the FDA. I have had more experience with supporting agencies that were being reviewed by the Government Accountability Office (GAO) and the Office of the Currency (OCC). The OCC reviews the practices in the banking industry, but it is the GAO that reviews government agencies and the subcontractors that work for them.

13.3.7 When the GAO Comes Knocking

The GAO describes the results of their reviews on their public website. For example, the GAO reviewed and commented on the configuration management practices used by the Federal Deposit Insurance Corporation (FDIC). The GAO cited several areas where the FDIC configuration management controls needed to be improved. For example, in May 2008, the GAO issued a report that said that there were weaknesses in configuration management controls in two key FDIC financial systems. The GAO report stated that the FDIC did not adequately (1) maintain a full and complete baseline for system requirements; (2) assign unique identifiers to configuration items; (3) authorize, document, and report all configuration changes; and (4) perform configuration audits. This was not the first time that the FDIC had come under scrutiny for inadequate configuration management controls. In 2005, the FDIC Office of Inspector General (OIG) retained the services of the International Business Machines (IBM) Business Consulting Services to audit and report on the effectiveness of the FDIC's configuration management controls over operating system software.[3]

---

[3] FDIC's Information Technology Configuration Management Controls over Operating System Software, report number 05-031, September 2005, Office of Inspector General

The report also noted that configuration management is a critical control for ensuring the integrity, security, and reliability of information systems. Absent a disciplined process for managing software changes, management cannot be assured that systems will operate as intended, that software defects will be minimized, and that configuration changes will be made in an efficient and timely manner. The objective of the audit was to determine whether the FDIC had established and implemented configuration management controls over its operating system software that were consistent with federal standards and guidelines and industry-accepted practices.[4]

13.3.8 Results of the Audit

The FDIC had established and implemented a number of configuration management controls over its operating system software that were consistent with federal standards and guidelines and industry-accepted practices. Such controls included a software patch management policy, a change control board, and periodic scanning of operating system software configurations. These actions were positive; however, control improvements were needed. Specifically, the FDIC needed to establish an organizational policy and system-specific procedures to ensure proper configuration of operating system software. The FDIC also needed to standardize and integrate the recording, tracking, and reporting of operating system software configuration changes to the extent practical.

In the report, IBM recommended that the FDIC

- Establish an organizational policy that defines roles, responsibilities, and overall principles and management expectations for performing configuration management of operating system software

- Develop configuration management plans that include system-specific procedures for managing the configuration of operating system software

- Ensure that the certification and accreditation of the FDIC's general support systems incorporate an evaluation and testing of the configuration management policy and plans referenced above

- Fully document the minimum required configuration settings for the operating systems covered in this review, and develop procedures to ensure that changes to baseline configuration settings are documented

- Standardize and integrate the recording, tracking, and reporting of configuration changes within and across operating system software platforms to the maximum extent practical

---

[4] *Ibid*

The GAO report on the FDIC is certainly a good example of a government agency being cited for having inadequate configuration management controls in practice. This was not the first time that the GAO had explicitly assessed and reviewed an agency's IT controls citing both inadequate configuration management practices and a failure to follow related IEEE standards.

13.3.9 GAO Reports on NARA's Configuration Management Practices

Since 2001, the National Archives and Records Administration (NARA) has been working to develop the policies and plans to build the Electronic Records Archives (ERA), a major information system intended to preserve and provide access to massive volumes of all types and formats of electronic records. Senate Report 108-146 directed GAO to provide a progress report on NARA's development of the ERA system. Specifically, the GAO's objective was to determine the agency's progress in implementing recommendations from previous assessments.[5]

13.3.10 ERA Configuration Management Plan

A configuration management plan establishes and maintains the integrity and control of the products through their lifecycles. The IEEE standard for configuration management plans has elements that include configuration activities and configuration schedules. Configuration management activities include the following:

- Listing items to be placed under configuration control

- Procedures for approving or disapproving changes

- A system for naming configuration items

- Verifying and implementing approved changes

- Assembling information for documenting a completed change

- Configuration status accounting (including data elements to be tracked; types and frequency of reports; how information is to be collected, stored, processed, and reported; and how access to status data is to be controlled)

- Analysis and evaluation of change requests, subcontractor control, and configuration audits and reviews

---

[5] United States Government Accountability Office Report to Congressional Committees, September 2004, RECORDS MANAGEMENT Planning for the Electronic Records Archives Has Improved - GAO-04-927

Overall, the ERA Configuration Management Plan fully satisfied 4 (21%), partially satisfied 11 (58%), and did not satisfy 4 (21%) of the 19 applicable subject areas in the IEEE standard.[6]

13.3.11 Areas for Improvement

The ERA Configuration Management Plan, however, only partially satisfies other areas of the standard, including the following, for example:

- The plan specifies the activities for verifying and implementing approved changes, but it does not specify any of the information needed to document completion of a change.

- Although it includes some of the information required for configuration status accounting, such as data elements to be tracked and types and frequency of reports, it does not mention the specific software package used to collect, store, process, and report the status of items under configuration control or how access to status data is to be controlled.

The plan does not satisfy several important aspects of the IEEE standards, including[7]

- Having a schedule for configuration management activities and for all events affecting the plan's implementation

- Specifying how subcontractor configuration management activities are to be monitored

- Including definitions of configuration audits and reviews such as the configuration items under audit or review, procedures for conducting the audit, and approval criteria

13.3.12 Understanding the Results of the Audit

There are a number of interesting results in this audit. The importance of having an SCM plan based on a recognized standard is highlighted in several places. For example, procedures for configuration identification and conducting a configuration audit were clearly a priority for both the GAO and the OIG. I also

---

[6] *Ibid*

[7] *Ibid*

find it interesting that the use of IEEE standards as a valid set of guidelines for implementing CM best practices was explicitly cited, too. This is not the only government agency directly concerned with compliance with configuration management best practices. I have also received calls from technology professionals who work for banks that have been cited by the OCC.

13.3.13 Office of the Comptroller of the Currency

The OCC was created by Congress to charter national banks, to oversee a nationwide system of banking institutions, and to ensure that national banks are safe and sound, competitive and profitable, and capable of serving in the best possible manner the banking needs of their customers. The OCC issued guidelines on internal controls.

The OCC has also identified cases resulting in bank losses in which internal control weaknesses included improper and untimely reconcilements of major asset or liability accounts. In others, the bank did not institute or follow normal separation of duties between the physical control of assets and liabilities and the record-keeping functions involving those assets and liabilities.[8]

In practice, banks need configuration management best practices to maintain a separation of duties between the software developers who write the code and the operations teams that maintain the production systems. The calls that I have received were about getting build engineers in place to compile, package, and deploy the code in a repeatable and traceable way. I have worked in organizations where the developers would do their own build and deployment, which was very bad for many reasons. In most cases, the procedure was not repeatable, and the developers relied on being able to access production to fix last-minute problems that had been overlooked. This meant that their build and deployment was just broken, the operations team could not roll back to a previous release, and there was little or no traceability into changes that were made to production systems. I am not blaming the developers. They were focused on writing great code. Another team was needed to provide traceability and repeatable deployment processes.

13.4 Essential Compliance Requirements

You will have to work with your own internal compliance experts to be certain that you know all of your own compliance requirements, but I will describe a few that I have personally come across in my own work and know are common

---

[8] Internal Controls - A Guide for Directors, Office of the Comptroller of the Currency, Washington, D.C., September 2000

in many organizations. The first is requirements traceability and the separation of controls between development and production.

13.4.1 Providing Traceability of Requirements to Releases

One of the most common compliance controls is to have traceability from the requirement as it was envisioned all the way through the lifecycle to the deployment of the release. In some organizations, this is a formal process with requirements tracking. In other environments, it is handled a little more loosely, with just some release notes that document exactly what went into a release. The goal is to make sure that requirements are never lost and changes deployed and promoted to production are fully traceable back to the authority who authorized the change.

13.4.2 Production Separation of Controls

We have already mentioned the requirement for a separation of controls. This is a particularly important requirement because it can avoid many of the problems central to the purpose of IT governance. Simply put, it is essential that the developers who write the code are not the people who operate and control the production environment. If this requirement is not met, the organization has a number of risks that could harm the firm and obviously the shareholders, too. It's been my personal observation that requiring a separation of duties improves quality and productivity by facilitating the implementation of a set of repeatable processes to support application release and deployment. If the procedures are implemented properly, the operations team should be able to promote a release into production and roll it back if necessary. This is a good example of where a compliance requirement can result in CM best practices that truly add value and help support the organization's critical systems. I also believe that there is a moral argument for why CM best practices should be adopted.

13.5 The Moral Argument for Supporting CM Best Practices

Society relies more on technology each day. I always use the following example when I consider the moral argument for establishing effective IT controls. Suppose you really need to get cash from your bank on a Saturday night and the system is down because the bank has cut corners that resulted in a CM-related error. In this example, I am suggesting financial institutions have an obligation to implement effective IT controls because of their impact on their customers, shareholders, and society as a whole. I strongly believe institutions should just be willing to implement these practices as good corporate citizens. I also believe that implementing IT controls and compliance is a great opportunity to improve organizational quality and productivity.

13.6 Improving Quality and Productivity Through Compliance

Focusing on compliance as a requirement to just pass an audit is, at best, a missed opportunity. Preparing for a compliance audit should always be an opportunity for an organization to identify what they are doing well and what practices they can improve. I have found it disappointing when the organization repeatedly focused on just getting past the yearly or quarterly audit. Instead, improving productivity and quality should be the goal of any review of existing practices and a central part of continuous process improvement. Of course, management must show leadership in this regard and provide time and resources to achieve these goals. Learning to conduct your own CM assessment is a great skill that will help you use this time to improve your organizational best practices and especially your organization's quality and productivity.

13.7 Conducting a CM Assessment

Conducting a configuration management assessment is a lot of fun. I have had this opportunity as both an internal member of the organization and an outsider coming in to essentially perform an audit and provide recommendations for improvement. In most cases, I worked closely with the organization's audit team in creating the criteria and framework for the assessment. Sometimes, I focused on teaching the auditors to look for items that were valid and to avoid minor issues that might sound important but were not really serious violations. In fact, I have seen assessments fail because there was too much of a focus on minor issues that really should not have been the focus of the audit at all. The best way to do a CM assessment is to use an established standard or framework. Understanding the text of the standard or framework is not always easy.

IT Standards Terminology

Some of the language in existing industry standards and frameworks is hard to understand, and I believe that improving this situation should be a priority for industry standards boards and the organizations that have established frameworks for supporting IT controls. I include myself in this problem. When writing a standard, we need to be precise because the document is often used in contractual agreements. The problem is that sometimes we also make the language difficult for technology professionals to understand and follow. We also have to be aware that changes must be done gradually because many organizations are already using the standards and rely on the existing terminology. I have recommended that standards working groups not only look closely at the language used in the standards, but also begin to include more examples that can make it easier to understand exactly how a standard can be implemented. Much of my own writing has focused on how to understand these tools in development organizations. For example, I don't think that *configuration status accounting* is an intuitive term, and I think that the phrase *following the status of a configuration item throughout its lifecycle* is also less than perfectly clear. I have also argued that *configuration change control* does not mean the same thing that it did 20 years when we did pick specific versions of Cobol programs for a specific release. It would be much easier for technology professionals to adopt and implement industry standards if the language were written in a more clear and descriptive way. That is precisely why I defined *configuration management* in six functions that I believe more closely reflect how CM is really practiced and that I believe make it easier for technology professionals to get started with implementing CM best practices.

13.7.1 Assessment First Steps

Getting started should always involve gaining senior management's support for the assessment, along with identification of the goals of the assessment and who will participate. Transparency is essential; otherwise, the team will likely be less cooperative because they will wonder about the purpose and agenda of the assessment. They might even be defensive and fearful that the assessment could potentially harm them personally. In truth, even the worst groups that I have seen usually had at least one excellent best practice that I had never seen before. For this and other reasons, I have learned to listen first when starting an assessment.

13.7.2 Listen First Regardless of How Bad the Situation Appears

When you start a CM assessment, always ask for a description of the best practices in place already. This not only shows the proper respect for the team, but it also always results in ascertaining the best practices that should likely not be impacted because they already work well for the team. I have also consistently found that when I ask for a description of existing best practices that work well, members of the team willingly give me plenty of information about areas that they know need to be improved. My approach seems to put people at ease and is a good example of "driving out fear" as recommended by Deming. Some assessments are very formal and often required as part of a contractual obligation.

SCAMPI and CMMI Configuration Management Practice Area

I have worked in organizations that used the Standard CMMI Appraisal Method for Process Improvement (SCAMPI) to assess existing configuration management practices and identify areas where improvement is needed. This is a formal approach to assessment and is generally used when the organizational has a commitment to use the CMMI for all of its lifecycle processes. The CMMI has been criticized as not providing enough constructive guidance on how to establish best practices where they do not yet exist. For this, I recommend using the extensive collection of IEEE standards, which provide an abundance of well-established industry guidelines on all aspects of software and systems development. Nonetheless, organizations worldwide delight is announcing that they have achieved recognition for being a Level 3, 4, or 5 organization under the CMMI framework. Whether you use a formal appraisal method or a more loose approach to looking at existing best practices and areas for improvement, CM assessments can significantly improve your organization's quality and productivity by providing a view into opportunities where the technology can improve on their existing configuration management best practices. Whether this is done in baby steps or as part of a well-sponsored organizational change effort, CM assessments can help your organization implement excellent IT controls and meet your compliance requirements.

Conclusion

In this chapter, we discussed a number of high-profile incidents where configuration management controls were found to be inadequate. We also discussed, in operational terms, how compliance controls can impact an organization on a day-to-day basis. The use of CM assessments to self-monitor and prepare for an external audit was discussed, and some of the common compliance frameworks were mentioned. It is my personal opinion that CM best practices add significant value to any organization and that there should be strong reasons for implementing CM best practices to help the organization truly comply with all appropriate requirements. I also believe that the approach should be to improve quality and productivity and not just focus on getting past an audit. The frameworks themselves should be improved over time so that their recommendations are valid and their adoption may be accomplished as efficiently as possible.

Chapter 14

Industry Standards and
Frameworks

Chapter Overview

14.1 Why Are Standards and Frameworks Important?   188

14.2 How Do I Get Started?   189

14.3 Terminology Required   189

14.4 Applying These Terms to the Standards and Frameworks   193

14.5 Industry Standards   193

14.6 Industry Frameworks   196

In this chapter, we start by reviewing the essential terminology required, including configuration item (CI), configuration identification, configuration control, interface control, configuration status accounting, configuration audit, subcontractor/vendor control, and conformance versus noncompliance. We also discuss applying these terms to the standards and frameworks. Next, we discuss specific standards, including the following: IEEE 828—Standard for Software Configuration Management Plans; ISO 10007—Quality Management Systems—Guidelines for Configuration Management; ANSI/ITAA EIA-649-A—National Consensus Standard for Configuration Management; and comprehensive lifecycle standards ISO/IEC/IEEE 12207 and 15288. Next, we discuss industry frameworks, such as ISACA Cobit, including my own journey with Cobit, with a focus on control practices. Then, we discuss implementing a comprehensive configuration and change control function and how continuous process improvement addresses common challenges and problems such as releases that fail. Next, I relate my own experience with the CMM/CMMI and ITIL frameworks, including change management, service asset and configuration management (SACM), and establishing a configuration management system (CMS), definitive media library (DML), configuration management database (CMDB), and integrating the CMS, DML, CMDB, and source code management systems. We also discuss best practices for implementing release management and deployment and home-spun environment monitoring. Then, we close the chapter by briefly touching on SWEBOK, Open Unified Process (OpenUP), Agile/SCRUM, and continuous integration (CI).

Goals of Using Industry Standards and Frameworks

The primary goal of industry standards and frameworks is to promote a consistent set of widely accepted best practices that consists of the combined knowledge and wisdom of industry experts. These practices help you get the job done right and improve the quality and productivity of your own processes. Another goal of using industry standards and frameworks is to implement continuous process improvement, resulting in overall excellence. This is accomplished by the fact that it is relatively easy for any technology professional to participate and contribute to many standards and frameworks. For configuration management, these best practices represent the essential things that you need to do to have your processes be effective and efficient. As with any specialized discipline, some terminology needs to be understood to work effectively with standards and frameworks. We will start by discussing why standards and frameworks are important along with how to get started. Then we will dive into some important terminology.

14.1 Why Are Standards and Frameworks Important?

Standards and frameworks are wisdom developed by experts. Standards and frameworks will help you get started faster and do a better job. For many, they are also a requirement for compliance, and they certainly make passing your next audit much easier. Standards and frameworks are essentially best practices that have been vetted and tested by many of your colleagues who volunteer considerable time to share their knowledge and experience. Please contact me if you would like to get personally involved with this effort.

14.2 How Do I Get Started?

If you have a requirement to establish IT controls and compliance, your audit/ compliance department may tell you exactly where you need to start. If you are just using standards and frameworks as best practices, start by considering your own goals and priorities. I have often suggested that taking a risk-based approach is pragmatic, which means that you consider what your own risks might be and then focus on addressing those requirements. Make sure that you start this journey with a focus on improving quality and productivity!

14.3 Terminology Required

The terminology used by CM experts can seem rather arcane. You will also find that some of the terminology is used differently in common standards (such as ISO 10007, IEEE 828) and frameworks (such as Cobit, CMMI, ITIL). I recommend using the IEEE's SEVOCAB: Software and Systems Engineering Vocabulary, which, at the time of this writing, can be found at www.computer.org/ sevocab. In this section, I discuss the most important technical terms that you need to know to read through the standards and frameworks. Terms such as *configuration status accounting* and *configuration audits* are often misunderstood, and I have seen them used incorrectly in CM plans used by large corporations. *Configuration change control* is another term that is often misunderstood and can actually have two different meanings! CM is certainly not the only discipline with specialized terminology, but I believe we can improve the situation by updating our terminology to be more consistent with other technology disciplines. This is easier said than done because there can also be difficulty in reaching consensus on what a particular term means. For example, *configuration items* may be defined at a very high level (for example, components) or a very granular level (for example, configuration files). What exactly is included in a configuration item?

14.3.1 Configuration Item

The first term that you need to understand is *configuration item* (CI). Unfortunately, this term is not always used in a consistent way. The question is this: What exactly constitutes a CI? Configuration items certainly include all components that are created during the build and packaging process. But, I would also consider configuration files, Word documents, and XML to be configuration items, too. Obviously, all hardware components are also configuration items. It starts to become difficult to determine exactly what is *not* a configuration item. Should a header file that is compiled into one or more components be considered a configuration item? I think so and, in fact, I cast a very wide net and consider almost anything required in a release a configuration item. In practice, CIs are selected, identified, and then tracked very closely. We discuss this further in the following section.

14.3.2 Configuration Identification

Configuration identification involves implementing a reliable way to select and identify the correct configuration items. Usually, this means that you are embedding an immutable version ID into a configuration item, such as a component, configuration file, Word document, or XML, along with providing a procedure to reliably retrieve this version ID. Configuration identification also involves creating a unique and reliable naming convention for baselines, packages and components, and so on. In practice, you are doing this in the version control or source code management tool. Configuration identification enables you to identify the exact version of a configuration item, regardless of whether it is in the source code management system. Many CM experts spend much of their time selecting, implementing, and supporting toolsets that facilitate effective configuration identification, including providing traceability to track requirements to changes. This is discussed further in Section 14.3.5, "Configuration Status Accounting."

14.3.3 Configuration Control

Configuration control is used to control all changes to configuration items, including exactly what the change was, who made the change, and authorization for the change. Configuration control also includes the capability to revert the change back, if necessary. Configuration control also involves controls to make certain that unauthorized changes do not occur. Configuration control has also been used to control the exact version of configuration items that will be part of a particular baseline of the code. In *a priori* change control, permission is requested to make a change before the change actually occurs. Many development teams do not really control changes up front. The project manager, tech lead, or even the developers implicitly decide which changes should be made and when they should occur. Many development teams practice change control very loosely in the beginning of a project and then more strictly when the application has been released and is being maintained.

14.3.4 Interface Control

Components often have interface dependencies that might be as simple as pointing to the correct database (such as QA, production) or they may be very complex. I have worked with applications that had interface requirements that included complex structures to support object persistence or behavior across complex firewalls and proxies. Many organizations will handle *interface control* as part of a configuration control function that will span all the groups impacted. For example, interface control may require that the security team authorize ports to be opened on a firewall while the systems administrators configure the systems to communicate on a specific port. In practice, configuration control and interface control must be managed very tightly together.

14.3.5 Configuration Status Accounting

Configuration status accounting (CSA) involves tracing a configuration item through its complete lifecycle. This can include tracking a requirement from the beginning of the application development effort through its development and eventual deployment as part of a release. CSA also involves providing status of the CIs at any point of time. It's been my experience that configuration status accounting is often misunderstood and frequently overlooked during the development effort. In practice, status accounting is often achieved through toolsets that associate work item (such as defects, tasks, change requests) tracking with the changesets stored in the source code management system.

14.3.6 Configuration Audit

Performing a *configuration audit* involves being able to verify both the physical and functional characteristics of any configuration item (CI). A common mistake is that developers believe that it is sufficient to track CIs while they are in a source code management system. The CI should still be identifiable even when the code is released to production (or QA). Many organizations rely on their own internal record keeping to trace when a baseline was promoted to production. They then mistakenly assume that they know exactly what version is running in production. I have seen code, even in highly secure production environments, accidentally modified (sometimes with disastrous results). When configuration items have embedded immutable version IDs, a configuration audit can be done is a reliable and efficient way. I usually write a small script to display the version ID of each CI and ship a copy of the list of CIs (and their respective version IDs). I call this list my *release map*. A configuration audit can then be done by regenerating the release map and comparing it to the copy shipped when the release was first deployed. There are more sophisticated ways of handling this issue involving cryptographic keys, which we discussed in Chapter 5, "Release Management."

14.3.7 Subcontractor/Vendor Control

It is common for a subcontractor to do work that needs to be under software configuration management, including version and change control. It is also increasingly common for subcontractors, including offshore resources, to be treated just like any other member of the team. This has become more practical as many robust source code management systems can be used for teams that are distributed across multiple locations. This might mean that there are a few extra security controls required because the onshore resource should review and accept work as it is being completed. In addition, subcontractors are sometimes producing complete products at another location, and only the completed baselined release needs to be version controlled. Many government agencies and defense contractors have a requirement to confirm that a subcontractor has appropriate IT controls in place, including configuration and release management. Sometimes, you will also need to manage customizations to the subcontractor's release. At a minimum, you need to be able to perform a configuration audit on the baselined release as it is delivered.

I have also seen open source projects handled as a vendor/third party release, too. In this case, the development team takes responsibility for a particular release of the product and handles it much like a third-party product. There are also times when one developer will provide code to another team, even within the same company, and handle the release as a third-party product. In practice, a common key issue is confirming that all copyright requirements have been met. In some cases, embedding an open source product into a commercial one may incur unforeseen or unintended obligations on the development team. Having the code secured in a source code repository makes it make easier to handle these issues. It also makes it much easier to affirm that your team is in compliance with the specific criteria established in the standard.

14.3.8 Conformance Versus Noncompliance

Some standards define specific criteria for claiming compliance with the standard. The implication is that if you follow the guidelines as specified, you have the right to state that your CM plans comply with the specific standard. However, if you do not include all the required practices, you cannot claim that your CM plans comply with the standard. Practices required for compliance are usually indicated by the word *shall,* whereas suggested practices are indicated with the word *should.* Some standards are intended to be guidance only and specifically indicate that they are not intended to be "compliance" standards. Depending on the industry that you are in, you might be required to show that you are in compliance with a particular standard. In other cases, you may just benefit from employing best practices and demonstrating during your audit that you have industry standard IT controls in place.

14.4 Applying These Terms to the Standards and Frameworks

Each of these terms is commonly cited in a number of different standards and frameworks. I have explained the basics, but you still need to read the entire standard to confirm your understanding of the terminology within the context of the particular standard. What follows is an overview of the CM-related standards and frameworks that you need to know about to confirm that your own best practices follow established industry guidelines. In some cases, I am permitted to quote only a small section of the standard verbatim, so I have to recommend that you legally obtain a copy of the actual standard or framework to get a complete picture and thus successfully implement these best practices. What follows is an overview that I hope will help get you started.

14.5 Industry Standards

Many excellent standards have been written to support configuration management. We discuss some of the most common standards in this section, but you should remember that standards are best practices that have been written and reviewed by a team of industry experts. I am going to play fast and loose by saying that standards are wisdom, and from time to time you may decide not to follow them or to tailor them to your own needs. But, I want to make sure that we start the discussion by noting that a lot of work goes into creating an industry standard and for the most part you would do well to follow them and benefit from you colleagues who took the time to create them. Incidentally, I also want to mention that many standards working groups consist of volunteers who receive no monetary benefit from their involvement and their sharing of substantial knowledge and experience. We all owe them a debt of gratitude for their corporate citizenship, and I hope that you will contact me to get involved with these efforts.

14.5.1 IEEE 828—Standard for Software Configuration Management Plans

The IEEE 828 CM planning standard is one of the most widely used guidelines for effective software configuration management. IEEE rules prohibit me from including more than 10% of the standard in this book, so I will give you an idea of how the standard can help you while encouraging you to go out and purchase your own copy from the IEEE. Here are the main sections of the Software Configuration Management Plan:

- The Introduction describes the plan's purpose, scope of application, key terms, and references.

- SCM Management identifies the responsibilities and authorities for accomplishing the planned activities.

- SCM Activities identifies all activities to be performed in applying to the project.

- SCM Schedules identifies the required coordination of SCM activities with the other activities in the project.

- SCM Resources identifies tools and physical and human resources required for execution of the plan.

- SCM Plan Maintenance identifies how the plan will be kept current while in effect.

The activities include configuration identification, configuration control, configuration status accounting, configuration audits and reviews, interface control, and subcontractor/vendor control. Release management and delivery describes how the build, release, and delivery of the software products and documentation will be formally controlled.[1]

14.5.1.1 Conformance with the Standard

I have worked in many and varied organizations, including private companies, government agencies, and defense contractors that had a contractual obligation to comply with the requirements specified in the IEEE 828 standard. CM plans that conform to the standard bear the coveted phrase, "This SCM plan conforms with the requirements of IEEE Std 828," which means that the plan includes the introduction, management, activities, schedules, resources, and plan maintenance as described above. In addition, all activities must have an assigned resource to perform the activities specified in the plan. It is also a requirement to have defined processes for creating baselines and change control for all configuration items (CI). As you read through the standard, you will also

---

[1] Note that in IEEE 828-2005, the SCM activities were grouped into five functions: configuration identification, configuration control, configuration status accounting, configuration evaluations and reviews, and release management and delivery.

notice that some activities are described with the word *shall* or *required*. This refers to activities that are minimally required for conformance to the standard. Other activities are described using the work *should,* which means that they are optional, although still best practices that you should employ to improve your quality and productivity. The IEEE 828 Standard for Software Configuration Management Plans is the most commonly used CM-related standard and is regarded as a "national consensus standard," but other standards and guidance documents are also widely used.

14.5.2 ISO 10007—Quality Management Systems—Guidelines for Configuration Management

ISO 10007 is part of the ISO 9001 family of standards, designed to support a quality management system (QMS). It provides guidance on the use of configuration management by outlining the configuration management process, including configuration management planning, configuration identification, change control, configuration status accounting, and configuration audit.

14.5.2.1 ISO 10007 Is a Guidance Document

ISO 10007 is a guidance document and is not intended to be used for certification purposes.

14.5.2.2 Understanding ISO 10007

To understand ISO 10007, you need to know that the ISO 9001 family of standards are intended to support a quality management system in both software and nonsoftware environments. Closely related is the ISO 9000 family of standards, which are intended to support quality management and quality assurance. It's helpful to note that these early standards were focused on establishing quality management but were not specifically geared toward software environments. ISO 9000-3 was the application of ISO 9001 to the specification, development, installation, and support of software. Under ISO 9000-3, configuration management included version control and identification of baselines, change control, and status reporting, along with well-defined roles and responsibilities. ISO 10007 and ISO 9000-3 are primarily high-level guidance documents and are often supplemented by other, more detailed, standards. Nonetheless, most standards groups will strive to be in alignment with the ISO 9000/9001 family of standards, including ISO 10007.

14.5.3 ANSI/ITAA EIA-649-A—National Consensus Standard for Configuration Management

This standard describes configuration management functions and also defines CM terminology. This standard focuses on establishing and maintaining consistency between the resulting product and the product requirements and attributes defined in product configuration information. The standard recommends processes and tools to perform the configuration management functions.

The plan includes schedules, resources, training required, and cost information that are all placed under configuration control. This standard is not as widely used as the IEEE 828 and describes itself as being a "noncompliance" standard.

14.5.4 ISO/IEC/IEEE 12207 and 15288

The ISO/IEC/IEEE 12207 standard describes the software engineering processes used throughout the entire lifecycle of any software system (with 43 processes), whereas ISO/IEC/IEEE 15288 covers the processes used during the entire lifecycle of any human-made system (with 25 processes). I like to call these standards an *umbrella standard* because they provide a comprehensive framework for the entire development effort. In practice, they contain brief treatment of any part of the development lifecycle. They are easily extended by plugging in any of the IEEE-specific standards such as testing, quality assurance, code reviews, or configuration management planning. These two standards provide an excellent starting point and are always harmonized with the other deeper function-specific standards mentioned earlier.

14.6 Industry Frameworks

Frameworks are written and supported by the industry group responsible for them. Frameworks do not generally require the stringent 75% vote that is more commonly required by standards boards. Standards are more commonly quoted in contractual agreements, although I have seen plenty of organizations that had contractual agreements to implement frameworks such as Cobit, ITIL, or the CMMI. It is my opinion that it is easier to get personally involved with standards boards,[2] although frameworks committees have the advantage of operating with more autonomy (which may sometimes result in better results because they do not have to worry about the voting process). This is my personal view and may be somewhat controversial. But, I have seen standards get mired in the consensus building process to get the required quorum (and get approved). In practice, frameworks typically quote standards, and my colleagues and I work

---

[2] Contact me personally if you would like to get involved with the IEEE standards work!

hard to help keep CM-related standards in harmony with frameworks. Wisdom should be shared, so let's explore the frameworks related to CM!

14.6.1 ISACA Cobit

Cobit is one of my favorite frameworks and is generally considered to be synonymous with compliance with section 404 of the Sarbanes-Oxley Act of 2002. There are 34 high-level IT processes described in the Cobit model, which combined provide comprehensive guidance in establishing IT controls, including those that support configuration management. To implement Cobit, you need to have studied the model and understand the IT controls that it prescribes. But even then, it is not easy to implement IT processes by just reading the Cobit framework. In fact, I have had many discussions with technology professionals who were responsible for IT compliance and audit professionals who were concerned about correctly interpreting the guidance specified in the Cobit framework. Some others just went through the motions to appear as if they had implemented the Cobit controls, saying that it was just too difficult and expensive to really implement the Cobit controls—even if they were understandable. So, then, if it's this difficult, what is wrong with Cobit?

14.6.1.1 The Problem with Cobit

Many people complain that Cobit, among other frameworks and standards, is just too complex and difficult (read *expensive*) to implement. I do not believe that this criticism is valid. Instead, I suggest that many people tend to approach Cobit the wrong way. Too often, technology professionals are forced to narrowly focus on passing an audit, versus improving processes along with quality and productivity. My view is that implementing Cobit should be a journey in improving your IT processes, including establishing effective IT controls. It is essential that you start with defining your goals in practical terms. Cobit is just a tool to help you get this job done, and if used well, it will save you lots of time and effort. Cobit provides you with plenty of guidance on how to define these goals and implement the controls themselves in practical terms. In short, there is nothing wrong with Cobit. It is a framework with expert guidance just like any other standard or framework. Written and developed by industry experts, although it may not be perfect, it is nonetheless a valuable tool when used to guide the implementation of IT processes in an effective and appropriate way.

14.6.1.2 My Own Journey with Cobit

In this section, I describe my own personal efforts to understand Cobit and how it can best be implemented in practical terms. It is true that I have had the distinct advantage of recognizing that Cobit is just guidance. Years ago, we worked on improving our processes without any available frameworks, and back then we just wished that we had a database of project-related metrics to guide us on our journey. Back in the 1980s, we used the tools of collaborative process consultation with the subject matter experts available to us. Now, with a comprehensive framework, we can accomplish a lot more and achieve our goals with considerably less effort. So my approach is to use Cobit as a tool, in conjunction with other frameworks and industry standards. To say this differently, I would never suggest that you just jump into the complexities of the framework without a specific goal-driven approach. I have also found that some sections of Cobit are just easier to grasp than others. Many people have complained to me that their first attempt at understanding Cobit was less than successful and that they found it almost impossible to implement the processes just based on the guidance described in the framework.

14.6.1.2.1 Control Practices Give Clarity

I have personally found that the key to success with Cobit is to analyze the detailed control practices described in the online model. I encourage you to get the original copy from ISACA directly, but I will describe what I have learned during my own journey and my own method for analyzing the guidance described. To start with an example, we'll look at change control, which is one of the most important IT processes described in the Cobit framework. The Cobit framework provides considerable guidance on change management. (Later in this book, we discuss the itSMF's ITIL change management function.) Let's start with analyzing this specific process, and then we'll look at scaling configuration and change control in a wider context.

14.6.1.2.2 Manage Changes

In this critical IT process area, changes are reviewed, approved (or rejected), controlled, and tracked. There is a heavy focus on requiring that all changes be reviewed and only permitted on being authorized by the Change Control Board (CCB). I have found that some individuals will work hard to bypass the change control process if they believe that it is too burdensome to follow. When an emergency occurs, these folks can usually gain enough political power to get authority to just make their changes without having to worry about the change control process. The problem here is twofold. Not only could that change result in a serious mistake, but even worse, others will stop taking change control seriously when these exceptions occur. As a result, an emergency change becomes a way to bypass the standard change control process. In some organizations, it almost becomes a badge of honor that you don't have to *waste time* following a burdensome change control process. The answer to this problem is to have a well-defined and manageable emergency change control process in place to handle legitimate emergency changes but to be extremely selective as to what constitutes a true emergency change.

14.6.1.2.3 What Makes Something an Emergency?

Sometimes, completely unforeseen incidents occur and impact critical IT infrastructure. In these situations, you need to have an emergency change control function in place to address the issue. I have also seen situations where someone made an emergency change that did go through change control and inadvertently made the problem even worse. Emergency changes could include patches for both infrastructure and all applications. The emergency change control process should require getting permission from a senior manager who demonstrates support for the change management process by ascertaining why the change cannot go through the normal channels. In practice, most professionals will use the emergency change control sparingly only if they have to explain themselves before a senior manager who has authority over the change control process (with the ability to approve or deny the change).

In addition, all changes should be logged and reviewed before and after the change is made. I have been in many change control meetings where we reviewed changes—approving or rejecting them (usually because of missing information) and also reviewed changes that had been completed already to ascertain whether there were any problems that could have been prevented. For example, if a change was approved, but resulted in an unexpected side affect or downstream impact, this dependency needs to be identified and documented to prevent a similar problem from occurring in the future. From these lessons learned, we could effectively improve our change control process.

14.6.1.2.4 Metrics Provide Visibility

The Cobit framework also provides guidance on the effective use of metrics to measure success. For example, tracking the number of problems and errors caused by "inaccurate specifications" or "incomplete impact assessment" (of the change) gives us valuable data to ascertain the root cause of the problems. These metrics help us to manage change better because it is common to get surprised by unexpected impacts that might directly result from a given change. Other recommended metrics include the amount of "application or infrastructure rework" caused by inadequate change specifications and the percent of changes that follow formal change control processes. The number of emergency changes and the reason for them bypassing the regular change control process are also important metrics to track. These metrics help us to recognize problems (and risks) and to try to avoid making the same mistake over again. Recognizing the practical value of the metrics gathered can help us become much more adept at managing change in the IT process.

14.6.1.2.5 Scaling Cobit to Improve Your IT Processes

In the previous section, I briefly described analyzing one of the 34 IT processes described in Cobit. In practice, you want to analyze a number of Cobit processes along with IEEE standards and other frameworks such as ITIL and the CMMI to design effective and comprehensive IT processes. I will now explain the way that I approach synthesizing three Cobit processes with support from other standards and frameworks to implement a comprehensive configuration and change control function. Note that while I am using Cobit for guidance, I am also tailoring the guidance to a typical company that I have imagined based on my own experiences.

14.6.1.3 *Implementing a Comprehensive Configuration and Change Control Function*

In practice, implementing configuration and change control involves a number of important processes. To accomplish this integration, I analyze the guidance in three Cobit processes:

1. Manage changes.

2. Manage the configuration.

3. Install and accredit solutions and changes.

14.6.1.3.1 Start with the Goals in Mind

Cobit lists many important goals that should be considered when designing any configuration and change control function. I usually recommend starting with your own list first. Here's my first cut:

1. Identify and plan for changes that are needed to support the business.

2. Assess and mitigate risk associated with the proposed changes.

3. Implement changes accurately and efficiently.

4. Provide traceability into changes, including who authorized them.

5. Test and verify that changes were implemented successfully.

6. Provide reliable procedures to back out changes if necessary.

7. Continuously improve our configuration and change control procedures.

After I create my own list, I review the goals listed in Cobit, along with other frameworks, and update my list with any goals that may help me get the job done better. Obviously, you also need to set priorities because, although certain functions might be nice to have, you should first address the most immediate needs.

14.6.1.3.2 Consider Metrics to Measure Success

Here are some metrics that may indicate poor to nonexistent configuration and change control procedures:

1. Number of mistakes or errors resulting from a change or configuration issue that resulted in an unexpected problem or higher risk to the business

2. Number of valid issues identified during an audit or compliance review

3. Number of requests for change that needed to be rejected because of inaccurate or incomplete specifications

4. Missing or unknown information about configuration items, including configuration issues such as patch or driver versions

5. Amount of downtown or service interruption caused by inaccurate change specifications or missed impact assessment

6. Number of emergency change requests or attempts to bypass the standard change management process

7. Amount of time in staff hours required to implement and support a change

Here are some metrics that should indicate that you have an excellent configuration and change control function:

1. Customer satisfaction as measured by survey and anecdotal information

2. Number of requests for change that were completed on time without unexpected incidents or problems

3. Changes that are handled by a third party without requiring developer intervention

4. Number of changes completed within a specified window

5. Number of changes that have well defined and repeatable change control processes (including automation)

6. Number of changes that can be easily backed out if necessary

7. Number of changes completed that included specific tests to validate and verify system functionality after changes have been completed

14.6.1.3.3 The Soft Indicators

I have personally found two other soft indicators are a clear indication of efficient and effective change management. The first is the ability to make many small changes flawlessly without significant risk, as opposed to saving all the changes up for a "big bang" window when you need developers on call to deal with mistakes and problems. The other soft indicator is the ability and confidence to make a change within a short window, as opposed to requiring a long window with a large number of staff on call to resolve problems. This may upset a few people, but I have seen organizations that had so many problems that they simply gave up on effective release management and required that all changes be made on Friday nights with the entire staff on call for the weekend. The organization just assumed that promoting a release would always be problematic and just required that everyone share the pain. In some other industries and work cultures, subpar performance is just accepted as the *norm*. For example, in some places, it is just assumed that trains and buses will not be able to stick to a schedule.

Buses and Trains Should Run on Time

W. Edwards Deming pointed out that transit systems should always run precisely on time. I have read descriptions of transit systems that ran precisely on time and others that were constantly unreliable. Deming's point was that there is no possible excuse for accepting poor quality as a norm. Similarly, release management should be automated, reliable, traceable, and verifiable. Sadly, many organizations just assume that release management cannot be controlled, just as trains and buses will be habitually late. For example, many organizations require that changes be made on a Friday night, allowing for lots of time to fix and deal with problems that should not occur in the first place. Some of these organizations are just being prudent, but I believe that many organizations are really admitting defeat and assuming that every release will be a problem that takes many hours to fix. These same organizations often do not have confidence that they can easily roll back a release after it has been deployed. Your release management process should be reliable, predictable, controlled, and traceable. In the next section, we take a closer look at the tasks and functions that need to be part of a robust configuration and change management function using the guidance described in Cobit. Intuitively, I look at this effort as starting with a set of primary configuration and change management functions, with a set of supporting functions essential for success. I also readily synthesize in concepts, functions and processes from other standards (e.g., IEEE, ISO) and frameworks (e.g., Cobit, CMMI).

14.6.1.3.4 Putting Together a Configuration and Change Management Framework

Organizations need to start by realizing that this effort involves creating and implementing a comprehensive change management framework, including well-defined processes and procedures to support the change request lifecycle. Much of what we are about to describe should be part of your change management framework. You will certainly want a clear and consistent way to submit change requests (CRs), which are then reviewed by the change control board (CCB) to assess impact and priority. This review process should be based on assessing and mitigating risk. Therefore, you should focus on those specific issues that might adversely impact your organization. It is essential to realize that emergencies do occur, and there needs to be a well-defined and repeatable emergency change control process. I recommend requiring that a very senior manager approve all emergency change requests so that you can confirm that people are not using the emergency change control process to simply bypass the standard change control process. An essential part of this review should include automated procedures to promote releases (and fallback to a previous release if necessary). The CCB should insist that deployment be automated, especially if there have been mistakes made in previous releases. Deployment also needs to be fully traceable so that you know exactly what is deployed at any particular point in time. After the review of the CRs has been completed, authority should be granted to promote the release. Changes to configurations are sometimes viewed as being "minor" changes but should be handled in essentially the same way because they are effectively the same as a release.

14.6.1.3.5 Do Configuration Changes Need to Be Handled by the Change Control Process?

People often ask whether configuration changes need to be handled in the same manner as releases. For the most part, the answer is yes, especially if the change has the potential to shut down the production system. Even seemingly "minor" configuration changes can have devastating impacts. Therefore, all configuration changes ideally should be handled by change control. Your change control processes will need to assess whether there are indeed "minor" changes that do not incur significant risk.

14.6.1.4 Continuous Process Improvement

Any configuration and change control process needs to build in a mechanism to assess itself and continuously improve. In my experience, it is often impossible to design a comprehensive change control process for a large-scale technology effort. There are often just too many moving parts, leading to a level of complexity that makes it almost impossible to specify the perfect change control process from the beginning. Yet, that is often exactly what I am asked to do. There are also usually good reasons for why the group is making mistakes, but it might not be easy to ascertain the root cause of these problems. It is my opinion that the best way to handle this is to continuously review and improve your processes with a special focus on implementing changes and improvements to address challenges and problems that occur in your environment. In the next section, we discuss the primary configuration and change management functions.

14.6.1.4.1 Primary Configuration and Change Management Functions

Figure 14.1 shows what should be included in your configuration and change management function.

Figure 14.1 *What you need to include in your change and configuration management function.*

14.6.1.4.2 Essential Support Configuration and Change Management Functions

Many functions described in the Cobit framework are essential for you to include in your configuration and change management function. You will recognize them because we have discussed most of them earlier in the book. Configuration identification must include embedding immutable version IDs in all configuration items so that you can successfully audit releases of the code in production in addition to having an efficient version control mechanism to manage your source code. Good source code and release management practices include the creation of baselines to know the exact versions of all source code and other configuration items that were included in a particular release. This practice is known as *baselining* your code and should result in well-packaged releases stored in a central release library. (In ITIL, we call this the *definitive media library* or DML.)

14.6.1.4.3 The Challenge of Asset Management

Tracking baselines and configuration items as software assets is an essential practice that can be complex to implement in large-scale environments. The configuration and change management function should include procedures to identify all software (and hardware) assets and any changes that are required (and, of course, vetted in the change control process).

Managing environments and environment dependencies (both compile and runtime) is an often overlooked function that is critical for your success. Training is also often overlooked and needs to be a key function that includes identifying changes required by the new release of the software. Verification and validation should be part of any process, too. As mentioned before, verification means that your processes have the intended results. Validation means that your processes yield the *correct* results! In the next section, we discuss how to plan and implement the processes described by the Cobit model.

14.6.1.4.4 Essential Change and Configuration Management Supporting Functions

Figure 14.2 shows the supporting functions that you need to implement to support your core functions (the core functions were shown previously in Figure 14.1).

14.6.1.4.5 Planning for Implementation

Planning for the implementation of Cobit can be very challenging. I have seen organizations attempt to adopt Cobit on a wide-scale basis to support the need for immediate Sarbanes-Oxley (SOX) compliance. This is tough and often results in less-than-spectacular success. Remember that you do not want your organization to just "pretend" to follow Cobit. The adoption of any standard or framework is an opportunity to assess your current best practices and then improve your processes by adopting well-defined industry best practices. Your implementation needs to start by defining your own goals and especially the risks that you need to mitigate. Make sure that you also plan for both support and training of all involved personnel. In practice, I look for the "low hanging fruit," where improvement can be shown easily. Getting some successes will make it much easier for you to tackle the tougher problems. For example, many organizations start by implementing a simple change control function to just act as a gatekeeper for reviewing releases that are going to be promoted to production. Usually, you will also review configuration changes, too. This might be enough to get you started with a basic change control function. You then need to decide which functions to add to improve your processes. I usually look at mistakes as a great way to evaluate and justify raising the bar.

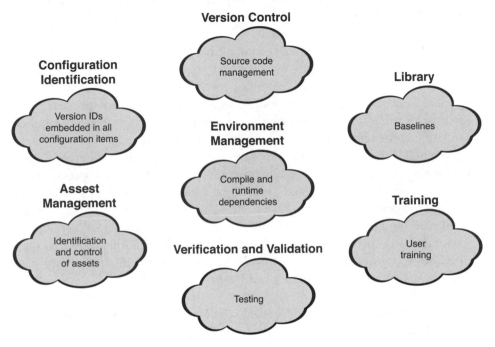

Figure 14.2 *Change and configuration supporting functions.*

14.6.1.4.6 Releases that Fail

People usually call me when the release management process is broken. This is always a great opportunity to look for ways to improve existing processes. I often find that many things are being done well, but there is always a reason why the team is making mistakes. Reviewing the functions described in the Cobit model, I might ask to review the testing that will be done when a release is promoted to production. I also ask to see the detailed release procedures, including scripts to automate the deployment. I ask to see the procedures for backing a release out should that be necessary. Mistakes and releases that fail are often the perfect opportunity to make things a little better. My advice is to review the best practices described in the standards and frameworks (including Cobit) and then pilot improving your processes by implementing a change that addresses the problem that you need to solve or the goal that you need to achieve. It is common for mistakes and failures to trigger a request for a complete assessment of existing practices.

14.6.1.4.7 Conclusion

Cobit is one of the best frameworks to use when you want to improve your IT processes. The best practices regarding configuration and change management can help you establish your own CM-related practices. Other excellent frameworks also provide guidance, including the CMMI and ITIL.

14.6.2 CMM/CMMI

The original Capability Maturity Model (CMM) and the newer Capability Maturity Model Integration (CMMI) provide guidance on effective processes, including configuration management. The Software Engineering Institute (SEI) at Carnegie Mellon states that the CMMI is a process-improvement approach that can be used to guide process improvement across a project, a division, or an entire organization. The CMMI helps integrate traditionally separate organizational functions, set process-improvement goals and priorities, provide guidance for quality processes, and provide a point of reference for appraising current processes. The CMMI can be implemented in a flexible continuous process-improvement manner or staged in a more formal way, similar to the original CMM. I have worked in many organizations that embraced process improvement, especially with the CMM/CMMI as a framework.

One of the most frustrating considerations was the traditional view that process areas had to be implemented in a specific order. In practice, this meant that you could not start code reviews before you had implemented subcontractor management. This was pretty silly because our pain points were just not really focused on subcontractor maintenance and code reviews gave us immediate return on our investment. This was a perfect example of where we really needed to tailor the framework to meet our organizational needs. Today, I often hear companies refer to implementing CMMI Levels 2/3, which means that they select only the process areas from Levels 2 and 3 that are most relevant to their organizations.

The CMMI configuration management process area states that "the purpose of configuration management is to establish and maintain the integrity of work products using configuration identification, configuration control, status accounting, and configuration audits." We have discussed what each of these terms means earlier in this chapter, but the real work of configuration management involves creating a means to identify everything from components to documentation that goes into creating a release of your code. You also need to baseline your code (sometimes called *establishing a control point*) so that you can get back to the exact versions of your source code and all other configuration items when you need to. You also need to control changes, provide status on all configuration items being created, and maintain a configuration management system that includes your source code and accurate records of all changes.

14.6.2.1 Subcontractor Management

The CMM and the CMMI always placed a strong value on managing contractors. This is also seen in the Cobit framework and many IEEE standards, too. For configuration management, this oversight is particularly important. It is common for companies to purchase systems that they then modify and extend as needed. Purchasing a product from a supplier does not mean that you don't need to establish configuration management controls. In fact, many times, we have asked the supplier to give us visibility into their own configuration management practices, especially their procedures for identifying configuration items that you will need to know to conduct a configuration audit. You also need to establish change control to handle configuration change issues, including opening firewall ports in production or managing interface dependencies with other systems.

The Capability Maturity Model has always been an excellent framework to use in assessing your existing processes and determining what still needs to be changed and be improved. I have found that most organizations need other help to establish these practices. One excellent approach is to use the CMMI and related IEEE standards to provide more information on how to actually establish the practices that you can then use to evaluate your progress and identify areas for improvement using assessment tools such as the CMMI Appraisal Method for Process Improvement (SCAMPI). While the CMM has been used for decades as a framework for establishing effective IT processes, a more recent model is the itSMF's ITIL framework, which focuses heavily on configuration management as it defines best practices for IT service management.

14.6.3 itSMF's ITIL Framework

The itSMF has developed an exhaustive framework that describes best practices for IT service management. ITIL has a strong emphasis on configuration management best practices and, in my view, is the most comprehensive description of CM practices that I have ever seen. ITIL can also be somewhat intimidating to tackle because it requires five rather large texts to present all the essential information. The volume that focuses most on CM is called *service transition* and includes guidance on change management, release and deployment management, and service asset and configuration management (SACM). ITIL has a strong focus on asset management and treats both hardware and software as *assets* that need to be placed under control. Throughout the framework, there is a heavy focus on planning activities and managing the implementation process. In fact, the title of the volume refers to transitioning an IT service or other configuration item from one lifecycle status to the next. I discuss some of the core concepts of ITIL here, but suggest that you obtain the framework directly from the itSMF so that you can read all the essential information described in this framework.

14.6.3.1 Change Management

Change management involves the review, impact assessment, approval, and possibly rejection of requests for change. ITIL describes change management in terms of being a repeatable process and a specific organizational function. All changes are managed through the change request, and there is a specific workflow suggested that can be modified to your organizational needs. ITIL is so detailed that it suggests a specific process flow for actions such as change request, deployments, and standard operational changes. There is also a list of items that you should include in your change document. I find this level of detail in a framework extremely helpful because it gives you a starting point to create your processes. Some organizations might adopt the entire framework because of contractual obligations or the desire to show that they are ITIL compliant. Ideally, your organization can pick which practices make the most sense and trim down to be as lean as possible.

14.6.3.2 Change Advisory Board

ITIL is the first standard or framework that I have seen that differentiates between the people who are responsible for the change control process and those technology experts who actually understand the impact of a particular change. The change advisory board is a group of subject matter experts (SMEs) who can provide guidance on what might happen if a particular change is authorized. In practice, this is very important, and I have seen many situations where the change control board was reviewing a request for change and really did not have anyone present who could fully advise them on what might happen if a particular change occurred. That might sound incredible, but it is common for the "process guru" to not have all the technical details (because this information is often highly specialized, with only a few experts really understanding all the essential details). The change advisory board helps to identify the technical experts who need to be consulted without trying to make them attend every CCB meeting. In practice, this makes a lot of sense and will lead to fewer mistakes and better control over changes.

14.6.3.3 Service Asset and Configuration Management

ITIL service asset and configuration management (SACM) provides a comprehensive approach to configuration management, including the management of all configuration items as "assets." The first time that I heard about software being managed as IT assets, I was rather surprised and puzzled. Asset management makes sense when it comes to counting desktop computers or printers, but I had some trouble adjusting to the idea that software applications were also considered assets. Over time, I realized that this was exactly how we should regard software applications.

14.6.3.4 Asset Management

Asset management needs to be handled as part of a complete lifecycle. In many ways, it includes many of the points that are intended by status accounting as described in the IEEE standards and the CMMI. Status accounting is intended to track the status of configuration items throughout their lifecycle. The ITIL framework describes the use of a configuration management system (CMS) to track the status of all related assets.

14.6.3.5 Configuration Management System

The configuration management system is used to track all assets and their related changes. In practice, it can be a challenge to keep the CMS up-to-date on a regular basis. If this requires that a person manually update a database, you might find that the CMS gets out-of-date pretty quickly. It's best to automate your processes as much as possible to update the CMS (or its equivalent) as part of the release management process.

14.6.3.6 Definitive Media Library

The definitive media library (DML) is the repository for all production releases. It is essential that the DML be kept secure and accessed only by authorized release management personnel. In Chapter 1, "Source Code Management," we discussed the use of source code management to manage all the source code that is part of a release. The ITIL framework does not describe the software development process because it is mostly focused on IT service management. For my description of ITIL, I need to include source code management because, in practice, the source code management system needs to be integrated with the DML. Developers interact daily with the SCM tools while the release management team builds and deploys the official *baselined* release.

14.6.3.7 Release Management and Deployment

The ITIL framework focuses on the planning effort required to accomplish release management and deployment. There is also a focus on reducing the impact on services that could be affected by the release. ITIL expects that releases are appropriately packaged, tracked, installed, tested, and if necessary, backed out through a well-defined uninstall process.

14.6.3.8 Integrating the CMS, DML, CMDBs, and SCM

Figure 14.3 shows the relationship between the configuration management system (CMS), configuration management databases (CMDBs), definitive media library (DML), and the source code management system (SCM). Note that the source code repository is not the same as the configuration management system; the latter is usually a database that tracks the status of configuration items throughout their lifecycle. Baselines are typically kept in the DML, which in some cases is a separate instance of the source code management system intended to be used for asset management.

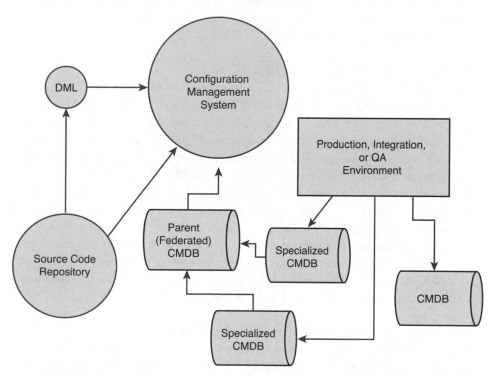

Figure 14.3 *The relationship between the CMS, CMDBs, DML, and SCM.*

14.6.3.9 *Configuration Management Database*

There are many different types of configuration management databases. CMDBs may be dedicated devices that monitor the environment or fully functional databases that receive input from a variety of sources (such as other CMDBs). In the latter case, we usually refer to the CMDB as being *federated,* because typically one or more specialized CMDBs feed their information to a parent CMDB that consolidates the information and provides an information console. Some types of CMDBs have been around for a long time. Nevertheless, some of my colleagues have criticized the ITIL concept of a CMDB as being impractical and not fully realized. In my opinion, the folks who criticize ITIL are missing the essential point that while ITIL provides valuable guidance, process improvement has to be driven from within the organization. A framework or standard is really just guidance. Obviously, your business may contractually require that you comply with a standard or framework, but process improvement has to start with defining the goals that matter most to you and your organization. Too many people focus on the perception that many CMDBs fall short of their expectations, instead of realizing the value that they provide and working toward making the best better. Here's how to approach implementing a CMDB as part of your process-improvement effort.

14.6.3.10 Process Improvement for CMDBs

In my experience, it is always best to define the goals of a process-improvement effort in very narrow terms. Trying to "boil the ocean" often falls short of expectations, which can adversely impact your process-improvement efforts. The key is to determine priorities by considering risks and goals. For example, a firewall provides an essential service to the organization in terms of preventing unauthorized access and the potential loss involved with such incidents. One of the most common CMDBs in place today is a dedicated device that monitors firewall access and reports on unauthorized attempted access. This information is often reported up to a console that is surveilled by data security personnel. Most organizations watch the firewall access closely in their production environments, although many also have an integration environment (possibly accessed by customers involved with beta testing) and QA environments, which, in my opinion, should be treated like a production environment.

14.6.3.11 Homespun Environment Monitoring

I have worked in organizations where the source code management repository was a full-featured production database. The organization's most valued assets were in the SCM repository, and losing that code would have been nothing short of a major disaster. To protect our code, we regularly ran integrity checks on the SCM repository. In one case, a misconfigured storage device resulted in the source code repository becoming corrupted. Fortunately, we did not lose a line of code because we had scripts in place that checked the integrity of the repository on a nightly basis. It took the two vendors involved months to find the problem and fix it, which turned out to be a rather trivial configuration error. In the meantime, none of our code was lost because we were able to immediately spot the problem and take measures to address the issue. Without this surveillance in place, we could have potentially lost years of work and put the firm's source code assets at risk.

14.6.3.12 Putting Together Your CMDB

I recommend that you consider your own risks and goals when you decide how to implement your CMDB. What assets do you need monitored? What events are essential to review and deal with immediately? Perhaps you need to monitor your environment for disk space and available resources, including connections to essential resources. Individual processes need to be monitored to see that they stay online and available. Some of your CMDBs may be dedicated devices with a narrow focus, and others may have a wider focus (often receiving input from the specialized devices). Make sure that when a mistake or problem occurs you consider whether adding another CMDB (or improved functionality to an existing CMDB) will help avoid the problem in the future. In pragmatic terms, you might not be able to prevent every incident from occurring, but you should address situations where the same problem occurs over and over again. CMDBs provide an excellent, cost-effective way to handle the surveillance of your environment. Closely related is the topic of automated testing. In fact, it is pretty common to use testing as part of your approach to monitoring and controlling your environments.

14.6.3.13 *Validation and Testing*

Configuration management and testing are closely related in many ways. The ITIL framework does a great job of pointing out that your configuration management processes need to include a testing function. Testing is implicit in everything that we do, and improving your automated and manual testing processes will significantly impact your quality and productivity. For example, the deployment of a release is never considered complete until a smoke test has been successfully executed. If the smoke test fails, you will most likely need to roll back the release. Configuration management best practices make backing out a change possible (without unexpected problems) and help to improve your quality and productivity. Even small changes should always be tested. The release baseline should also be validated by conducting a configuration audit, as described previously in this book. The validation process must be automated; otherwise, it will likely not be practical to conduct it on a regular basis. Some good tools automate this process, and you should consider validation and testing to be part of your required CM best practices.

14.6.3.14 *Conclusion*

In my opinion, the itSMF's ITIL framework raises the bar in many ways by recommending excellent CM best practices. You might find that it requires a journey to implement all of these best practices. You absolutely should use ITIL in concert with other frameworks such as Cobit or the CMMI. You should also make use of existing standards from the standards organizations such as the IEEE to provide the detailed guidance to support all of your processes (especially development where ITIL is less focused). It is certainly a great time to be in the process-improvement industry, when good processes are so critical to organizational productivity and there are so many excellent sources of CM best practices. Another excellent source is the IEEE's Software Engineering Body of Knowledge (SWEBOK).

14.6.4 SWEBOK

The purpose of the guide to the Software Engineering Body of Knowledge (SWE-BOK) is to provide a consensually validated characterization of the bounds of the software engineering discipline and to provide topical access to the body of knowledge supporting that discipline. The body of knowledge is subdivided into ten software engineering knowledge areas (KAs) plus an additional chapter providing an overview of the KAs of strongly related disciplines. The descriptions of the KAs are designed to discriminate among the various important concepts, permitting readers to find their way quickly to subjects of interest. On finding a subject, readers are referred to key papers or book chapters selected because they succinctly present the knowledge.[3]

The SWEBOK knowledge areas include

- Requirements

- Design

- Construction

- Testing

- Maintenance

- Configuration management

- Engineering management

- Engineering process

- Engineering tools and methods

- Software Quality

14.6.4.1 *Software Configuration Management in SWEBOK*

For SWEBOK, software configuration management (SCM) is the discipline of identifying the configuration of software at distinct points in time for the purpose of systematically controlling changes to the configuration and maintaining the integrity and traceability of the configuration throughout the system lifecycle. The CM KA comprises six subareas:

- **Management of the SCM process.** Management of the SCM process covers the topics of the organizational context for SCM, constraints and

---

[3] SWEBOK, 2004

guidance for SCM, planning for SCM, the SCM plan itself, and surveillance of SCM.

- **Software configuration identification.** Software configuration identification identifies items to be controlled, establishes identification schemes for the items and their versions, and establishes the tools and techniques to be used in acquiring and managing controlled items. The first topics in this subarea are identification of the items to be controlled and the software library.

- **Software configuration control.** Software configuration control is the management of changes during the software lifecycle. The topics are (first) requesting, evaluating, and approving software changes; and (second), implementing software changes; and (third), deviations and waivers.

- **Software configuration status accounting.** Software configuration status accounting includes topics such as software configuration status information and software configuration status reporting.

- **Software configuration auditing.** This consists of software functional configuration auditing, software physical configuration auditing, and in-process audits of a software baseline.

- **Software release management and delivery.** This subarea covers software building and software release management.

SWEBOK is available for free in HTML form and is harmonized with all the IEEE standards on an ongoing basis. It's expected that SWEBOK will mature and develop into a comprehensive framework.

14.6.5 Open Unified Process (OpenUP)

The Open Unified Process (OpenUP), part of the Eclipse Process Framework, is an iterative process model that strives to be both agile and lean. The Open Unified Process applies iterative and incremental approaches within a structured lifecycle that even in its lighter forms provides a comprehensive development framework. OpenUP embraces a pragmatic, agile philosophy that focuses on the collaborative nature of software development. It is a tools-agnostic, low-ceremony process that can be extended to address a broad variety of project types. The Unified Process has taken many forms over the years and has evolved over time. I am resisting going into the history of the Unified Process (and its open source implementation known as OpenUp) in this book, and instead will discuss its evolution on the supporting website. The Unified Process is iterative but curiously supported by many documents (known as *artifacts*). Too often, people believe that they are required to include more artifacts than are really necessary (making this approach more verbose than necessary). Some of the essential artifacts are the configuration management plan, change request management, support for continuous integration, and overall project planning. I have personally found the topology for organizing testing to be particularly helpful.

Overall, the organization and topology of the OpenUP documents is excellent, and many organizations rely heavily on the Unified Process in one of its many forms. It has often been said that the key to success with the Unified Process is to only use the artifacts that are absolutely necessary and to guide and limit your selection by repeatedly asking yourself this question: What bad thing could happen if we do not include this artifact?

14.6.6 Agile/SCRUM

Agility just works. If you are not yet working on becoming more agile, you need to start today. Agile refocuses on what really matters in the software development effort. There are many good books on Agile development, and that is not the focus of this book. However, I do want to include a few important points in this chapter as they relate to CM best practices. Agile focuses us on realizing that we might not be able to know all of our requirements up front. Being honest about what we know and what we don't yet understand is essential in any process-improvement effort. By the same token, you need to realize when documenting your requirements is necessary. Many times, document traceability is an absolute requirement for regulatory purposes. I believe that you can become agile and still pass your audit. Providing standards to support Agile is an important part of this effort. I am working with other technology professionals to provide additional industry standards to support Agile so that you can enjoy the benefits of agility and still pass your next audit.

14.6.6.1 Rapid Build and Deploy Support Agility

Configuration management best practices help support Agile development by providing rapid (automated) procedures to build, package, and deploy applications on an iterative basis. In my opinion, Agile development is not possible without excellent CM best practices. One of the most well-respected CM best practices is continuous integration.

14.6.6.2 Continuous Integration

Martin Fowler and others have done an excellent job of promoting continuous integration (CI) as a best practice that is implicit in Agile development. CI is usually implemented as an automatic build (and deploy to a test environment) that is triggered by code being checked in (or committed) to the source code management repository. This is the classic approach to CI, although I have seen organizations where nightly builds were preferable to immediate builds triggered by a code check-in (or commit). Nonetheless, integrating your code early and often is implicit in becoming agile and a core CM best practice, too. Agile CM is evolving quickly and could easily be the subject of a complete book by itself.

Conclusion

Technology professionals are fortunate to enjoy many excellent industry standards and frameworks that help to guide their process-improvement efforts. You need to assess your own organizational goals and choose wisely when you begin your own process-improvement journey. My advice is to always trim down your process to what is absolutely required and necessary. This is consistent with the very popular Lean development practices. You should also freely harmonize standards and frameworks to gain valuable guidance on how to implement CM best practices!

Index

A

a priori change control, 58, 62
active listening, 148-149
after-action reviews, 71
Agile, 118, 216-217
ALM (application lifecycle management), 26
ANSI/ITAA EIA-649-A standard, 196
Ant, 38
  for complex builds, 39-40
  Maven versus, 39
Appleton, Brad, 121
application architecture. *See* architecture
application lifecycle management (ALM), 26
applying psychology. *See* psychology
approval process in change control,
    forged approvals example, 69
architecture, CM (configuration management) and, 94-99
  build engineering in, 103
  changes to architecture, 101-102
  CMDD (configuration management-driven development), 101
  goals of, 98
  importance of, 99
  source code management in, 102-103
  starting point for, 99
  testing, role of, 99-101
  training, 102-103
assessments, configuration management, 183-185. *See also* audits
asset management in ITIL framework, 210
audits. *See also* assessments; configuration audits
  FDIC audit, 177-179
  NARA audit, 179-181

B

bad builds, 31
balancing risk, 158
baselines in source code management, 8-10
Berczuk, Steve, 121
best practices. *See also* compliance
  in build engineering, 47
  in deployment, 87-90
  in environment configuration, 57
  moral argument for, 182-183
birth order roles in personality, 150-152
  firstborns as leaders, 150-151
  middle-borns as compromisers, 151
  only children, 151-152
  self-expression, 152
  youngests as initiators, 151
blackbox testing, 154
blindness example (process improvement), 116
"Bob method" for training, 24-25
branching in source code management, 11-12
  bugfixes, 12-13
  copybranches versus deltas, 12-13
branding executables, 32
breaking rules in workplace culture, 157-158
budget for source code management, 23-24
bugfixes in source code management, 12-13
build engineering, xxxiv, 27-30
  in architecture development, 103
  best practices, 47
  build process improvements, 42-44
  compile dependency management, 33-34
  continuous integration (CI) versus nightly builds, 47-48
  cost of quality, 42

ethical issues, 36-37
future of, 48
goals of, 30
importance of, 31
independent builds, 34-35
organizational structure, 37-38
overengineering, 35-36
as part of development team, 153-154
principles of, 30-31
release management and, 79
responsibilities in, 32
role of build engineer, 44-46
starting point for, 32
technology architecture, importance of, 46-47
tool selection, 38-42
version IDs, 32-33
build frameworks, 41

C

CAB (change advisory board), 63, 209
Capability Maturity Model (CMM), 116-117, 207-208
Capability Maturity Model Integrated (CMMI), 116-117, 128, 185, 207-208
CCB (change control board), 61. *See also* change control
centralized environment CMDBs, 55-56
change advisory board (CAB), 63, 209
change control, xxxiv, 58-60
    a priori change control, 62
after-action reviews, 71
    change advisory board (CAB), 63
    as CM process driver, 69-70
    in Cobit framework, 198-203
    configuration control, 62-63
    creating change control function, 65
    e-change control, 67
    emergency change control, 64
    entry/exit criteria, 70
    environment configuration and, 56
    evaluating, 71
    examples
        forged approvals example, 69
        investment bank example, 66-67
        team conflict, 65
        trading firm example, 67

gatekeeping, 62
goals of, 60
hierarchy of, 67
importance of, 61
in ITIL framework, 209
principles of, 60-61
process engineering, 64
risk in, 69
senior management oversight of, 64-65
specialized change control, 67
starting point for, 61
system integration, 70
time management of, 66
change control board (CCB), 61. *See also* change control
changesets in source code management, 16
checkouts, reserved versus unreserved, 10-11
CI (continuous integration), 40, 47-48, 216-217
CI servers, 40
CIs (configuration items), xxxiii, 6, 32
    defined, 189-190
    in hardware configuration management, 107-108
    release maps of, 77
CM (configuration management)
    architecture and, 94-99
        build engineering in, 103
        changes to architecture, 101-102
        CMDD (configuration management-driven development), 101
        goals of, 98
        importance of, 99
        source code management in, 102-103
        starting point for, 99
        testing, role of, 99-101
        training, 102-103
    assessments, 183-185
    change control as process driver, 69-70
    core functional areas, xxxiv
    defined, xxxiv-xxxvi
    goals of, xxxvii
    hardware configuration management. *See* hardware configuration management
    personality and. *See* personality
    terminology, xxxiv-xxxvi

CMDB (configuration management database)
centralized environment CMDBs, 55-56
in ITIL framework, 211-213
CMDD (configuration management-driven development), 101
CMM (Capability Maturity Model), 116-117, 207-208
CMMI (Capability Maturity Model Integrated), 116-117, 128, 185, 207-208
CMS (configuration management system)
in ITIL framework, 210
Cobit framework, 176-177, 197-207
change control, 198-203
emergency change control, 199
metrics, 199
problems with, 197
process improvement, 203-207
scaling, 200
cockpit of plane example, 44
code management. *See* source code management
code promotion support in environment configuration, 52
code regression, avoiding, 33
code variants. *See* variant management
collaboration, psychology of, 153
commercial tools, open source tools versus, 21
Committee of Sponsoring Organizations (COSO), 175-176
communicating release status, 80
communication styles, 147
active listening, 148-149
consultation methods, 148
gender differences in, 147-148
communications planning in deployment, 92-93
compile dependency management in build engineering, 33-34
compliance, 168-172. *See also* best practices
Cobit framework, 176-177
configuration management assessments, 183-185
conformance versus, 192-193
COSO (Committee of Sponsoring Organizations), 175-176
GAO (Government Accountability Office) FDIC audit, 177-179

GAO (Government Accountability Office) NARA audit, 179-181
goals of, 172-173
HIPAA (Health Insurance Portability and Accountability Act of 1996), 177
importance of, 173
improving quality and productivity via, 183
moral argument for, 182-183
OCC (Office of the Comptroller of the Currency), 181
requirements, 181-182
SOX (Sarbanes-Oxley Act of 2002), 174-175
starting point for, 173-174
compromisers, middle-borns as, 151
"conducting bakeoffs," 42
configuration audits, xxxvi, 90, 191
configuration control, 62-63
defined, 190
release management and, 81
configuration identification, xxxvi, 190
configuration items (CIs), xxxiii, 6, 32
defined, 189-190
in hardware configuration management, 107-108
release maps of, 77
configuration management. *See* CM (configuration management)
configuration management assessments, 183-185
configuration management database (CMDB)
centralized environment CMDBs, 55-56
in ITIL framework, 211-213
configuration management driven development (CMDD), 101
configuration management system (CMS)
in ITIL framework, 210
configuration management-driven development (CMDD), 101
configuration status accounting (CSA), 191
conflict between teams in change control, 65
conflict of interest in build engineering, 37

conformance, noncompliance versus, 192-193
consensus, failing to gain, 165
consultation methods for communication improvement, 148
continuous integration (CI), 40, 47-48, 216-217
coordination function, release management as, 80-81
copybranches in source code management, 12-13
corporate culture. *See* culture
COSO (Committee of Sponsoring Organizations), 175-176
cost of quality
  for build engineering, 42
  for source code management, 23-24
cryptography, signing release packages with, 82
CSA (configuration status accounting), 191
culture
  matching process to, 127-128
  personality and, 156-159
    acceptance of others, 157
    loose cannons, 157-158
    standards, following, 156, 158
CVS, 4

D

database dependencies in environment configuration, 52-55
Davidson, James Duncan, 38
defect tracking in source code management, 16-17, 26
definitive media library (DML) in ITIL framework, 210
deltas in source code management, 12-13
Deming, W. Edwards, 71, 114, 119, 162, 163, 202
dependencies
  in build engineering, 33-34
  in hardware configuration management, 108
  runtime dependencies. *See* environment configuration

deployment, 83-86. *See also* release management

best practices, 87-90
communications planning, 92-93
configuration audits, 90
of firmware changes, 109
goals of, 86
importance of, 87
improvements to, 93-94
interface control, 92
in ITIL framework, 210
principles of, 86-87
responsibility for, 93
smoke test, 92
staging process, 87-89
starting point for, 87
"trust, but verify,"93
deployment frameworks, 89
design documents in hardware configuration management, 107-108
DML (definitive media library) in ITIL framework, 210
DSM-IV R psychiatric diagnostic manual, 146

E

e-change control, 67
EIA. *See* ANSI/ITAA EIA-649-A standard
Electronic Records Archives (ERA) audit, 179-181
emergency change control, 64, 199
entry criteria in change control, 70
environment configuration, xxxiv, 48-50
  best practices, 57
  centralized environment CMDBs, 55-56
  change control and, 56
  code promotion support, 52
  dependency management, 52-55
  environment management in, 57
  future of, 57-58
  goals of, 50-51
  importance of, 51
  principles of, 51
  starting point for, 51-52
environment management in environment configuration, 57
environment monitoring in ITIL framework, 212
ERA (Electronic Records Archives) audit, 179-181

ergonomics of release management, 77-80

Erikson, Erik, 144

errors. *See* human error

ethical issues in build engineering, 36-37

evaluating change control, 71. *See also* selecting

exit criteria in change control, 70

extensibility of source code management tools, 22

F

"failure is not an option,"138-139

family dynamics in personality, 155

FDIC (Federal Deposit Insurance Corporation) audit, 177-179

feature branching in source code management, 12-13

Federal Deposit Insurance Corporation (FDIC) audit, 177-179

Feldman, Stuart, 38

firmware changes, deployment of, 109

firstborns as leaders, 150-151

forged approvals example (change control), 69

forgetting to ask for help, 166

fostering teamwork, 131

Fowler, Martin, 216

frameworks

  Agile/SCRUM, 216-217

  CMM/CMMI, 207-208

  Cobit framework, 197-207

    change control, 198-203

    emergency change control, 199

    metrics, 199

    problems with, 197

    process improvement, 203-207

    scaling, 200

  goals of, 188

  importance of, 188

  ITIL framework, 208-213

    asset management, 210

    change advisory board (CAB), 209

    change control, 209

    CMS (configuration management system), 210

    configuration management database (CMDB), 211-213

    definitive media library (DML), 210

    environment monitoring, 212

    process improvement, 212

    relationships among systems, 210-211

    release management and deployment, 210

    service asset and configuration management (SACM), 209

    validation and testing, 213

  Open Unified Process, 215-216

  standards versus, 196-197

  starting point for, 189

  SWEBOK framework, 214-215

  terminology, 189-193

G

gaining consensus, 165

GAO (Government Accountability Office)

  FDIC audit, 177-179

  NARA audit, 179-181

gatekeeping change control, 62

gender differences in communication styles, 147-148

globally distributed teams, source code management in, 17-18

GNU Make, 38

governance. *See* compliance

Government Accountability Office (GAO)

  FDIC audit, 177-179

  NARA audit, 179-181

graybox testing, 154

group dynamics, 154

guerrilla tactics for overcoming resistance to change, 138-139

H

hardware configuration management, 103-106

  changes to firmware, deploying, 109

  dependencies in, 108

  future of, 109

  goals of, 106

  importance of, 106

  interface control in, 108

  starting point for, 107

  traceability in, 108-109

  version control in, 107-108

Health Insurance Portability and Accountability Act of 1996 (HIPAA), 177
hierarchy of change control, 67
HIPAA (Health Insurance Portability and Accountability Act of 1996), 177
honesty, need for, 168
human error, avoiding in release management, 78-79

I

IDEs (integrated development environments), 25, 40-41
IEEE 828 standard, 193-195
immutable version IDs
    in build engineering, 33
    in release management, 76-77
implementation time for source code management, 25
incremental changes in process improvement, 136
indecisiveness, 155
independent builds, 34-35
industrial psychology. *See* psychology
industry frameworks. *See* frameworks
industry standards. *See* standards
information processing preferences, 149-150
initiative of youngest-borns, 151
inner merges in source code management, 15
input from stakeholders, 132-133
integrated development environments (IDEs), 25, 40-41
interface control, 92
    defined, 190-191
    in hardware configuration management, 108
investment bank example (change control), 66-67
ISACA. *See* Cobit framework
ISO 10007 standard, 195
ISO/IEC/IEEE 12207 standard, 196
ISO/IEC/IEEE 15288 standard, 196
IT controls, 168-172. *See also* best practices
    Cobit framework, 176-177
    configuration management assessments, 183-185

COSO (Committee of Sponsoring Organizations), 175-176
GAO (Government Accountability Office) FDIC audit, 177-179
GAO (Government Accountability Office) NARA audit, 179-181
goals of, 172-173
HIPAA (Health Insurance Portability and Accountability Act of 1996), 177
importance of, 173
improving quality and productivity via, 183
moral argument for, 182-183
OCC (Office of the Comptroller of the Currency), 181
requirements, 181-182
SOX (Sarbanes-Oxley Act of 2002), 174-175
starting point for, 173-174
IT standards. *See* standards
ITIL framework, 208-213
    asset management, 210
    change advisory board (CAB), 209
    change control, 209
    CMS (configuration management system), 210
    configuration management database (CMDB), 211-213
    definitive media library (DML), 210
    environment monitoring, 212
    process improvement, 212
    relationships among systems, 210-211
    release management and deployment, 210
    service asset and configuration management (SACM), 209
    validation and testing, 213
itSMF. *See* ITIL framework
ivory tower, remaining in, 167

J-K

just-in-time process improvement, 120

L

language barriers, 78
leadership
    failing to show, 165

of firstborns, 150-151
in process improvement, 133
Lean Software Development, 119-120
learning from mistakes. *See* mistakes, learning from
lessons learned. *See* mistakes, learning from
lifecycle. *See* ISO/IEC/IEEE 12207 standard; ISO/IEC/IEEE 15288 standard
listening to organizational rhythm, 134-136

M

MAC SHA1,82
Make, 38
Maven, 38-39
MBI (Myers-Briggs Inventory), 144
MD5, 82
merging in source code management, 15-16
message verification, 148-149
metadata, 10
metrics in Cobit framework, 199
middle-borns as compromisers, 151
missing the big picture, 163-164
mistakes, learning from, 161-162
    examples of mistakes, 163-168
        becoming part of problem, 165-166
        failing to gain consensus, 165
        failing to show leadership, 165
        lack of honesty, 168
        missing big picture, 163-164
        not asking for help, 166
        promoting process improvement, 165
        remaining in ivory tower, 167
        writing release automation, 164
    goals of, 162
    importance of, 162
    lessons learned, 166-167
    starting point for, 162
    understanding mistakes, 163
moral argument for IT controls, 182-183
Myers-Briggs Inventory (MBI), 144

N

NARA (National Archives and Records Administration) audit, 179-181

National Archives and Records Administration (NARA) audit, 179-181
nightly builds, CI (continuous integration) versus, 47-48
noncompliance, conformance versus, 192-193

O

OCC (Office of the Comptroller of the Currency), 181
OCEAN personality assessment, 144
Office of the Comptroller of the Currency (OCC), 181
only children, personality of, 151-152
open API for source code management tools, 22
open source tools, commercial tools versus, 21
Open Unified Process, 118-119, 215-216
operating systems, release management support, 82
Optimistic checkout model, 10
organizational structure in build engineering, 37-38
outer merges in source code management, 16
overengineering
    in build engineering, 35-36
    in process improvement, 120-121
    of source code management tools, 22-23

P

packaging technology, understanding of, 78-79

personality. *See also* psychology; resistance to change
    assessments for understanding, 144
    birth order roles, 150-152
        firstborns as leaders, 150-151
        middle-borns as compromisers, 151
        only children, 151-152
        self-expression, 152
        youngests as initiators, 151
    communication styles, 147
        active listening, 148-149
        consultation methods, 148

gender differences in, 147-148
defined, 143
family dynamics in, 155
goals of understanding, 142-143
information processing preferences,
    149-150
workplace culture and, 156-159
    acceptance of others, 157
    loose cannons, 157-158
    standards, following, 156, 158
Poppendieck, Mary and Tom, 119
procedural justice, 132
process consultation, 122
process engineering, 64
process improvement, 109-114
    Agile, 118
    blindness example, 116
    CMMI (Capability Maturity Model
        Integrated), 116-117
    in Cobit framework, 203-207
    goals of, 114-115
    importance of, 115
    in ITIL framework, 212
    just-in-time process improvement, 120
    Lean Software Development, 119-120
    Open Unified Process, 118-119
    overengineering, avoiding, 120-121
    process consultation, 122
    promoting, 165
    resistance to change, overcoming,
        123-126
        combining with technology training,
            134-135
        goals of, 126-127
        guerrilla tactics for, 138
        importance of, 127
        improvement from within company,
            129-130
        incremental changes, 136
        leadership, 133
        legitimate opposition, 132
        listening to organizational rhythm,
            134-136
        matching process to culture, 127-128
        pick your battles, 131
        practicality of processes, 133-134
        procedural justice, 132
        promoting process improvement, 137
        psychology and, 129
        self-interest, addressing, 137

stakeholder input, 132-133
starting point for, 127
teamwork, encouraging, 131
scene surveys, 130
as service, 137-138
SPIN (Software Process-Improvement
    Network), 115
starting point for, 115
sustainability of, 122
technology and, 121
test-driven process improvement
    (TDPI), 136
testing in, 121
too little process, 120
verbose processes, 115, 118
processing preferences, 149-150
processing speed, 149-150
processing styles, 149
product maturity for source code man-
    agement tools, 21-22
productivity improvement via compli-
    ance, 183
promoting code in environment configu-
    ration, 52
promoting process improvement, 137,
    165
psychology. See also personality
    listening to organizational rhythm,
        134-136
    process improvement and, 129
    workplace applications of, 152-155
        collaboration, 153
        group dynamics, 154
        teamwork, 153
        testers and build engineers in develop-
            ment team, 153-154

Q

quality improvement via compliance, 183

R

RCS, 4
regression. See code regression
release automation, writing, 164
release calendars, 80-81
release engineering, xxxiv
release management, 71-74. See also
    deployment

build engineering and, 79
configuration control and, 81
as coordination function, 80-81
ergonomics of, 77-80
future of, 81-82
goals of, 74
importance of, 75
in ITIL framework, 210
principles of, 74-75
requirements tracking, 81
starting point for, 75
version IDs, 76-77
release maps, 77
release status, communicating, 80
requirements for compliance, 181-182
requirements tracking
  in release management, 81
  in source code management, 16-17, 26
reserved checkouts, unreserved checkouts
  versus, 10-11
resistance to change, overcoming, 123-
  126. *See also* personality
  combining with technology training,
    134-135
  goals of, 126-127
  guerrilla tactics for, 138
  importance of, 127
  improvement from within company,
    129-130
  incremental changes, 136
  leadership, 133
  legitimate opposition, 132
  listening to organizational rhythm,
    134-136
  matching process to culture, 127-128
  pick your battles, 131
  practicality of processes, 133-134
  procedural justice, 132
  promoting process improvement, 137
  psychology and, 129
  self-interest, addressing, 137
  stakeholder input, 132-133
  starting point for, 127
  teamwork, encouraging, 131
rhythm of organization, listening to,
  134-136
rightsizing CM processes. *See* process
  improvement
risks
  balancing, 158

in change control, 69
in source code management, 25
RM. *See* release management
runtime dependencies. *See* environment
  configuration

S

Sachs, Benjamin K., 119
SACM (service asset and configuration
  management), 209
sandboxes, 11
Sarbanes-Oxley Act of 2002, 174-175
scaling, in Cobit framework, 200
SCAMPI (Standard CMMI Appraisal
  Method for Process Improvement),
  185
SCCS, 4
scene surveys, 130
SCM (source code management). *See*
  source code management
scripts for source code management tools,
  22-23
SCRUM, 216-217
selecting
  build tools, 38-42
  source code management tools, 19-23
self-expression in birth order roles, 152
self-managed teams, 42
senior management oversight of change
  control, 64-65
senior management support for source
  code management, 9
sensory modalities, 149
separation of controls in compliance
  requirements, 182
SEPG (software engineering process
  group), 122
service asset and configuration management (SACM), 209
services
  build engineering as, 103
  process improvement as, 137-138
  source code management as, 103
signing release packages, 82
smoke test, 92
*Software Configuration Management Pat-
  terns: Effective Teamwork, Practical
  Integration* (Berczuk), 121

Software Engineering Body of Knowledge (SWEBOK), 214-215
software engineering process group (SEPG), 122
Software Process-Improvement Network (SPIN), 115
source code management, xxxiii-xxxiv
    in architecture development, 102-103
    baselines, 8-10
    changesets, 16
    defect and requirements tracking, 16-17, 26
    in globally distributed teams, 17-18
    goals of, 4-6
    implementation time, 25
    importance of, 6
    principles of, 6
    reserved versus unreserved checkouts, 10-11
    risks in, 25
    sandboxes, 11
    senior management support for, 9
    starting point for, 7-8
    support process for, 25-27
    tool selection, 19-23
    total cost of ownership, 23-24
    training, 24-25
    usage model definition, 25
    user empowerment, 27
    variant management, 11-12
        bugfixes, 12-13
        copybranches versus deltas, 12-13
        merging, 15-16
        streams, 14-15
SOX (Sarbanes-Oxley Act of 2002), 174-175
specialized change control, 67
SPIN (Software Process-Improvement Network), 115
staging process, 87-89
stakeholder input, 132-133
Standard CMMI Appraisal Method for Process Improvement (SCAMPI), 185
standards
    ANSI/ITAA EIA-649-A standard, 196
    frameworks versus, 196-197
    goals of, 188
    IEEE 828 standard, 193-195
    importance of, 188

ISO 10007 standard, 195
ISO/IEC/IEEE 12207 standard, 196
ISO/IEC/IEEE 15288 standard, 196
    personality and workplace culture, 156, 158
    starting point for, 189
    terminology, 184, 189-193
static code analysis, 41
status accounting, xxxvi
streams in source code management, 14-15
subcontractor control
    in CMM/CMMI, 208
    defined, 192
support process for source code management, 25-27
sustainability of process improvement, 122
SWEBOK framework, 214-215
system integration of change control, 70
systems architecture. See architecture

T

Tannen, Deborah, 147-148
TDD (test-driven development), 101
TDPI (test-driven process improvement), 136
team conflict in change control, 65
teams, self-managed, 42
teamwork
    encouraging, 131
    psychology of, 153
technology, process improvement and, 121
technology architecture in build engineering, importance of, 46-47
technology training, process improvement and, 134-135
test-driven builds, 43
test-driven development (TDD), 101
test-driven process improvement (TDPI), 136
testing
    blackbox versus whitebox versus graybox, 154
    deployment, 92
    in ITIL framework, 213
    as part of development team, 153-154
    in process improvement, 121, 136

role in architecture and CM (configuration management), 99-101
third-party training, vendor training versus, 24
time management in change control, 66
token substitution, 54-55
tool selection
in build engineering, 38-42
in source code management, 19-23
total cost of quality
for build engineering, 42
for source code management, 23-24
traceability
in compliance requirements, 182
in hardware configuration management, 108-109
trading firm example (change control), 67
training
in architecture development, 102-103
in build engineering, 42
importance of, 17, 23, 167
in source code management, 24-25
technology training, process improvement and, 134-135
transparency in process improvement, 122
"trust, but verify," 43-44, 93

U

unreserved checkouts, reserved checkouts versus, 10-11
usage model definition in source code management, 25
user empowerment in source code management, 27

V

validation, 136, 213
variant management, 11-12
bugfixes, 12-13
copybranches versus deltas, 12-13
merging, 15-16
streams, 14-15
vendor commitment for source code management tools, 21-22
vendor control, 192
vendor training, third-party training versus, 24

verbose processes, 115, 118
verification, 136
verifying the message, 148-149
version control in hardware configuration management, 107-108. *See also* source code management
version IDs
in build engineering, 32-33
in release management, 76-77

W-X

whitebox testing, 154
workplace applications of psychology, 152-155
collaboration, 153
group dynamics, 154
teamwork, 153
testers and build engineers in development team, 153-154
workplace culture. *See* culture
workspaces. *See* sandboxes

Y-Z

youngests as initiators, 151

Addison
Wesley

REGISTER

THIS PRODUCT

informit.com/register

Register the Addison-Wesley, Exam Cram, Prentice Hall, Que, and Sams products you own to unlock great benefits.

To begin the registration process, simply go to **informit.com/register** to sign in or create an account. You will then be prompted to enter the 10- or 13-digit ISBN that appears on the back cover of your product.

Registering your products can unlock the following benefits:

- Access to supplemental content, including bonus chapters, source code, or project files.
- A coupon to be used on your next purchase.

Registration benefits vary by product. Benefits will be listed on your Account page under Registered Products.

About InformIT — THE TRUSTED TECHNOLOGY LEARNING SOURCE

INFORMIT IS HOME TO THE LEADING TECHNOLOGY PUBLISHING IMPRINTS Addison-Wesley Professional, Cisco Press, Exam Cram, IBM Press, Prentice Hall Professional, Que, and Sams. Here you will gain access to quality and trusted content and resources from the authors, creators, innovators, and leaders of technology. Whether you're looking for a book on a new technology, a helpful article, timely newsletters, or access to the Safari Books Online digital library, InformIT has a solution for you.

informIT.com

THE TRUSTED TECHNOLOGY LEARNING SOURCE

Addison-Wesley | Cisco Press | Exam Cram
IBM Press | Que | Prentice Hall | Sams

SAFARI BOOKS ONLINE